"One goal of theology is to make us ready to offer an account of the hope that is in us as Christians (1 Pet 3:15). *A Sacramental-Prophetic Vision* meets this goal with impressive scope, discriminating concision, and refreshing clarity. Eggemeier brings together thinkers not often treated in the same work (von Balthasar and Sobrino; Benedict XVI and Foucault; Heidegger and Dillard) to offer such an accounting for hope. Even more, he translates the book's demanding vision into a set of spiritual exercises that make up a 'micropolitics' to counter the enervating apathy that too often results from seeing clearly the grim realities of our suffering world. He also shows how figures such as Aldo Leopold, Dorothy Day, or Martin Luther King demonstrate in wonderful variety that persons formed by such a micropolitics into the practice of seeing those realities against a broader horizon of hope suggest and provide warrants for 'macropolitical' solutions as well. In short, Eggemeier provides a concrete proposal for what a 'mysticism of open eyes' (J. B. Metz) should look like in our world."

—J. Matthew Ashley
University of Notre Dame

"Many theologians today are calling our attention to the devastating effects of global capitalism, the destruction of the environment, and the church's present spiritual malaise. Far fewer seem equipped to offer intellectual resources and spiritual practices for sowing resistance and hope in ourselves and in the next generation. Matthew Eggemeier's new book is a *tour de force* of prophetic imagination grounded in sacramental wonder and hope. In the midst of competing cultural claims on our hearts, Eggemeier sees Christian spirituality as a means of retraining and reorienting our deepest human desires. His attention to the best critical minds and spiritual writers of the modern and postmodern era is masterful and, in a refreshingly clear and understated way, symphonic. I found this book difficult to put down, but even more, I believe my students will resonate deeply with the transformative vision of the Christian life that Eggemeier advances. This is a fabulous book."

—Christopher Pramuk
Xavier University

A **Sacramental-Prophetic Vision**

Christian Spirituality in a Suffering World

Matthew T. Eggemeier

A Michael Glazier Book

LITURGICAL PRESS
Collegeville, Minnesota

www.litpress.org

A Michael Glazier Book published by Liturgical Press

Cover design by Jodi Hendrickson. Photo: Thinkstock.

1   2   3   4   5   6   7   8   9

Library of Congress Cataloging-in-Publication Data

Eggemeier, Matthew T.
    A sacramental-prophetic vision : Christian spirituality in a suffering world / Matthew T. Eggemeier.
       pages   cm
    "A Michael Glazier book."
    Includes bibliographical references.
    ISBN 978-0-8146-8067-4 — ISBN 978-0-8146-8092-6 (ebook)
    1. Christian life—Catholic authors.   2. Poverty—Religious aspects—Catholic Church.
3. Human ecology—Religious aspects—Catholic Church.   4. Christian stewardship—Catholic Church.   5. Catholic Church—Doctrines.   I. Title.
    BX2350.3.E35   2014
    248—dc23   2013045667

Contents

Acknowledgments

Although much of this book was written in solitude, I have incurred many debts in the process. It is with deep gratitude that I acknowledge these debts here. Thank you to the following:

To the College of the Holy Cross for granting me a junior leave in 2011–2012 during which this book project was conceived and several of the chapters drafted. Thanks also to my colleagues in the department of Religious Studies at Holy Cross who warmly welcomed me into the department five years ago and who have been a constant source of support and encouragement. The opportunity to work as a member of such a vibrant and engaging community of scholars and teachers has been an immense privilege. I owe a particular debt to my friend and colleague Peter Fritz, who has been a constant dialogue partner since our time as doctoral students at Notre Dame. Peter was generous enough to read the entire manuscript and offer constructive criticism as well as stylistic suggestions. This work has benefited immeasurably from his keen editorial eye, thoughtful comments, and encouragement.

To my students at the College of the Holy Cross, thank you for your passion, intellectual curiosity, and critical engagement. The classroom is often the setting in which my research ideas first emerge, and my students at Holy Cross have been invaluable as interlocutors and critics. In particular, special thanks to my 2012–2103 Montserrat students who embarked with me on a yearlong exploration of Christian responses to environmental degradation and global poverty.

To my undergraduate mentors, Jim Heft and Mike Barnes, I owe a special debt of gratitude. Jim and Mike cultivated my interest in theology at the University of Dayton and since then have been a significant source of intellectual support. I am grateful for their friendship. Thanks also to my mentors during my doctoral studies at Notre Dame, Matt Ashley and Cyril O'Regan, who during comprehensive exams set me on a path for thinking about the relationship between the sacramental and the prophetic that is expressed in this book.

To the people at Liturgical Press, specifically to Hans Christoffersen for supporting this project since its inception, Linda Maloney for her careful and attentive editorial work, and Lauren L. Murphy for overseeing the entire editorial process. I am grateful for the important work they do and for seeing this work through to publication.

To Caroline Castleforte; Chris, Sara, Jonah, and Bea Eggemeier; Tom, Katie, Libby, and Will Eggemeier; and Vedi Patel who reminded me at critical junctures that there is more to life than research and writing. Your presence in my life during this period filled the process with grace, joy, and laughter.

Finally, I dedicate this book to my parents, Tom and Judy Eggemeier. There are no words that can adequately express my gratitude for their constant encouragement, friendship, and loving support. Their faith, compassion, and love for one another is a vibrant example of the sacramental-prophetic ethos described in this work. Thank you, Mom and Dad, for your witness.

Parts of this book have appeared in earlier form in journal articles. I am grateful to the following publishers for granting me permission to use excerpts from the following works:

"A Mysticism of Open Eyes: Compassion for a Suffering World and the *Askesis* of Contemplative Prayer," *Spiritus: A Journal of Christian Spirituality* 12, no. 1 (2012): 43–62.

"A Sacramental Vision: Environmental Degradation and the Aesthetics of Creation," *Modern Theology* 29, no. 3 (July 2013): 338–60.

"Ecology and Vision: Contemplation as Environmental Practice," *Worldviews* 18 (2014): 54–76.

I am also thankful to Orion Press for permission to reprint excerpts from R. S. Thomas, "Sea-Watching," *Collected Poems: 1945–1990* (London: Phoenix, 2000).

Introduction

Over 1.3 billion human beings survive on less than $1.25 a day; 2.7 billion live on less than $2 a day. Extreme global poverty causes the death of 50,000 people each day, approximately 34,000 of whom are children under the age of five.[1] This means that a third of the total number of deaths each year (18 million out of 57 million) is caused by poverty. These statistics are deeply troubling. But the deeper scandal is that this form of extreme poverty could be eliminated, and it would not be enormously difficult to do so.[2] Jeffrey Sachs argues that if the developed world increased its total foreign aid to combat global poverty to $200 to $250 billion a year, that would be enough to eliminate its most devastating consequences.[3] Thomas Pogge contends that if we placed a one percent tax on aggregate global income, this would raise sufficient funds to eliminate extreme global poverty. Pogge observes that 2.8 billion "people together have about 1.2 percent of aggregate global income, while 903 million people of 'high income economies' together have 79.7 percent. Shifting merely one percent of aggregate global income—$300 billion annually—from the first group to the second would eradicate severe poverty worldwide."[4] More dramatically, Peter Singer argues that all that would be needed in order to meet the development aid goals set by United Nations Millennium Development Goals agreed to in 2000 would be for the top 0.1 percent of income earners in the United States to give away a third of their income. This is an astonishing number. To meet the

---

[1] Thomas Pogge, *World Poverty and Human Rights* (Malden, MA: Polity Press, 2008), 2.

[2] See Jeffrey D. Sachs, *The End of Poverty: Economic Possibilities for Our Time* (New York: Penguin Books, 2005); Peter Singer, *The Life You Can Save* (New York: Random House, 2009); Paul Collier, *The Bottom Billion: Why the Poorest Countries are Failing and What Can Be Done About It* (New York: Oxford University Press, 2007).

[3] Nina Munk, "Jeffrey Sachs's 200 Billion Dollar Dream," *Vanity Fair* (July 2007); http://www.vanityfair.com/politics/features/2007/07/sachs200707. See also Sachs, *End of Poverty*, 288–308, and idem, *Common Wealth: Economics for a Crowded Planet* (New York: Penguin, 2008), 246.

[4] Pogge, *World Poverty and Human Rights*, 2.

entire additional global aid necessary to respond to extreme global poverty (in 2006 Jeffrey Sachs set it at $121 billion, rising to $189 billion in 2015) there would be no need for a non-US citizen to contribute anything. Indeed, it would be unnecessary for 99.9 percent of the US population to contribute anything at all. According to Singer, if the top 0.1 percent of income earners in the United States would each contribute a third of their income, the yield would be $126 billion (exceeding the requisite $121 billion), and the entire world would be placed on a path to eliminating extreme global poverty.[5] In this sense it is not a question of whether we have the resources to prevent the most devastating consequences of extreme global poverty. It is rather a question of whether we have the collective will to do so.

Overall, the crisis of global poverty has been met with indifference and ideological resistance in the developed world. While the United States (like the rest of the developed world) tends to respond with enormous vigor to crises that affect the affluent (the financial crisis of 2007–2008) or appear to represent a threat to its way of life (the War on Terror), those crises that threaten the most vulnerable populations in the world often fail to register as realities that demand action. In 2009 Jeffrey Sachs framed the spending priorities of the United States in this way: "out of every $100 of US national income, our government currently provides the grand sum of 5 cents in aid to all of Africa. Out of that same $100, we have found around $10 for the stimulus package and bank bailouts and another $5 for the military."[6]

This same point can be framed in different terms. On September 11, 2001, almost 3,000 people died as a result of the terrorist attacks on the World Trade Center. UNICEF released statistics a few days later that showed that 30,000 children under the age of five died on that same day (9/11/2001) as a result of preventable poverty-related causes.[7] The subsequent war on terror as a response to 9/11 will cost the United States somewhere between $2.5 and $5 trillion when all the costs are calculated (including medical care and disability for veterans).[8] This includes

---

[5] Peter Singer, "What Should a Billionaire Give—and What Should You?" *New York Times*, 17 December 2006. See also the discussion of Singer's (and Pogge's) approaches in David Schweickart, "Global Poverty: Alternative Perspectives on What We Should Do—and Why," *Journal of Social Philosophy* 39 (2008): 471–91.

[6] Jeffrey Sachs, "Aid Ironies," *The Huffington Post*, 24 May 2009, http://www.huffingtonpost.com/jeffrey-sachs/aid-ironies_b_207181.html.

[7] Peter Singer, *One World: The Ethics of Globalization* (New Haven: Yale University Press, 2002), 150–51.

[8] Mark Thompson, "The $5 Trillion War on Terror," *Time*, 29 June 2011, http://nation.time.com/2011/06/29/the-5-trillion-war-on-terror.

approximately $200 to $400 billion spent annually on the wars in Afghanistan and Iraq (2001–2013).[9] The contribution of the United States to foreign aid over this period ranged from $16.3 billion in 2003 to $30.5 billion in 2012. Only a small portion of this aid is dedicated to fighting global poverty. To put the issue more concretely, it costs approximately $775,000 per year to send one soldier to Afghanistan or Iraq.[10] Peter Unger has concluded that it costs approximately $200 to save the life of a child suffering under conditions of extreme poverty. This $200 would provide the child with the inoculations necessary to prevent the most common causes of poverty-related deaths.[11] The cost of sending just one soldier to Afghanistan or Iraq could save almost 4,000 children a year from the type of extreme poverty that leads to preventable death. Quite apart from questions about the morality of the War on Terror from a just war perspective or the wisdom of bailing out the excesses of Wall Street with 700 billion taxpayer dollars, these spending priorities are deeply worrisome from a Christian point of view. Indeed, these budgetary decisions express values that appear to stand in tension with the commitment to peace and the elimination of poverty that are at the core of the Gospel message.

Global poverty is not the only crisis we face in the present. The environmental crisis is urgent and becomes more severe every year. Furthermore, environmental crisis is linked to the crisis of global poverty insofar as the disasters that result from climate change will most profoundly affect the poor around the world.[12] The environmental crisis manifests a number of interrelated dimensions—deforestation, decline in the diversity of species, ocean acidification, and pollution—but none of these is more serious and urgent than climate change. One reason climate change is uniquely challenging is that all that needs to take place for the earth to continue to warm is for individuals in the developed world to go on living the same lifestyle they live right now. Although the global population is currently seven billion, it is estimated that if the rest of the world

---

[9] Overall, in 2012 the US spent over 20 times as much on military expenditures ($645.7 billion) as on foreign aid to eliminate global poverty ($30.5 billion). The 2012 budget of the United States military ($645.7 billion) was 6 times as much as that of China at $102 billion (the second-highest military budget in the world), 11 times as much as that of Russia at $59.9 billion, and 27 times as much as that of Iran at $23.9 billion: http://armscontrolcenter.org/issues/securityspending/articles/2012_topline_global_defense_spending.

[10] Mark Thompson, "The 1 Trillion Bill for Bush's War on Terror," *Time*, 26 December 2008, http://www.time.com/time/nation/article/0,8599,1868367,00.html.

[11] Peter Unger, *Living High and Letting Die: Our Illusion of Innocence* (New York: Oxford University Press, 1996), 148.

[12] James Gerken, "Climate Change-Poverty Link Highlighted in World Bank Report," *The Huffington Post*, 19 June 2013, http://www.huffingtonpost.com/2013/06/19/climate-change-poverty-link_n_3463748.html.

drew from natural resources at the same rate as the United States it would be able to accommodate only 1.4 billion people.[13] This is simply to say that on a finite planet the lifestyle of the developed world—and the United States in particular—is unsustainable. The world cannot absorb the continued expansion of the modern economy because its growth is dependent on the fossil fuels that are the primary cause of the overall increase in global temperatures. If serious changes are not made, the results will be catastrophic: widespread drought, water shortages, natural disasters, the submersion of coastal cities like New York, London, Shanghai, and Mumbai under a rising ocean tide, mass migration of hungry and water-deprived populations, and increasing conflict over scarce resources.

The United States could be an international leader in responding to the environmental crisis. The level of affluence in the United States makes it uniquely qualified to do so. Furthermore, this would be a fitting role for the nation that has contributed more than any other to the increase of CO_2 emissions into the atmosphere since the industrial revolution—approximately 25 percent.[14] The United States has failed, however, at every turn to support international treaties that would represent a substantial effort to limit the types of activities that contribute to climate change. For instance, while George W. Bush pulled the United States out of any commitment to the Kyoto protocol in 2001, halting international momentum in relation to climate change, Barack Obama did not do much better in 2009 at the Copenhagen climate accords when he only committed the United States to voluntary agreements on carbon reduction. This type of voluntary agreement amounts to a statement of goodwill that does little to confront the crisis with any seriousness. In addition to this failure, the United States has done little to support the development of the type of infrastructure that would enable a transition from an environmentally destructive economy to a sustainable one. By way of contrast, places like Germany have made real efforts to support the development of renewable sources of energy, and those efforts have produced tangible results. Last summer there were days on which the power generated by solar panels produced more than half of Germany's energy needs. This is all the more remarkable in view of the fact that Germany does not boast the sun-soaked climates of places like California, Florida, and Texas.[15] These examples could be multiplied endlessly, but even a brief summary points to the fact that the United States has refused time and again to face up

---

[13] Fred Magdoff and John Bellamy Foster, *What Every Environmentalist Needs to Know About Capitalism* (New York: Monthly Review Press, 2011), 28.

[14] http://abcnews.go.com/blogs/technology/2012/07/whos-most-to-blame-for-global-warming.

[15] http://creativetimereports.org/2013/05/20/dj-spooky-and-bill-mckibben-350-org.

to the severity of the environmental crisis. As noted above, this failure is all the more problematic because the United States has contributed disproportionately in the modern era to the dramatic rise in CO_2 in the atmosphere.

If nothing else, these crises demonstrate that we live in a suffering world. The goal of this book is to retrieve resources from the sacramental and prophetic traditions of Christianity in response to these crises. This task of putting the crises of global poverty and environmental degradation at the center of Christian spirituality is made difficult, however, by the fact that Christians are habituated to forms of life that often contribute to the social, political, and economic conditions that have caused these crises. Johann Baptist Metz suggests that we live in a situation in which broader economic and political forces have come to dominate the formation of the identities of individuals. The result is that Christianity has been relegated to the realm of an individual piety that has little to do with political, economic, and social life.[16] Indeed, the current situation is characterized by a tendency for the economic and political commitments of individuals to determine the way in which they appropriate religious traditions in their lives.[17] The result is that religion has become a mere superstructure placed over a preformed market or consumer identity that privatizes any values that do not fit within the logic of the market.[18]

As a privatized dimension of human existence, religion becomes yet another commodity used for therapeutic or consumer purposes.[19] Vincent Miller argues that consumer spirituality harbors within it an apolitical agenda in which "traditions are pillaged for their symbolic content, which is then repackaged and recontextualized in ways that jettison their communal, ethical, and political consequence."[20] He suggests that it is not simply the case that consumerism is in competition with Christianity, but more deeply that consumer culture trains believers to function as consumers in their religious activities. The result is that

[16] Johann Baptist Metz, *Faith in History and Society*, trans. J. Matthew Ashley (New York: Crossroad, 2007), 47.

[17] Metz observes: "Religion does not lay claim to the bourgeois; instead, the bourgeois lays claim to religion. Religion does not transform society; rather, bourgeois society does not rest until religion fits in within itself and with what it considers reasonable." Johann Baptist Metz, *The Emergent Church: The Future of Christianity in a Post-Bourgeois World*, trans. Peter Mann (New York: Crossroad, 1981), 83.

[18] Metz, *Faith in History and Society*, 49.

[19] See L. Gregory Jones, "A Thirst for God or Consumer Spirituality: Cultivating Disciplined Practices of Being Engaged by God," *Modern Theology* 13 (1997): 2–28, at 3–4.

[20] Vincent J. Miller, *Consuming Religion: Christian Faith and Practice in a Consumer Culture* (New York: Continuum, 2004), 84. See also Jones's analysis of this phenomenon, "A Thirst for God or Consumer Spirituality," 4.

Christian rituals and symbols are abstracted from their original context in the communal life of a living tradition and placed on the market to serve the needs of consumer culture.[21] This move is representative of the overarching process of commodification in contemporary culture in which all things—including religion—have been reduced to mere expressions of consumer preference.

The form of spirituality that is valorized in contemporary culture is not one that challenges or disrupts the values of the broader culture. Instead, society has become well versed in the methods necessary to weaken the radicalism of the Gospel by reducing Christianity to what is viewed as reasonable by the logic of the market and by a culture committed to a largely post-Christian, consumerist vision of human life.[22] Thus the disruptive character of Christianity is silenced and Christian spirituality is repackaged as a soothing therapeutic exercise that serves the needs of a culture committed above all else to the enjoyment of consumer activities.[23] Jeremy Carrette and Richard King observe: "the most troubling aspect of many modern spiritualities is precisely that they are not troubling enough. They promote accommodation to the social, economic, and political mores of the day and provide little in terms of a challenge to the status quo or to a lifestyle of self-interest and ubiquitous consumption."[24] Carrette and King contend that "instead of the more traditional emphasis upon self-sacrifice, the disciplining of desire and a recognition of community, we find productivity, work-efficiency, and the accumulation of profit put forward as the new goals" of this spirituality.[25] Thus we live in a cultural situation in which Christian spirituality has been marginalized as a vehicle of identity formation; when it is engaged it serves merely as a means of legitimating preformed political commitments or of optimizing the capacity of individuals to become more productive agents in the marketplace.[26]

It is in response to this situation of privatization, depoliticization, and commodification that a number of theologians have called for the retrieval of the mystical-prophetic spirituality of the Christian tradition. This mystical-prophetic

---

[21] See, e.g., Mara Einstein, *Brands of Faith: Marketing Religion in a Commercial Age* (London and New York: Routledge, 2008).

[22] See Johann Baptist Metz, "God: Against the Myth of the Eternity of Time," 26–46 in idem et al., *The End of Time? The Provocation of Talking about God*, trans. J. Matthew Ashley (Mahwah, NJ: Paulist Press, 2004), 40.

[23] Naomi Klein, *No Logo* (London: Flamingo, 2001).

[24] Jeremy Carrette and Richard King, *Selling Spirituality: The Silent Takeover of Religion* (New York: Routledge, 2005), 5.

[25] Ibid., 23.

[26] Johann Baptist Metz, *Memoria Passionis: Ein Provozierendes Gedächtnis in pluralistischer Gesellschaft* (Freiburg: Herder, 2006), 146.

spirituality is oriented toward the cultivation of forms of life that not only contest the privatization and commodification of religion but also engender practices of resistance to a culture that commits itself to actions that destroy the environment and contribute to the ongoing crisis of poverty. This renewal of Christian spirituality has been described in various ways in contemporary theology in terms of the unity between mysticism and politics (Edward Schillebeeckx, Johann Baptist Metz, Jon Sobrino), contemplation and prophecy (Gustavo Gutiérrez), mysticism and resistance (Dorothee Soelle), the mystical and prophetic (David Tracy), being a contemplative in liberation (Leonardo Boff) or a contemplative in action for justice (Ignacio Ellacuría).[27] This book is an attempt to extend this conversation on the relationship between Christian spirituality and sociopolitical transformation by attending to the importance of cultivating a sacramental-prophetic vision of reality as a means of responding to the crises of environmental degradation and global poverty. Before turning to the outline of the argument made chapter by chapter, three elements of the overall argument should be discussed briefly: (1) spirituality as disciplined seeing; (2) the centrality of witness in the cultivation of a sacramental-prophetic spirituality; (3) the relationship between spirituality and sociopolitical transformation.[28]

First, the sacramental-prophetic approach to spirituality described here is rooted in an interpretation of spirituality as a disciplined way of seeing.[29] The importance of vision for the spiritual life is a pervasive theme in Scripture (e.g., Isa 6:10; Matt 5:8; John 20:24-39) and is prominent in various Christian theologians from

---

[27] See Edward Schillebeeckx, *Christ: The Experience of Jesus as Lord* (New York: Seabury, 1980); Gustavo Gutiérrez, *On Job: God-Talk and the Suffering of the Innocent*, trans. Matthew J. O'Connell (Maryknoll, NY: Orbis Books, 1987); idem, *We Drink from Our Own Wells: The Spiritual Journey of a People*, trans. Matthew J. O'Connell (Maryknoll, NY: Orbis Books, 1984); Dorothee Soelle, *The Silent Cry: Mysticism and Resistance*, trans. Barbara and Martin Rumscheidt (Minneapolis: Fortress Press, 2001); David Tracy, *Dialogue with the Other: The Inter-Religious Dialogue* (Grand Rapids: Eerdmans, 1990); Leonardo Boff, *Faith on the Edge: Religion and Marginalized Existence*, trans. Robert Barr (Maryknoll, NY: Orbis Books, 1991); Ignacio Ellacuría "Fe y justicia," *Christus* (August 1977): 26–33.

[28] See Frederick Bauerschmidt, "The Politics of the Little Way: Dorothy Day Reads Thérèse of Lisieux," 77–95 in *American Catholic Traditions: Resources for Renewal*, ed. Sandra Yocum Mize and William L. Portier (Maryknoll, NY: Orbis Books, 1997). See also Wendell Berry, "Think Little," 81–92 in idem, *The Art of the Commonplace: The Agrarian Essays of Wendell Berry* (Washington, DC: Counterpoint, 2002).

[29] See Brian Goldstone and Stanley Hauerwas, "Disciplined Seeing: Forms of Christianity and Forms of Life," *South Atlantic Quarterly* 109 (2010): 765–90; Stanley Hauerwas, "The Significance of Vision: Toward an Aesthetic Vision," 51–60 in idem, *Vision and Virtue: Essays in Christian Ethical Reflection* (Notre Dame, IN: University of Notre Dame Press, 1981).

St. Augustine to Nicholas of Cusa. In contemporary philosophy and theology, Iris Murdoch and Stanley Hauerwas have developed an important set of reflections on the significance of the cultivation of a proper vision of reality in the moral and spiritual life.[30]

In her philosophy Murdoch reflects on the way in which individuals engage in different moral actions not because of different individual choices made but because the world is perceived differently. She argues that, prior to any moral decision, there exists a background horizon of habits and practices that condition how one sees the world and that shape the choices available in concrete moral situations.[31] According to Murdoch we act differently in the world because we have been trained into different visions of it: "we differ not only because we select different objects out of the same world but because we see different worlds."[32] The task of morality, therefore, is quite simply to perceive the real. Murdoch argues, however, that we engage in a variety of evasion strategies that prevent us from coming to see the real and responding to the demands reality places on us.[33] She observes: "by opening our eyes we do not necessarily see what confronts us. . . . [O]ur minds are continually active, fabricating an anxious, usually self-preoccupied, often falsifying veil which partially conceals the world."[34] In response to this situation Murdoch recommends an engagement with moral and spiritual exercises as a means of increasing the capacity of the self to perceive reality properly: "moral changes comes from an *attention* to the world whose natural result is a decrease in egoism through an increased sense of reality."[35] Murdoch's argument is that, over time, spiritual exercises cultivate a selfless disposition that opens it to an authentic perception of reality, making it

---

[30] This approach also comports with that of Pope Francis in his recent encyclical, *Lumen fidei*, in which it is repeatedly argued that faith is a form of gazing or seeing in which we are called to share "Jesus' way of seeing things" (§19), http://www.vatican.va/holy_father/francesco/encyclicals/documents/papa-francesco_20130629_enciclica-lumen-fidei_en.html.

[31] Murdoch explicitly links this background horizon to how one sees the world: "Virtue is good habit and dutiful action. But the background condition of such habit and such action, in human beings, is a just mode of vision." Iris Murdoch, *The Sovereignty of Good* (New York: Schocken, 1971), 91.

[32] Iris Murdoch, *Existentialists and Mystics: Writings on Philosophy and Literature*, ed. Peter Conradi (New York: Penguin Books, 1998). In this regard "moral differences look less like differences of choice, given the same facts, and more like differences of vision" (p. 82).

[33] Murdoch, *Sovereignty of Good*, 91.

[34] Murdoch, *Existentialists and Mystics*, 368–69.

[35] Iris Murdoch, *Metaphysics as a Guide to Morals* (New York: Penguin Books, 1994), 52. Emphasis in original.

possible that at the time of moral decision-making the choice about the proper course of action has already been made.[36]

Stanley Hauerwas transposes Murdoch's philosophical reflections into a theological idiom by arguing that "the central aim of the Christian life is not so much a matter of right action" as it is a training in "a truthful vision of the world."[37] Hauerwas suggests that the fundamental task of Christian spirituality is "to help us see. For we can only act within the world we can see."[38] Thus when Christian formation is done successfully it grants Christians a vision of the world that contrasts with broader patterns of cultural perception. According to Hauerwas "Christians can see things that other people cannot see, we can notice what others fail to notice, and we can make connections that otherwise would be overlooked."[39] He locates the reason for this in the fact that the Christian is trained "'to see' the world under the mode of the divine."[40]

Hauerwas argues that this process of seeing the real under the mode of the divine does not come about naturally and involves training because "we can only see the world rightly by being trained to see. We do not come to see just by looking, but by disciplined skills developed through initiation."[41] Thus, for him, the rituals and practices of the Christian community take on a particular significance in the formation of Christians in a truthful vision of the world. For instance, he contends that the sacraments of the church constitute the rituals and gestures through which Christians develop both the embodied and imaginative skills to be Christians. Hauerwas believes that "nothing in life is more important than gestures, as gestures embody as well as sustain the valuable and the significant. Through gestures we create and form our worlds."[42]

This is a central point and will be emphasized throughout this book. The second chapter and sections in both the fourth and sixth chapters focus on the

---

[36] Murdoch, *Sovereignty of Good*, 37.

[37] Stanley Hauerwas, "The Significance of Vision: Toward an Aesthetic Ethic," 30–47 in idem, *Vision and Virtue*, at 31.

[38] Idem, "The Demands of a Truthful Story: Ethics and the Pastoral Task," *Chicago Studies* 21 (1982): 59–71, at 65–66.

[39] Idem, *War and the American Difference: Theological Reflections on Violence and National Identity* (Grand Rapids: Baker Academic, 2011), xiii.

[40] Hauerwas, "Significance of Vision," 45–46. Jon Sobrino similarly claims that the task of Christian spirituality is to see "the real world with God's eyes." Jon Sobrino, *Witnesses to the Kingdom: The Martyrs of El Salvador and the Crucified Peoples* (Maryknoll, NY: Orbis Books, 2003), 69.

[41] Hauerwas, "The Demands of a Truthful Story," 65–66.

[42] Stanley Hauerwas, *Christian Existence Today: Essays on Church, World, and Living in Between* (Durham, NC: Labyrinth Press, 1988), 106.

importance of embodied spiritual exercises as a means of forming the human person in a Christian vision of reality. The logic that animates this argument is that in order to respond effectively to present social crises of environmental degradation and global poverty it is necessary to form the self so that it can be honest with the real.[43]

In addition to the emphasis placed on the relationship between spirituality and vision, we will also focus on the centrality of concrete witness as an important feature of the development of a sacramental-prophetic spirituality. Recent philosophy and theology has shown a renewed interest in the cultivation of virtues through the imitation of others.[44] The emphasis placed on virtue ethics underscores the extent to which the lives of others have the capacity to reform our imagination and desire. Because we desire what we see in others, the task is to produce countercultural witnesses (or saints) who provide us with authentic pictures of the Christian life. These lives serve as alternatives to the dominant pictures of the good life presented in the lives of film stars, sports heroes, or politicians. Additionally, more often than not it is the case that we become convinced of the truthfulness of religious claims not because of their logical coherence or inherent rationality but because we see that a religion has been embodied provocatively in concrete lives.[45] The lives of individuals, who in varied ways embody contemplative, sacramental, and prophetic spiritualities, represent a serious challenge to the forms of life to which we commit ourselves in contemporary culture. As James McClendon puts it, these lives present to us "a oneness, a wholeness, a holiness not otherwise available to them or to us. Their lives witness to their vision, even as they challenge the depth of our own.

---

[43] The significance of being honest with the real to Christian spirituality is a focus of the works of Ignacio Ellacuría, SJ, and Jon Sobrino, SJ. See, for instance, Jon Sobrino, *Spirituality and Liberation: Toward Political Holiness* (Maryknoll, NY: Orbis Books, 1988), 13.

[44] This emphasis is present in von Balthasar's theology in a variety of ways, from his attempt to retrieve aesthetic pictures of the world in the second and third volumes of *The Glory of the Lord: A Theological Aesthetics*, 7 vols. (San Francisco: Ignatius Press; New York: Crossroad, 1983–1991) to his consistent emphasis on the saints in the Christian life. In the Protestant world, James McClendon, Jr. has a been a central figure in the revitalization of the importance of witness in contemporary theology, arguing that "the only relevant critical examination of Christian beliefs may be one which begins by attending to lived lives." James McClendon, Jr., *Biography as Theology* (Nashville: Abingdon, 1974), 22, and idem, *Systematic Theology,* vol. 3, *Witness* (Nashville: Abingdon, 2000). See also Stanley Hauerwas, *With the Grain of the Universe: The Church's Witness and Natural Theology* (Grand Rapids: Brazos Press, 2001).

[45] Roberto Goizueta, *Christ Our Companion: Toward a Theological Aesthetics of Liberation* (Maryknoll, NY: Orbis Books, 2009), 3.

So there comes the question, not so much of the suitability of their own vision to their own circumstances, but of the justification of our present way of life when held against theirs."[46] In subsequent chapters we will examine the writings of Annie Dillard and Wendell Berry (chapter four) and Dorothy Day and Martin Luther King, Jr. (chapter six) as concrete witnesses to the sacramental and prophetic commitments of the Christian tradition.

Finally, this book will emphasize Christian spirituality as a politics of the little way or "micropolitics" that is focused on the transformation of the personal and the local as a means of responding to these social crises. This focus on Christian spirituality as micropolitical activity serves to accent the fact that transformation at the level of affect, sensibility, and perception is central to the project of broader macropolitical transformation. Jane Bennett and Michael Shapiro observe: "to engage in micropolitics is to pay attention to the connections between affective registers of experience and collective identities and practices. The aim is to encourage a more intentional project of reforming, refining, intensifying, or disciplining the emotions, aesthetic impulses, urges, and moods that enter into one's political programs, party affiliations, ideological commitments, and policy preferences."[47] Because spiritual exercises constitute a set of practices and rituals that transform the desire, sensibilities, and dispositions of individuals, it follows that these exercises are political because the transformation that takes place at the micropolitical level has an effect on what is deemed possible at the macropolitical level. As Melissa Orlie observes of micropolitics: "if current schemes of power can be changed, they can only be changed politically, by means of significant coordinated, collaborative action. However, the collective political movements that can change systemic powers can emerge only if there are shared changes of conviction and everyday conduct."[48]

In addition to drawing this link between micropolitical and macropolitical transformation, this emphasis on the micropolitical represents an attempt to reclaim a sense of human agency in the face of what are often perceived to be unmanageable global crises. The enormity of the challenges of environmental degradation and global poverty creates a very real sense of hopelessness, a resignation to the conclusion that change is impossible. While confronting this sense of hopelessness is a critical task of the Christian imagination, that task

[46] McClendon, *Biography as Theology*, 110.

[47] Jane Bennett and Michael Shapiro, "Introduction," *The Politics of Moralizing*, ed. Jane Bennett and Michael Shapiro (New York: Routledge, 2002), 5.

[48] Melissa Orlie, "Political Capitalism and the Consumption of Democracy," 138–60 in *Democracy and Vision: Sheldon Wolin and the Vicissitudes of the Political*, ed. Aryeh Botwinick and William E. Connolly (New Jersey: Princeton University Press, 2001), 144.

can be aided by attending to the importance of concrete local action as a form of resistance to the distorted features of broader culture.

Outline of the Book

The argument of this book unfolds in six chapters. The first two establish the methodological basis for the argument made in chapters four and six on sacramental and prophetic vision. In the first chapter I analyze Charles Taylor's description of the social imaginary. For Taylor, the social imaginary (or what I will describe as the cultural imaginary) represents those images, narratives, and symbols that provide a culture with a tacit understanding of the world and give it a sense of what is valuable and meaningful. In this chapter I will argue that the market economy is at the root of two of the most pervasive features of the contemporary cultural imaginary: technological and consumerist forms of life (these points will be elaborated in chapters three and five). In contrast to these distorted features of the contemporary cultural imaginary, Christian spirituality is committed to a way of imagining existence that is rooted in the sacramental-prophetic commitments of the Christian tradition. The broad description of the sacramental and prophetic imagination offered in this chapter will be treated in more detail in the fourth and sixth chapters on sacramental vision and prophetic vision.

In the second chapter I will examine the significance of Christian asceticism and spiritual exercises as a means of training persons in a vision of the world that surpasses the restrictive technological and consumerist features of the cultural imaginary. In particular this chapter focuses on the significance of adopting embodied practices as a means of resisting the broader discipline of cultural formation. The first section elucidates the widespread turn to the significance of the body in anthropological, sociological, and philosophical discourse by analyzing two points from the philosophical writings of Michel Foucault: the disciplinary character of culture and the way in which this discipline is resisted through the training of the self through *askesis*. The second section extends Foucault's retrieval of ancient *askesis*, as a form of resistance to cultural discipline, into Christian discourse and practice by examining Christian asceticism as a resource for the production of Christian selves. At their center, spiritual exercises cultivate a form of self-emptying attentiveness to the world that trains individuals to see what lies outside the self: God, creation, and the human other. In the final section of this chapter I examine four spiritual exercises that can cultivate this sacramental-prophetic spirituality in the present: liturgical worship, the remembrance of past suffering (*memoria passionis*), embodied encounter, and contemplative prayer. Finally, I will analyze these spiritual exercises as a micropolitics of resistance to the discipline of culture.

In the third chapter I explore the contemporary ecological crisis by examining its symptoms and root causes, with a particular focus on the crisis of climate change. Next, I will examine the market economy and the technological culture of modernity as social processes that have created conditions ripe for the degradation of the natural world. The authors whose work is presented in this section contend that the current ecological crisis is rooted in a way of perceiving the world that commodifies the natural world and exploits it for the purposes of technological development and economic growth. In different ways these thinkers assert that resisting the grip of this technological-instrumental vision requires a fundamental reorientation of values as well as a transformation of the manner in which individuals perceive the world. Thus, for instance, Martin Heidegger has argued that the recovery of a contemplative-aesthetic sensibility is necessary to engender a non-instrumental relationship with reality. In the final section of this chapter I examine the theological roots of the environmental crisis by analyzing the writings of Pope Benedict XVI and Norman Wirzba. Both argue that the instrumental ethos of the modern world is rooted in a forgetfulness of the relationship between Creator and creation. As a result both thinkers maintain that an antidote to the present crisis should be grounded in the remembrance of God and a retrieval of the experience of the world as creation.

In the fourth chapter I turn to a sacramental vision of creation as a means of responding to the ecological crisis. First I analyze the turn to aesthetics in contemporary theology and examine its significance for ecological theology. Specifically, I will examine Hans Urs von Balthasar's theological aesthetics, which focuses on the task of seeing the beauty of creation as a manifestation of the glory of God. In this section I will also link von Balthasar's theological aesthetics with Aldo Leopold's land aesthetic and land ethic in order to describe the relationship between theological aesthetics and environmental ethics. Next, I will turn to the practices that cultivate this aesthetic-sacramental vision of reality by examining the significance of liturgical worship, mourning, immersion in the natural world, and contemplative prayer. In the third section of this chapter I present concrete sacramental witnesses by analyzing the nature writings of Annie Dillard and the reflections of Wendell Berry on the environmental crisis.

In the fifth chapter I will describe the crisis of global poverty and analyze the contemporary cultural situation in terms of the dominance of market and consumer values in the present. First I will describe the character of global poverty and examine some of the root causes of inequality and then analyze the market as an ersatz religion in contemporary culture. In this context in which the market has become the dominant religion, human relationships have been reduced to exchange principles and the value of an activity is assessed exclusively in terms of its profitability and its capacity to serve the self-interest of individuals. The ethos of consumerism supports these market values by producing a form of desire that reduces goodness to the pleasure of aesthetic consumption. Consumerism, which replaces the Christian desire for the reign of God with the endless desire for commodities, represents a dangerous alternative to an authentic Christian spirituality. Specifically, the values of the market and the practices of consumer culture present critical obstacles to seeing the truth of the world from a Christian perspective—a truth rooted in the capacity to perceive and be affected by the suffering of others.

In the sixth chapter I will describe a prophetic vision of reality as a resource for responding to the crisis of global poverty and the suffering of the innocent. In the first section I examine the way in which the political and liberation theologies of Johann Baptist Metz and Jon Sobrino foreground the suffering of the innocent as the foundational reality to which Christian spirituality must respond. In this section I analyze the parable of the Good Samaritan as a story that describes the focus of Christian spirituality in terms of responding to painful contradictions with a praxis of responsibility. This constitutes a mysticism of open eyes that sets itself the task of making visible all forms of suffering and permitting this suffering to disturb and interrupt strategies of evasion that excuse individuals from taking responsibility for it. In the second section I turn to the ascetical practices that can cultivate this mysticism of open eyes by again examining the importance of the spiritual exercises of liturgical worship, *memoria passionis*, the embodied encounter with the suffering flesh of the other, and contemplative prayer. Where the practices of consumer culture cultivate an ethos in which the suffering of the innocent is placed at a faceless distance, these ascetical practices train the self in a practice of attention that views the suffering of the innocent as a scandal that demands ethical and political attention. Finally, I turn to the writings of Dorothy Day and Martin Luther King Jr. as concrete witnesses to prophetic spiritualities that represent different responses to the suffering of the poor.

In conclusion I will argue that, while the sacramental and prophetic commitments of the Christian tradition can be seen as moving in different directions, it is necessary to hold these spiritualities in productive tension. This is required of us because in an age of environmental degradation and global poverty a sacramental-prophetic spirituality is best able to endow Christians with the vision of reality necessary to respond to these crises.

Chapter 1

The Sacramental-Prophetic Imagination

Introduction

In this chapter I will examine the significance of the Christian tradition's sacramental-prophetic imagination for the development of spiritualities responsive to the social crises of environmental degradation and global poverty. The imagination plays a pivotal role in the cultivation of this vision because it gives us new ways of perceiving the world.[1] Paul Ricoeur writes: "our imagination is the power to open us to new possibilities, to discover another way of seeing."[2] Similarly, Iris Murdoch argues that: "the world which we confront is not just a world of 'facts' but a world upon which our imagination has, at any given moment, already worked."[3] From this perspective the imagination is the faculty that permits individuals to construe the world prior to explicit reflection and to interpret its significance without sustained deliberation.[4] But, as noted in

[1] Paul Ricoeur, "Myth as the Bearer of Possible Worlds," 36–45 in *Dialogues with Contemporary Continental Thinkers*, ed. Richard Kearney (Dover, NH: Manchester University Press, 1984), 44–45.

[2] Paul Ricoeur, "The Logic of Jesus, the Logic of God," 279–83 in *Figuring the Sacred*, trans. David Pellauer and ed. Mark Wallace (Minneapolis: Fortress Press, 1995), 281. See also Wendell Berry, *It All Turns on Affection: The Jefferson Lecture & Other Essays* (Berkeley, CA: Counterpoint, 2012), 14.

[3] Iris Murdoch, *Existentialists and Mystics: Writings on Philosophy and Literature*, ed. Peter Conradi (New York: Penguin Books, 1999), 199.

[4] James K. A. Smith, *Imagining the Kingdom* (Grand Rapids: Baker Academic, 2013), 17, 34.

the introduction, it is also important to acknowledge that the imagination is itself formed by a broader culture that shapes the way people perceive reality by habituating them to a specific vision of things. From a Christian perspective this situation is problematic because often the collective imagination of Christians has been formed by a culture whose values are in tension with the foundational commitments of the Christian tradition.[5] James Davison Hunter describes the situation this way: "the problem for Christians—to restate the broader issue once more—is not that their faith is weak or inadequate . . . but while they have faith, *they have also been formed by the larger post-Christian culture*, a culture whose habits of life less and less resemble anything like the vision of human flourishing provided by the life of Christ and witness of scripture."[6]

This chapter and the next describe this tension between Christianity and culture by examining the formation individuals receive from the broader culture, directing their lives toward ends that are often in opposition to Christian commitments. In this chapter I will first examine Charles Taylor's use of the social imaginary in order to interpret culture as a reality that is produced imaginatively and that works on individuals at a level prior to explicit theoretical reflection, in the form of shared images, narratives, and stories.[7] Next I will analyze the role the imagination plays in the work of social transformation by examining the threefold process by which a culture and its values are critically questioned, alternatives imagined, and imagined possibilities become embodied in history. Finally I will examine the sacramental-prophetic imagination as a distinctively Christian way of seeing the world that serves as an alternative to the dominant cultural imaginary.

The Cultural Imaginary

In a number of recent works Charles Taylor has examined the significance of the modern social imaginary for understanding Western culture. For Taylor a

---

[5] Stanley Hauerwas writes that the task is "to see the world as it is, and not as it appears," but "if we get our theology wrong, we get the world wrong." Stanley Hauerwas, *With the Grain of the Universe: The Church's Witness and Natural Theology* (Grand Rapids: Brazos Press, 2001), 183.

[6] James Davison Hunter, *To Change the World: The Irony, Tragedy, and Possibility of Christianity in the Late Modern World* (New York: Oxford University Press, 2010), 227. Emphasis in original.

[7] On this point see Benedict Anderson's *Imagined Communities* (New York: Verso, 2006). While Taylor chooses the term "social imaginary," Arjun Appadurai uses "social imagination," Cornelius Castoriadis "instituting imaginary," Anderson "imagined communities," and Ricoeur "cultural imagination."

social imaginary is a reality that enables ordinary people to perceive their collective existence through shared images, stories, and narratives.[8] Taylor maintains that a social imaginary is characterized by "the ways people imagine social existence, how they fit together with others, how things go on between them and their fellows, the expectations that are normally met, and the normative notions and images that underlie these expectations."[9] The social imaginary represents a tacit understanding of the world that enables individuals to make sense of their place in the world and to learn both "how things usually go" and also "how they ought to go."[10] This implicit sense of the world shapes perception at a deep level that escapes the scrutiny of rational analysis.[11] Taylor maintains that a social imaginary "is in fact that largely unstructured and inarticulate understanding of our whole situation, within which particular features of our world show up for us in the sense they have."[12]

The social imaginary constitutes the horizon for what is seen in a particular culture and sets the parameters for what is deemed to be meaningful in that culture. Because it is the taken-for-granted vision of things in a culture, it is difficult to question its legitimacy without calling into question the entirety of the social, political, and religious life of a culture.[13] Taylor observes: "once we are well installed in the modern social imaginary, it seems the only possible one, the only one which makes sense."[14]

Although the social imaginary is contingent and therefore revisable, it is presented as universal and normative. Taylor specifically suggests that the modern social imaginary has "become so self evident to us that we have trouble seeing it as one possible conception among others."[15] Social imaginaries often serve the function of defending the status quo and marginalizing alternatives to the present order of society. This dimension of social imaginaries can be productive because it enables society to function without detailed instructions about how things should proceed in relation to every feature of daily life. But, as Taylor acknowledges, social imaginaries also possess ideological dimensions that can

---

[8] Charles Taylor, *Modern Social Imaginaries* (Durham: Duke University Press, 2004), 23.

[9] Ibid., 24, and Charles Taylor, *A Secular Age* (Cambridge, MA: Belknap Press, 2007), 172.

[10] Taylor, *Modern Social Imaginaries*, 24.

[11] Ibid., 23. On this point see James K. A. Smith, *Desiring the Kingdom: Worship, Worldview, and Cultural Formation* (Grand Rapids: Baker Academic, 2009), 64–67, and Hunter, *To Change the World*, 24–27.

[12] Taylor, *A Secular Age*, 173.

[13] Smith, *Desiring the Kingdom*, 28.

[14] Taylor, *Modern Social Imaginaries*, 17.

[15] Ibid., 2.

serve to defend a distorted vision of reality and perpetuate unjust social structures and cultural practices. He observes: "we regularly come across the ways in which the modern social imaginaries, no longer defined as ideal types but as actually lived by this or that population, are full of ideological and false consciousness."[16]

Taylor's acknowledgment of the presence of ideology and false consciousness in the social imaginary is critical. It points to the fact that although we are installed in a social imaginary it does not follow that the culture into which we are habituated trains us in an authentic vision of the world. This becomes particularly evident when the values present within the contemporary cultural imaginary are examined in relation to the standards of the Christian tradition. In subsequent chapters I will analyze the distorted character of the cultural imaginary in terms of its technological (chap. 3) and consumerist dimensions (chap. 5). At the root of the technological and consumerist dimensions of the cultural imaginary is the all-pervasive logic of the market. This logic and its reduction of life to the values of self-interest, competition, and the profit motive has become so pervasive in contemporary culture that we live in the midst of what can only be described as a "market imaginary."[17]

Taylor makes the argument that there are three distinct features of the modern social imaginary: the market economy, democratic citizenship, and the public sphere.[18] While Taylor's description of the modern social imaginary is instructive, the position adopted here is that the market has eroded the role that democratic citizenship and the public sphere play in the contemporary cultural imaginary. Cornelius Castoriadis properly interprets the situation when he argues that the market is "the central social imaginary of our times, which shapes the regime, its orientation, values, what it is worth living and dying for, the thrust of society, even its affects, and the individuals."[19]

The critical point here is that the market imaginary not only decisively shapes the logic of the economy but also trickles down into every feature of life.[20] This phenomenon is often characterized as the marketization of life and involves the

[16] Ibid., 183.

[17] See Cornelius Castoriadis, *The Imaginary Institution of Society*, trans. Kathleen Blamey (Cambridge: Polity Press, 1987), 358; Ivan Petrella, *The Future of Liberation Theology* (Burlington, VT: Ashgate, 2004); Manfred Steger, *The Rise of the Global Imaginary: Political Ideologies from the French Revolution to the Global War on Terror* (New York: Oxford University Press, 2008).

[18] Taylor, *Modern Social Imaginaries*, 2.

[19] Cornelius Castoriadis, *Figures of the Unthinkable*, trans. Helen Arnold (Stanford, CA: Stanford University Press, 2007), 137.

[20] See Hunter, *To Change the World*, 264.

transition from a market economy to a market culture. In theological terms, the market has eclipsed God as the ultimate reality around which cultural life is organized. In this sense the problem is not with the market itself insofar as the market possesses the capacity to generate goods and services that can be productive when its activity is guided toward responsible and humane ends. Rather, the issue is with the way in which the market dominates every sphere of life, overtakes all other values, and marginalizes alternative ways of organizing society.

Because the market imaginary generates technological and consumerist visions of the world that contribute to the degradation of the environment and perpetuate cycles of extreme poverty, it is important to understand the dynamics of resistance to these dimensions of the cultural imaginary. In the remainder of this section I will examine the threefold process by which the cultural imaginary can be resisted: (1) discursive and imaginative resistance to the present order (hermeneutics of suspicion); (2) the creative or utopic use of the imagination in order to picture alternatives to the present order (hermeneutics of retrieval); (3) the embodiment of what is imagined through practices that create spaces for Christians to witness to the sacramental-prophetic commitments of the Christian tradition (hermeneutics of praxis).

First it is necessary to name and unmask distorted cultural values as not only contingent and unnecessary but inconsistent with the basic values of the Christian tradition. Discursive resistance takes form in terms of the application of a hermeneutics of suspicion to the configuration of the present social, political, and economic order. This means that we must unthink the inevitability of the way things are now. Paul Ricoeur views this as the critical dimension of the imagination in its utopian form: "utopia is the mode in which we radically rethink the nature of family, consumption, government, religion, and so on. From 'nowhere' emerges the most formidable challenge to what is."[21] Ricoeur writes that utopia "performs the function of social subversion," so that its primary task is "the preservation of *opposition*" to the present social order.[22] Religion is one of the primary sites of this opposition to the cultural imaginary insofar as it is grounded in a utopian critique of what is (e.g., by imagining the reign of God).

This critical subversion of the social order is linked inextricably to the creative use of the imagination to describe an alternative to this order.[23] If imaginative

[21] Paul Ricoeur, *From Text to Action*, trans. Kathleen Blamey and John B. Thompson (Evanston, IL: Northwestern University Press, 1991), 184.

[22] Ibid., and Paul Ricoeur, *Ideology and Utopia*, ed. George H. Taylor (New York: Columbia University Press, 1986), 180. Emphasis in original.

[23] See Gustavo Gutiérrez, *A Theology of Liberation: History, Politics, and Salvation*, trans. Caridad Inda and John Eagleston (Maryknoll, NY: Orbis Books, 1988), 136.

resistance unmasks the contingency and distorted character of the cultural imaginary, it is the creative use of the imagination that opens the possibility of a new relation to the world. This future-oriented dimension of the imagination is described variously as the creative imagination (Elisabeth Schüssler Fiorenza, Gustavo Gutiérrez), the radical imagination (Castoriadis), the poetic imagination (Graham Ward, Rebecca Chopp, Kathryn Tanner), and the utopian imagination (Ricoeur, Gutiérrez).[24] Elisabeth Schüssler Fiorenza observes that this use of the imagination

> seeks to generate utopian visions that have not yet been realized, to "dream" a different world of justice and well-being. The space of the imagination is that of freedom, a space in which boundaries are crossed, possibilities are explored, and time becomes relativized. What we cannot imagine will not take place. The imagination is a space of memory and possibility where situations can be re-experienced and desires re-embodied.[25]

For Schüssler Fiorenza the creative capacity of the imagination to describe an alternative to the present is linked to the remembrance of subversive memories from the past.[26] She argues specifically that it is necessary for communities to retrieve liberating fragments from the past "in order to articulate creative visions and transcending imaginations for a new humanity, global ecology, and religious community."[27] In this sense the project of remembrance serves not only to relativize the present but also to reimagine the future.[28]

---

[24] See Elisabeth Schüssler Fiorenza, *Rhetoric and Ethics: The Politics of Biblical Studies* (Minneapolis: Fortress Press, 1999); Gutiérrez, *Theology of Liberation*; Castoriadis, *The Imaginary Institution of Society*, 145–47, and idem, "Radical Imagination and the Social Instituting Imaginary," 136–54 in *Rethinking Imagination: Culture and Creativity*, ed. Gillian Robinson and John Rundell (New York: Routledge, 1994); Graham Ward, *Cultural Transformation and Religious Practice* (New York: Cambridge University Press, 2005); Rebecca Chopp, "Theology and Poetics of Testimony," 56–70 in *Converging on Culture: Theologians in Dialogue with Cultural Analysis and Criticism*, ed. Delwin Brown, Sheila Greeve Davaney, and Kathryn Tanner (New York: Oxford University Press, 2001); Kathryn Tanner, *Theories of Culture* (Minneapolis: Fortress Press, 1997).

[25] Schüssler Fiorenza, *Rhetoric and Ethics*, 53.

[26] Elisabeth Schüssler Fiorenza, *But She Said: Feminist Practices of Biblical Interpretation* (Boston: Beacon Press, 1992). On this point see also Frederic Jameson, *Archaeologies of the Future: The Desire Called Utopia and Other Science Fictions* (New York: Verso, 2005), 4–9.

[27] Elisabeth Schüssler Fiorenza, *Democratizing Biblical Studies: Toward an Emancipatory Educational Space* (Louisville: Westminster John Knox, 2009), 124.

[28] On the retrieval of subversive memories see Johann Baptist Metz, *Faith in History and Society*, trans. J. Matthew Ashley (New York: Crossroad, 2007).

Finally, these imagined alternatives must be concretely embodied in the world. In his reflections on the significance of the imagination for Latin American liberation theology, Gustavo Gutiérrez examines the twofold process described above in terms of denunciation (hermeneutics of suspicion) and annunciation (hermeneutics of retrieval). He observes that "denunciation and annunciation can be achieved only *in* praxis. This is what we mean when we talk about a utopia which is the driving force of history and subversive of the existing order. If utopia does not lead to action in the present, it is an evasion of reality."[29] Indeed, for Gutiérrez, when the utopic imagination fails to find some form of embodiment in history its denunciation devolves into pessimistic forms of resentment and becomes little more than fanciful projection.

The second chapter will focus on the practices or spiritual exercises that concretize these imagined alternatives to the present. In the context of this chapter the central task of the Christian imagination is to retrieve subversive memories from the past in order to contest the ideologically sanctioned forgetfulness of alternatives to the present. This act of remembrance has been performed in a variety of ways in contemporary theology, from the retrieval of the sacramental imagination of patristic and medieval theology in *nouvelle théologie* to the retrieval of the prophetic dimensions of the Christian tradition in political, liberationist, and feminist theologies.[30] In the next two sections I will set forth a

---

[29] Gutiérrez, *A Theology of Liberation*, 136. Emphasis in original. The construction of alternatives has often been focused on the reformation of the church or the emergence of a new charism in the church: Latin American base communities (Daniel Bell Jr. and William Cavanaugh), the radically democratic ethos of the early *ekklēsia* (Schüssler Fiorenza), the beloved community/black church (Martin Luther King Jr.), Catholic Worker houses of hospitality (Dorothy Day). But it can also take form in the practice of the "institutional imagination" described by Roberto Unger in a variety of texts (e.g., *False Necessity: Anti-Necessitarian Social Theory in the Service of Radical Democracy* [New York: Cambridge University Press, 1987]) and elaborated in a theological context by Ivan Petrella in *The Future of Liberation Theology: An Argument and Manifesto* (Burlington, VT: Ashgate, 2004).

[30] These are only two important trajectories in contemporary theology that have made the use of the imagination as central to theological method. More broadly, see David Tracy, *The Analogical Imagination: Christian Theology and the Culture of Pluralism* (New York: Crossroad, 1981); Mary Catherine Hilkert, *Naming Grace: Preaching and the Sacramental Imagination* (New York: Continuum, 2008); William T. Cavanaugh, *Torture and Eucharist: Theology, Politics, and the Body of Christ* (Malden, MA: Blackwell, 1998); idem, *Theopolitical Imagination: Discovering the Liturgy as a Political Act in an Age of Global Consumerism* (London and New York: T & T Clark, 2002); Willie James Jennings, *The Christian Imagination: Theology and the Origins of Race* (New Haven: Yale University Press, 2010); Kwok Pui-lan, *Postcolonial Imagination and Feminist Theology* (Louisville: Westminster John Knox, 2005).

broad description of the sacramental and prophetic imaginations as elements of a Christian vision capable of producing forms of resistance to the contemporary cultural imaginary.

The Sacramental Imagination

The sacramental imagination views creation as a manifestation of the glory of God. While the term "sacrament" is often understood exclusively in terms of the seven sacraments of the church, a narrow focus on specific ecclesial sacraments obscures the broader significance of the role of the sacramental imagination in the Christian life. The sacramental imagination is grounded in a distinctive approach to the relationship between God and creation. This relationship is described in classical terms as the analogy of being (*analogia entis*), which affirms that God is both other than creation (concealed) and simultaneously present in all of creation (revealed).[31] To put it otherwise, the analogy of being sustains the paradox that while God is transcendent to creation, God is also found in the immanence of creation.[32] The affirmation made by Christians that God became incarnate in the person of Jesus Christ constitutes the definitive expression of the analogy of being. Hans Urs von Balthasar has described Jesus Christ as the "concrete analogy of being" through which the glory of God became manifest in the materiality of creation.[33]

This understanding of the relationship between God and creation sustains a vision of creation in which all of reality manifests the grace of God. In contrast to an episodic approach to grace in which God intervenes from time to time in an otherwise profane or graceless world, the sacramental imagination affirms the omnipresence of God's grace in the world.[34] Indeed, for Michael Himes, becoming aware of God's grace in the world is synonymous with an experience of the sacramentality of creation:

> we call the occasions when grace is made effectively present for us *sacra-ments* . . . by sacrament I mean any person, place, thing, or event, any sight, sound, taste, touch, or smell, that causes us to notice the love which

[31] Tracy, *The Analogical Imagination*, 405–21.

[32] Kevin Irwin, "Sacramentality and the Theology of Creation: A Recovered Paradigm for Sacramental Theology," *Louvain Studies* 23 (1998): 159–79, and idem, "The Sacramental World: The Primary Language for the Sacraments," *Worship* 76 (May 2002): 197–211.

[33] Hans Urs von Balthasar, *A Theology of History* (San Francisco: Ignatius Press, 1994), 69–70. See also, Tracy, *The Analogical Imagination*, 413.

[34] Karl Rahner, *The Practice of Faith: A Handbook of Contemporary Spirituality* (New York: Crossroad, 1983), 84.

supports all that exists, that undergirds your being and mine and the being of everything about us. How many such sacraments are there? The number is virtually infinite, as many as there are things in the universe. There is nothing that cannot be a sacrament, absolutely nothing.[35]

The sacraments of the church are concrete communal celebrations of the presence of God in all of creation. In this sense ecclesial sacraments serve to train individuals in a sacramental vision of reality at the level of embodiment and imagination that, in turn, permits them to perceive the sacramentality of creation beyond the confines of the church.[36] The Eucharist, in particular, constitutes the central sacrament of the Christian tradition in which God's grace becomes both visible and tangible to the Christian community.[37]

This point will be treated in much greater detail in the fourth chapter, but it should be noted here that theological aesthetics is rooted in this affirmation of the sacramentality of creation as well. Broadly stated, theological aesthetics emphasizes that perception (*aisthesis*) of God is possible in and through the five senses. Catholic theological aesthetics is grounded in an aesthetic interpretation of the analogy of being, so that there exists an aesthetic analogy between the beauty of creation and the glory of God. Von Balthasar, in particular, has emphasized the centrality of form and beauty, against the denigration of the visual and the aesthetic in Catholic neo-scholasticism and modern Protestant theology.[38] This emphasis on form and the beautiful lends itself naturally to the use of the arts as a form of theological expression. And the history of Christianity points to the fact that many of the most important works of "theology" have not been produced by theologians, but rather have been created or performed by painters (Michelangelo and Caravaggio), musicians (Mozart and Vivaldi), poets (Dante and Gerard Manley Hopkins), and prose writers (Flannery O'Connor and Graham Greene).

---

[35] Michael Himes, "'Finding God in All Things': A Sacramental Worldview and its Effects," 91–105, in *As Leaven in the World: Catholic Perspectives on Faith, Vocation, and the Intellectual Life*, ed. Thomas Landy (Franklin, WI: Sheed and Ward, 2001), at 99. Emphasis in original. This view is also expressed by Orthodox theologian Alexander Schmemann in *The Eucharist: Sacrament of the Kingdom* (Crestwood, NY: St. Vladmir's Seminary Press, 1988), 61.

[36] See Karl Rahner, "Personal and Sacramental Piety," *Theological Investigations,* vol. 2, *Man in the Church,* trans. Karl-Heinz Krüger (Baltimore: Helicon Press, 1963), 109–33.

[37] Anthony Godzieba, "The Catholic Sacramental Imagination and the Access/Excess of Grace," *New Theology Review* 21/3 (August 2008): 14–26.

[38] See Hans Urs von Balthasar, *The Glory of the Lord: A Theological Aesthetics*, vol. 1, *Seeing the Form*, trans. Erasmo Leva-Merikakis (San Francisco: Ignatius Press, 1982).

The sacramental imagination supports a spirituality that is aesthetic and doxological in its structure. Indeed, the proper disposition toward the gift of God's presence in the sacraments, icons and the arts, and the entirety of creation is one of gratitude, praise, wonder, and thanksgiving. The argument that follows in subsequent chapters is that the aesthetic and sacramental orientation of the Christian tradition (chap. 4) is an important corrective to the vision of the world dominant in contemporary culture, in which creation has been reduced to a mere commodity for human use (chap. 3). The task of these chapters on environmental degradation and sacramental vision is to examine the way in which a retrieval of the sacramental spirituality of finding God in all things—specifically in the beauty of creation—serves as an alternative to the market reduction of the world to a commodity for industrial use.

The Prophetic Imagination

While the sacramental imagination is rooted in the experience of wonder, gratitude, and thanksgiving before God's presence in creation, the prophetic imagination emerges out of a different experience of the world. In *The Prophets*, Abraham Joshua Heschel suggests that for the prophets "history is a nightmare."[39] The starting point of prophetic discourse is not, therefore, the contemplation of the splendor of beauty in creation. Instead, it is rooted in the encounter with the burning flesh and tortured bodies of victims of oppression. From the perspective of the prophetic imagination the world is described as a catastrophe (Walter Benjamin), a disaster (Heschel), or a crucified people (Ignacio Ellacuría).[40] While the prophet is consumed by the catastrophic, the broader culture is characterized by indifference and apathy toward the suffering of the innocent. Heschel argues that cultural perception is dominated by a "conventional seeing" in which "our eyes are witness to the callousness and cruelty of man, but our heart tries to obliterate the memories, to calm the nerves, and to silence our conscience."[41] A prophetic vision entails a definitive rupture with this mode of seeing and supports what Heschel terms a "genuine perception, seeing anew."[42] He argues that this vision of reality is rooted in an extreme pathos for the suffering of the

---

[39] Abraham Joshua Heschel, *The Prophets* (New York: Harper & Row, 1969), 231.

[40] Walter Benjamin, "Theses on the Philosophy of History," 253–64 in idem, *Illumina-tions* (New York: Schocken Books, 2007); Heschel, *Prophets*; Ignacio Ellacuría, "The Crucified People," 580–603 in *Mysterium Liberationis: Fundamental Concepts of Liberation Theology*, ed. Ignacio Ellacuría and Jon Sobrino (Maryknoll, NY: Orbis Books, 1993).

[41] Heschel, *Prophets*, 5.

[42] Ibid., xvi.

innocent. The prophet expresses this concern for the poor and the oppressed in a manner that is perceived by the broader culture as hyperbolic. Heschel observes: "to us a single act of injustice—cheating in business, exploitation of the poor—is slight; to the prophets, a disaster. To us injustice is injurious to the welfare of the people; to the prophets it is a deathblow to existence: to us an episode; to them, a catastrophe, a threat to the world."[43]

In *The Prophetic Imagination*, Walter Brueggemann extends the basic orientation of Heschel's description of the prophetic imagination, describing it as a tension between two modes of perception: the dominant and the prophetic. Brueggemann suggests that from the perspective of the prophetic imagination the mode of perception dominant in contemporary culture is distorted: "our consciousness has been claimed by false fields of perception and idolatrous systems of language and rhetoric."[44] In a way similar to Taylor's analysis of the conserving character of the social imaginary, Brueggemann argues that the way things are "has been imagined for so long and with such certitude that we come to regard it as a substantive given. It is in fact a consensus of signs, symbols, and gestures that we take as a given."[45] In response to this cultural situation, Brueggemann maintains that the most basic task of the prophetic imagination is to configure alternatives to this taken-for-granted view of things and to contest the way existence is imagined by dominant culture. The prophetic imagination seizes on the insight that social change begins with the recognition that there is an alternative to the present: "human transformative activity depends upon a transformed imagination . . . what the prophetic tradition knows is that it could be different, and the difference can be enacted."[46] For Brueggemann this "act of immense imagination" subverts all settled social, economic, and political arrangements and involves a critical confrontation with the idols that dominate the culture.[47]

Gustavo Gutiérrez and Jon Sobrino have applied the prophetic criticism of idols to the economic and political situation in Latin America. Gutiérrez and Sobrino argue that the fundamental challenge in the present is not the modern

---

[43] Ibid., 4.

[44] Walter Brueggemann, *The Prophetic Imagination* (Minneapolis: Fortress Press, 2001), 1.

[45] Walter Brueggemann, *Disruptive Grace: Reflections on God, Scripture, and the Church* (Minneapolis: Fortress Press, 2011), 301.

[46] Brueggemann, *The Prophetic Imagination*, xx–xxi.

[47] Brueggemann, *Disruptive Grace*, 297. On the relationship between utopianism and prophecy see also Ignacio Ellacuría, "Utopia and Prophecy in Latin America," 290–328 in *Mysterium Liberationis*, and Jon Sobrino, *No Salvation Outside the Poor: Prophetic-Utopian Essays* (Maryknoll, NY: Orbis Books, 2008).

preoccupation with the issue of faith and atheism. Instead, it is the biblical issue of the relationship between faith and idolatry.[48] The central question is not whether we devote our lives to a god, because we all invest our lives and give our time and attention to something we take to be ultimate. Instead, the critical question is which god we serve. Sobrino observes: "it is clear that the true God is at war with other gods. These are the idols, the false divinities—though they are real enough."[49] For Sobrino, idols represent those historical realities that take the place of God in a culture and "display the characteristics of divinity: ultimacy, self-justification, untouchability. They offer salvation to those who adore them . . . their most salient characteristic is that, like the god Moloch of mythology, they demand human victims to survive."[50] Thus for Sobrino the implication of this view of idolatry is "that to believe in God means to cease having faith in idols and to struggle against them."[51] Because the criticism of idols serves to unmask those contemporary realities that both justify and perpetuate the suffering of the innocent, the prophetic imagination supports a spirituality of interruption that dismantles ideologies that silence the cries of the victims.[52]

If we place the orientation of the sacramental imagination alongside that of the prophetic imagination, a number of important differences emerge. For instance, where the sacramental imagination perceives the glory of God in the beauty of creation and the incarnation, the prophetic imagination perceives the hiddenness of God on the cross and in the midst of the suffering of the innocent.[53] From the perspective of the sacramental imagination the proper response to the gift of creation is a disposition of gratitude, praise, wonder, and

---

[48] Gustavo Gutiérrez, *The God of Life*, trans. Matthew J. O'Connell (Maryknoll, NY: Orbis Books, 1991), 48.

[49] Jon Sobrino, *The Principle of Mercy: Taking the Crucified Down from the Cross* (Maryknoll, NY: Orbis Books, 1994), 9.

[50] Jon Sobrino, "Ignacio Ellacuría, the Human Being and the Christian: 'Taking the Crucified People Down from the Cross,'" 1–67 in *Love That Produces Hope: The Thought of Ignacio Ellacuría*, ed. Kevin Burke and Robert Lasalle-Klein (Collegeville, MN: Liturgical Press, 2006), at 55.

[51] Sobrino, *The Principle of Mercy*, 9.

[52] In one of his aphorisms Metz observed: "the shortest definition of religion: interruption." Metz, *Faith in History and Society*, 158. For an elaboration of Christianity as a religion of interruption see Lieven Boeve, *God Interrupts History: Theology in a Time of Upheaval* (New York: Continuum, 2007).

[53] David Tracy suggests that the hidden God is revealed in "cross and negativity, above all in the suffering of all those others whom the grand narrative of modernity has too often set aside as non-peoples, non-events, non-memories, in a word, non-history." David Tracy, "The Hidden God: The Divine Other of Liberation," *Cross Currents* 46 (Spring 1996): 5–16.

thanksgiving. By way of contrast, the prophetic imagination supports spiritualities that respond to the reality of oppression and innocent suffering with mourning, lamentation, protest, and resistance. Finally, where the sacramental imagination finds a potent expression of God's presence in icons, the prophetic imagination sets itself the task of dismantling all idols that serve to justify the suffering of the innocent.

In subsequent chapters I will argue (chap. 6) that the prophetic orientation of the Christian tradition represents an important corrective to the consumeristic vision of the world in which poverty and suffering are placed at a faceless distance (chap. 5). In the chapters on consumerism and prophetic vision it is argued that a retrieval of the prophetic roots of the Christian tradition is central to the task of contesting contemporary forms of life devoted exclusively to economic principles of exchange and the aesthetic pleasures of consumption.

Conclusion

This chapter has examined the centrality of the imagination to both the process of cultural formation and resistance to this formation. We noted the dominant character of the technological and consumerist dimensions of the cultural imaginary and explored the manner in which these elements stand in tension with the sacramental and prophetic imaginations of the Christian tradition. Although the sacramental and prophetic imaginations appear to be in tension with one another in terms of their respective emphases, these two forms of imagination do share the common commitment to a spirituality that is honest with reality—a reality that discloses itself as both beautiful and catastrophic, as graced and unreconciled, as sacramental and prophetic. Thus, while these two forms of imagination diverge in the ways they name reality, from a Christian perspective the sacramental and prophetic imaginations are held together because both are grounded in a commitment to seeing the real.

See also idem, "The Post-Modern Naming of God as Incomprehensible and Hidden," *Cross Currents* 50 (Spring/Summer 2000): 240–47.

Chapter 2

Asceticism and Spiritual Exercises

Introduction

The previous chapter examined the role played by the cultural imaginary in shaping the way individuals imagine existence and perceive the world. In response to the distorted character of contemporary market imaginary, I described the role of imaginative resistance in social change by focusing on the significance of the sacramental and prophetic commitments of the Christian tradition. In this chapter I will look at the formation that takes place in terms of the embodied habits of a culture, or what Pierre Bourdieu describes as *habitus*. While the use of the imagination is essential to resisting the social order, this chapter will argue that ascetical or spiritual exercises concretize imaginative resistance to the engrained habits of a culture at the level of embodiment and desire.

In the first section of this chapter I will examine Michel Foucault's work on the disciplinary character of cultural formation. Next, I will turn to a Christian approach to asceticism and analyze the capacity of ascetical practices to train individuals in distinctively Christian forms of life. The third section of the chapter looks at a set of contemporary spiritual exercises as forms of resistance to the discipline of contemporary culture: liturgical worship, the memory of past suffering (*memoria passionis*), embodied encounter, and contemplative prayer. Finally, in conclusion, I will discuss the manner in which spiritual exercises constitute a practice of micropolitics capable of contributing to the concrete work of social transformation.

Discipline and *Askesis*

In recent continental philosophy (Emmanuel Lévinas and Maurice Merleau-Ponty), cultural anthropology (Mary Douglas and Catherine Bell), feminist theory (Julia Kristeva and Judith Butler), and religious and theological studies there has been a widespread turn to the significance of the body as a locus of a meaning that is irreducible to the theoretical.[1] Representative of this turn toward embodiment is the work of Pierre Bourdieu on *habitus*. For Bourdieu *habitus* constitutes a network of embodied dispositions and ways of perceiving the world that are sustained by a set of social practices and rituals. It is through these practices and rituals that the "whole social order imposes itself at the deepest level of the bodily dispositions."[2] Bourdieu argues that *habitus* is written onto the body through mundane, everyday activities. The significance of these everyday activities is that they serve as an "implicit pedagogy" that trains the body in a mode of perception through postures, gestures, and rituals.[3] It is through this process that social convention becomes "internalized as a second nature."[4] Thus the simple acts of walking and talking instill a "whole cosmology, an ethic, a metaphysic, a political philosophy, through injunctions as insignificant as 'stand up straight' or 'don't hold your knife in your left hand.'"[5]

In this sense *habitus* represents an embodied analogue to the cultural imaginary discussed in the first chapter.[6] Indeed, for Bourdieu *habitus* "is political mythology realized, *em-bodied*, turned into a permanent disposition, a durable way of standing, speaking, walking, and thereby feeling and thinking."[7] As will

---

[1] On the turn to the body in religious studies see Miguel Vasquez, *More than Belief: A Materialist Theory of Religion* (New York: Oxford University Press, 2011).

[2] Pierre Bourdieu, *Pascalian Meditations*, trans. Richard Nice (Stanford, CA: Stanford University Press, 2000), 152. See the discussion of body pedagogics in Philip Mellor and Chris Shilling, "Body Pedagogics and the Religious *Habitus*: A New Direction for the Sociological Study of Religion," *Religion* 40 (2010): 27–38.

[3] For an extensive analysis of the significance of Bourdieu for Christian theology and spirituality see James K. A. Smith, *Imagining the Kingdom* (Grand Rapids: Baker Academic, 2013), 75–100.

[4] Pierre Bourdieu, *The Logic of Practice*, trans. Richard Nice (Stanford, CA: Stanford University Press, 1990), 56. See also idem, *In Other Words: Toward a Reflexive Sociology* (Stanford, CA: Stanford University Press, 1990), 63.

[5] Pierre Bourdieu, *Outline of a Theory of Practice*, trans. Richard Nice (New York: Cambridge University Press, 1977), 94.

[6] In a certain sense the analyses of Bourdieu (and Foucault) represent the embodied analogue to Charles Taylor's description of the social imaginary insofar as these thinkers specifically focus on how the body constitutes the site of cultural inscription, whereas Taylor's emphasis is on images, narratives, and stories. There is, of course, overlap between their approaches insofar as Foucault is very much concerned with discursive formation and Taylor does point to the significance of the body. See Charles Taylor, "Two Theories of Modernity," *Public Culture* 11/1 (1999): 153–74, at 167–68.

[7] Bourdieu, *The Logic of Practice*, 69–70. Emphasis in original.

be evident in our discussion of Christian asceticism, Talal Asad and others insist on the same point Bourdieu makes in his analyses of *habitus*, but they do so in relation to the rituals, routines, and practices of Christian spirituality. However, where Bourdieu tends to view the body as a passive site at which society imposes its norms, Asad (following Marcel Mauss) argues that the self is capable of generating new dispositions, affects, and modes of perception through the adoption of embodied practices. This, of course, is a central point in relation to the work of resisting broader cultural formation by producing distinctively Christian selves.

Although Bourdieu's analysis represents an important contribution to the description of the role of embodied practices in the process of shaping and forming subjects, I will focus in this section on Foucault's analysis of disciplinary formation. There are important similarities between Bourdieu on *habitus* and Foucault on power, insofar as both thinkers describe the way society habituates individuals into very specific forms of life through stigma and praise (Bourdieu) or discipline and punishment (Foucault).[8] For our purposes, however, Foucault's analysis is more significant because of his retrieval of ancient *askesis* as the means by which individuals resist cultural discipline.

Like Bourdieu, Foucault examines the significance of both discursive and embodied forms of socialization with a specific focus on the way individuals are disciplined into forms of life by institutions and structures of power in society. Foucault's use of the term "power" denotes the way in which realities external to the individual (institutions, governments, culture, etc.) shape and guide the individual's activity and delimit her or his "field of action."[9] Importantly, for Foucault the body is the primary site at which power is exercised on individuals. He observes: "it is always the body that is at issue—the body and its forces, their utility and their docility, their distribution and their submission."[10] While Foucault is concerned with the role that ideology plays in discipline, he insists that the fundamental way power is exerted on individuals is through their bodies.[11]

---

[8] For a broader comparison of Foucault and Bourdieu see David Couzens Hoy, "Critical Resistance: Foucault and Bourdieu," 3–22 in *Perspectives on Embodiment: The Intersections of Nature and Culture*, ed. Gail Weiss and Honi Fern Haber (New York: Routledge, 1999).

[9] Michel Foucault, "Afterword: The Subject and Power," 208–26 in *Michel Foucault: Beyond Structuralism and Hermeneutics*, ed. Hubert Dreyfus and Paul Rabinow (Chicago: University of Chicago Press, 1982), at 220.

[10] Michel Foucault, *Discipline and Punish: The Birth of the Prison*, trans. Alan Sheridan (New York: Vintage Books, 1995), 25.

[11] Thus, in relation to what we described as the market imaginary in the first chapter, Foucault claims: "one must set aside the widely held thesis that power, in our bourgeois, capitalist societies, has denied the reality of the body in favor of the soul, consciousness,

In *Discipline and Punish* Foucault illustrates these claims by describing the transition in the early nineteenth century from punishment as a public spectacle of torture and execution to a focus on incarceration as a means of disciplining criminality. This transition represents the birth of the prison and the emergence of new techniques of discipline as a means of social control. Foucault famously made use of Jeremy Bentham's description of the panopticon as a metaphor for the practices by which bodies are made "docile" and individuals are disciplined into certain forms of life. The panopticon was a model for a prison in which cells were arranged around a central tower that enabled the security personnel in the tower to observe the activities of individuals in the cells without the prisoners being aware of this surveillance. Foucault observes:

> We know the principle, at the periphery, an annular building; at the center, a tower; this tower is perceived with wide windows that open onto the inner side of the ring; the peripheric building is divided into cells, each of which extends the whole width of the building; they have two windows, one on the inside, corresponding to the windows of the tower; the other, on the outside, allows the light to cross the cell from one end to the tower. All that is needed, then, is to place a supervisor in a central tower and to confine in each cell a madman . . . by the effect of backlighting, one can observe from the tower, standing out precisely against the light, the small captive silhouettes in the cells of the periphery. They are like so many cages, so many small theatres, in which each actor is alone, perfectly individualized and constantly visible.[12]

The panopticon demonstrates the way in which docile bodies are produced by specific types of spatial organization. In particular, the organization of the prison in this way served to engender "a state of conscious and permanent visibility."[13] The result of the prisoner's awareness of this generalized spectre of surveillance is that the individual who is watched begins to engage in self-observation and self-discipline. The experience of uncertainty about whether one is being watched creates an environment in which the individual begins to desire to comply with the norms of the institution. Foucault observes: "discipline 'makes' individuals; it is the specific technique of a power that regards individ-

---

ideality. In fact nothing is more material, physical, corporal than the exercise of power." Michel Foucault, *Power/Knowledge: Selected Interviews and Other Writings, 1972–1977*, ed. Colin Gordon (New York: Pantheon Books, 1980), 58.

[12] Foucault, *Discipline and Punish*, 200.

[13] Ibid., 201.

uals as its objects and as instruments of its own exercise."[14] The modern prison system is a conspicuous example of the panopticon model of social control in which a particular use of power (in this case, surveillance) is used to normalize the bodies and souls of individuals.[15] Foucault observes that "in my book on the birth of the prison, I tried to show precisely how the idea of a technology of individuals, a certain type of power, was exercised over individuals in order to tame them, shape them, and guide their conduct."[16] Foucault suggests that this use of discipline as a means of producing particular types of individuals takes place in schools, hospitals, the military, and religious orders as well.[17]

In this sense Foucault's analysis of discipline constitutes a description of the way subjects are produced by the mechanisms of power in society.[18] Although the dominant sites of discipline Foucault describes in his writings—prisons, hospitals, factories, and schools—still influence society and contribute to the production of particular types of subjects in the present, they no longer retain the dominance they once possessed. Foucault points to the fact that in the present human beings are made subjects by cultural forces different from the bureaucratic discipline of the eighteenth and nineteenth centuries. In this sense Foucault argues that we should view the panopticon as a metaphor for broader processes of disciplinary formation in society: "on the whole, therefore, one can speak of the formation of a disciplinary society in this movement that stretches from the enclosed disciplines, a sort of social 'quarantine,' to an indefinitely generalizable mechanism of 'panopticism.'"[19] In particular Foucault suggests that there exists an "infinitely minute web of panoptic techniques" outside the enclosed structures of discipline (prisons, schools, hospitals, etc.) and concludes that we live "inside the panoptic machine, invested by its effects of power, which we ourselves reactivate since we are part of its mechanism."[20]

In his later writings Foucault became interested in how subjects come to participate in the "panoptic machine" through a discipline that takes place at the micro or "capillary" level. For Foucault this form of power and discipline is

---

[14] Ibid., 170.

[15] Ibid., 25–26.

[16] Quoted in James Miller, *The Passion of Michel Foucault* (New York: Simon & Schuster, 1993), 222.

[17] Foucault, *Discipline and Punish*, 135–37.

[18] Foucault observes that the central focus of his philosophy "has not been to analyze the phenomena of power, nor to elaborate the foundations of such analysis. My objective, instead, has been to create a history of the different modes by which, in our culture, human beings are made subjects." Foucault, "Afterword: The Subject and Power," 208–28, at 208.

[19] Foucault, *Discipline and Punish*, 216.

[20] Ibid., 224, 217.

self-imposed and infiltrates "our bodies, our lives, our day-to-day existence."[21] In a series of lectures delivered at the Collège de France, entitled *The Birth of Biopolitics* (1977–1978) Foucault analyzed the process by which individuals have come to consent to disciplinary formation in and through the micropractices of the modern economy.[22] In these lectures Foucault argues that the emergence of a particular set of economic discourses and practices known as neoliberalism in the 1970s served to colonize the state, reason, religion, and cultural life and submit these realities to the discipline of the economic logic of self-interest. According to Foucault the goal of neoliberalism is to create conditions in society that guarantee that competitiveness and market principles become the dominant values of both the public and the private sphere and that individuals come to view themselves primarily as products to be optimized, marketed, and sold. Foucault argues that the type of subject produced by the modern economy is *homo economicus*, for whom competition, cost-benefit analysis, and self-interest represent the very "grid of intelligibility."[23]

Because Foucault claims power is most potent when it infiltrates the body and "produces effects at the level of desire," the social production of desire represents one of the primary sites at which neoliberalism exerts its disciplinary power.[24] In this vein Zygmunt Bauman has argued that in the contemporary world a "new consumer discipline" has emerged and has been "transformed into

[21] Foucault, *Power/Knowledge*, 187.

[22] Stephen Gill, *Power and Resistance in the New World Order* (New York: Palgrave Macmillan, 2008).

[23] Michel Foucault, *The Birth of Biopolitics: Lectures at the Collège de France, 1978–1979*, trans. Graham Burchell (New York: Palgrave Macmillan, 2008). See also Wendy Brown, "American Nightmare: Neoliberalism, Neoconservatism, and De-Democratization," *Political Theory* 34 (December 2006): 690–714; eadem, "Neoliberalism and the End of Liberal Democracy," *Theory and Event* 7 (2003): 1–23; Jason Read, "A Genealogy of Homo Economicus: Neoliberalism and the Production of Subjectivity," *Foucault Studies* 6 (February 2009): 25–36; Trent H. Hamann, "Neoliberalism, Governmentality, and Ethics," *Foucault Studies* 6 (February 2009): 37–59.

[24] Foucault, *Power/Knowledge*, 59. In a different register Gilles Deleuze makes a similar argument by extending Foucault's analysis beyond the scope of disciplinary society into the realm of control society in "Postscript on the Societies of Control," 177–82, in idem, *Negotiations: 1972–1990*, trans. Martin Joughin (New York: Columbia University Press, 1995). Deleuze's basic point is that the mechanisms of control have shifted from factories, prisons, and schools to corporations, and from machines to computers and televisions. More broadly, on the relationship between Foucault, Deleuze, and Bauman see Nicholas Gane, "The Governmentalities of Neoliberalism: Panopticism, Post-Panopticism and Beyond," *The Sociological Review* 60 (November 2012): 611–34.

a self-sustained and self-perpetuating pattern of life."[25] Bauman argues that it is through this new discipline that the market accomplishes the goal of "making consumers dependent on itself." He suggests that this dependency is "guaranteed and self-perpetuating once men and women, now consumers, cannot proceed with the business of life without turning themselves to the logic of the market," so that "bit by bit, problem by problem, the consumer attitude refers the whole of life to the market; it orients every desire."[26] What at one time was achieved by the repressive powers of bureaucratic institutions is now accomplished through the allure of advertising, marketing, and the purported freedom of consumer choice. For Bauman this shift is representative of the fact that we have moved from a society of *panopticon* in which the few watch the many to a society of *synopticon* in which the many watch the few.[27] Bauman maintains that the "pan-optical drill" of schools, prisons, and hospitals has grown dull and no longer represents the dominant means of discipline.[28] Instead, a new form of discipline has emerged; it is introduced to individuals by consumer culture, through which the "many" watch the successful "few" (stars, celebrities, athletes, politicians, the affluent, etc.). As the many watch the few, their desire is both trained and directed toward the seductive appeal of the "good life" presented through the icons—or, better put, idols—of consumer culture.[29] Thus, for Bauman, the most basic mechanism of discipline in the present is not Bentham's panopticon or other bureaucratic surveillance mechanisms, but rather television with its endless stream of images that direct desire toward a consumerist vision of human flourishing. Bauman argues that "the Panopticon *forced* people into the position where they could be watched. The Synopticon needs no coercion—it *seduces* people into watching."[30]

Whether one characterizes the discipline of contemporary culture in terms of Foucault's *panopticon* or Bauman's *synopticon*, the critical point is that technologies of power exert a formative influence over individuals and serve to produce subjects driven by economic and consumer interests. In the late 1970s and early

---

[25] Zygmunt Bauman, *Memories of Class: The Pre-History and After-Life of Class* (Boston: Routledge, 1982), 140.

[26] Zygmunt Bauman, *Intimations of Postmodernity* (New York: Routledge, 1992), 98; idem, *Thinking Sociologically* (Malden, MA: Wiley-Blackwell, 2001), 204.

[27] Zygmunt Bauman, *Liquid Modernity* (Malden, MA: Polity Press, 2000), 85; idem, *Globalization: The Human Consequences* (New York: Columbia University Press, 1998), 51–54. For this point Bauman is dependent on Thomas Mathiesen's "The Viewer Society: Michel Foucault's 'Panopticon' Revisited," *Theoretical Criminology* 1 (1997): 215–34.

[28] Bauman, *Intimations of Postmodernity*, 194.

[29] Zygmunt Bauman, *Society under Siege* (Malden, MA: Polity Press, 2002), 171.

[30] Bauman, *Globalization*, 52. Emphasis in original.

1980s Foucault began to focus on the practices of resistance or technologies of the self that permit individuals to liberate themselves from the discipline of culture.[31] He described these techniques as a means of resisting the disciplinary power of the state: "the political, ethical, social, and philosophical problem of our days is not to try to liberate the individual from the state, and from the state's institutions, but to liberate us both from the state and from the type of individualization which is linked to the state. We have to promote new forms of subjectivity through the refusal of this kind of individuality which has been imposed on us for several centuries."[32] In Foucault's lexicon the state (or govern-mentality) represents the ensemble of discourses, institutions, laws, and cultural practices in a society that serves to produce particular kinds of subjects. It is in response to the diffuse and widespread character of disciplinary formation that Foucault claims that the fundamental task is to "refuse what we are" and to develop the "art of not being governed."[33]

In his work on technologies of the self Foucault specifically retrieves the *askesis* of the ancient Greeks as a set of techniques of counter-discipline that resist the discipline of culture.[34] Foucault argues that, because cultural discipline is omni-present, individuals must engage in intentional exercises of counter-formation as a means of resisting this discipline.[35] In his analysis of *askesis* Foucault drew from the historical investigations of Pierre Hadot on the ancient spiritual exercises practiced in Stoicism, Epicureanism, and Neo-Platonism. Hadot argued that in ancient philosophical schools spiritual exercises represented "voluntary, personal practices meant to bring about the transformation of the individual, a transforma-tion of the self."[36] Hadot specifically contended that for these philosophers spiritual

---

[31] Michel Foucault et al., *Technologies of the Self: A Seminar with Michel Foucault* (Amherst: University of Massachusetts Press, 1988), 18.

[32] Foucault, "Afterword: The Subject and Power," 216.

[33] Ibid., and idem, "What Is Critique?" 382–98 in *What Is Enlightenment? Eighteenth-Century Answers and Twentieth Century Questions*, ed. James Schmidt (Berkeley: University of California Press, 1996), 384.

[34] According to Foucault "for the Greeks the word does not mean 'ascetic,' but has a very broad sense denoting any kind of practical training or exercise. For example, it was commonplace to say that any kind of art or technique had to be learned by *mathesis* and *askesis*—by theoretical knowledge and practical training." Foucault, *Fearless Speech*, ed. Joseph Pearson (Cambridge: MIT Press, 2001), 143.

[35] Foucault, "On the Genealogy of Ethics," 340–72 in *The Foucault Reader*, ed. Paul Rabinow (New York: Pantheon Books, 1984), 364.

[36] Pierre Hadot, *The Present Alone is Our Happiness: Conversations with Jeannie Carlier and Arnold I. Davidson*, trans. Marc Djaballah (Stanford, CA: Stanford University Press, 2009), 87.

exercises were viewed as a therapy intended to effect a radical transformation that inaugurates a shift from an "inauthentic condition of life" to "an authentic state of life."[37] According to Hadot each school had "its own therapeutic method, all of them linked their therapeutics to a profound transformation of the individual's mode of seeing and being. The object of the spiritual exercises was to bring about this transformation."[38] Hadot argued that a variety of spiritual exercises were employed in ancient philosophy as a means of training and transforming the self: research (*zetesis*), thorough investigation (*skepsis*), reading (*anagnosis*), listening (*akroasis*), attention (*prosoche*), self-mastery (*enkrateia*).[39]

Following Hadot, Foucault argued that *askesis* is a form of training that allows individuals to engage in tactical operations on the body and the soul that transform the self.[40] For Foucault the goal of *askesis* is to establish mastery over the self in relation to broader forms of cultural discipline. He observed that *askesis* "has as its goal the establishment of a specific relation to oneself: a relationship of self-possession and self-sovereignty."[41] In his use of *askesis* as a means to obtain this self-possession Foucault places a particular emphasis on its aesthetic character. According to Foucault, *askesis* is characterized by "intentional and voluntary practices by which men not only fix rules of conduct for themselves, but seek to transform themselves, to modify themselves in their singular being, and to make of their life a work that bears certain aesthetic values and responds to certain criteria of style."[42] Foucault's use of "aesthetic" here serves to underscore the extent to which he views the development of the identity of an individual as most basically a creative act.[43] He observed: "from the idea that the self is not given to us, I think there is only one practical consequence: we have to create ourselves as a work of art."[44] Thus Foucault attempted to expand the meaning of art beyond the narrow confines of objects in a museum or a

---

[37] Pierre Hadot, *Philosophy as a Way of Life*, trans. Michael Chase (New York: Blackwell, 1995), 83.

[38] Ibid.

[39] Ibid., 84.

[40] Michel Foucault, *Technologies of the Self*, 18. See also Arnold Davidson, "Spiritual Exercises and Ancient Philosophy: An Introduction to Pierre Hadot," *Critical Inquiry* 16 (1990): 475–82.

[41] Foucault, *Fearless Speech*, 144.

[42] Michel Foucault, *The Use of Pleasure*, trans. Robert Hurley (New York: Vintage Books, 1990), 10–11.

[43] Michel Foucault, "An Aesthetics of Existence," in *Politics, Philosophy, Culture: Interviews and other Writings of Michel Foucault, 1977–1984*, trans. Alan Sheridan et al. (New York: Routledge, 1988), 49. See also Michel Foucault, *Fearless Speech*, 166.

[44] Foucault, "On the Genealogy of Ethics," 351.

gallery and, with Nietzsche, to apply it to the creation of the human person. According to Foucault, "what strikes me is the fact that in our society, art has become something which is related only to objects and not to individuals, or to life. That art is something which is specialized or which is done by experts who are artists. But couldn't everyone's life become a work of art? Why should the lamp or the house be an art object, but not our life?"[45]

Foucault drew a sharp distinction between his own Greco-Roman retrieval of *askesis* as a liberating aesthetics of existence and Christian asceticism, in which the individual is disciplined by the rules, the codes, and the power of the institutional church. He wrote: "from Antiquity to Christianity, we pass from a morality that was essentially a search for personal ethics to a morality as obedience to a system of rules."[46] Elsewhere Foucault described this distinction in terms of the difference between the aesthetic re-creation of the self (*askesis*) and the renunciation of the self (Christian asceticism): "in Christianity asceticism always refers to a certain renunciation of the self and of reality because most of the time your self is part of that reality you have to renounce in order to get access to another level of reality. This move to attain the renunciation of the self distinguishes Christian asceticism."[47] In this sense Foucault framed the difference between a technology of the self that frees the self to engage in the project of re-creating itself (Foucault's *askesis*) and a technology of domination that submits the self to the discipline of an external structure of normalization (Christian asceticism).

Although Foucault's retrieval of *askesis* has been central to the resurgent interest in asceticism in contemporary Christian theology, we can see that there are a number of important differences between his *askesis* and Christian asceticism. First, it is questionable whether care for the self and the act of renunciation of the self need to be set in opposition in the manner Foucault suggested. Within the Christian tradition the renunciation of the self or the *kenotic* emptying of the self is linked to the emergence of a transformed self.[48] The Christian tradition is concerned quite specifically with the creation of a new self, but the precondition for the production of this converted self (*metanoia*) is the stripping away of the false self.

Second, and related to this point, Foucault insisted that his own model of resistance to normalization disavows any vision of what form of life or which type of self should replace the subject that is produced by cultural discipline, because that would be to exchange one form of normalization for another.

---

[45] Ibid., 350.

[46] Foucault, "An Aesthetics of Existence," 49.

[47] Foucault, *Technologies of the Self,* 35.

[48] For an important feminist defense of *kenosis* see Sarah Coakley, *Powers and Submissions* (Malden, MA: Blackwell, 2002).

Instead, Foucault pointed to an aesthetics of existence in which each individual is called to create a new form of selfhood as a means of resisting the disciplinary power of society. From a Christian perspective Foucault's account is deficient with regard to the emergence of a transformed self insofar as the project of becoming a subject is turned over to the *jouissance* of postmodern freedom.[49] Hadot similarly argues that there is too much self in Foucault's *askesis* and that he failed to realize that both ancient and Christian spiritual exercises were concerned with a transformation of the self in relation to a transcendent reality.[50] Thus while there is much that can be drawn from Foucault's critical project of both diagnosing and contesting cultural discipline, it is necessary to adopt a critical posture toward the antidote he offers because it is *kenosis* and not the aesthetics of existence that constitutes the goal of asceticism from a Christian perspective.[51] In other words, it is openness to the mystery of God and not openness to the mystery of one's own freedom that is the ultimate *telos* of the Christian life.

Finally, because he was committed to the aesthetics of existence in which the task of each individual is to re-create herself, Foucault viewed all disciplinary formation with suspicion. The result was that Foucault did not adequately account for the possibility that disciplinary institutions can create spaces of authentic liberation. To state this in theological terms, just as there exist structures of discipline that deform desire, it is also possible that there exist disciplinary structures of grace that liberate individuals from distorted cultural formation and reorient their lives toward God.[52]

Christian Asceticism

As we have seen, Bourdieu and Foucault argue that the body is disciplined into forms of life by institutions and broader networks of power in culture. Although they name the disciplinary dimension of culture in different terms as either *habitus* (Bourdieu) or power (Foucault), they converge in their view that individuals are trained or disciplined into particular forms of life at the level of embodiment and desire. Thus, similar to what was said about the imagination in the first chapter, the question is not whether we are formed by the disciplin-

---

[49] See Hadot, *Philosophy as a Way of Life*, 211.

[50] Ibid., 207.

[51] Charles Taylor makes the same criticism philosophically in "Foucault on Freedom and Truth," 69–102 in *Foucault: A Critical Reader*, ed. David Couzens Hoy (Cambridge, MA: Blackwell, 1986).

[52] Talal Asad, *Genealogies of Religion: Discipline and Reasons of Power in Christianity and Islam* (Baltimore: Johns Hopkins University Press, 1993), 125–26.

ary power of culture; we are so formed in every conceivable way. The question, rather, is to what ends the discipline orients our lives. In contrast to Foucault's approach, which views all forms of discipline with suspicion, this way of framing the issue enables Christians to distinguish between authentic and inauthentic forms of discipline. In this section I will analyze the work of a number of contemporary theorists of Christian asceticism who have defended the centrality of discipline in Christian spirituality as a means of retraining and reorienting desire toward its proper *telos* in God. In particular, this section will focus on the necessity of working on the self at the level of embodiment and desire because, as Margaret Miles argues, "in our fascination with intellectual insight, [we] often forget that to be a Christian is to affirm an incarnational orientation to life whereby what we *do* is as important as what we *think*."[53]

In her analysis of Christian asceticism Miles describes the disciplinary power of culture as an "unconscious asceticism" and contends that resistance to this unconscious training into specific forms of life can be practiced through a conscious retrieval of Christian asceticism as a set of "dehabituating practices."[54] For Miles the task of asceticism is to locate cultural conditioning and "either to act out of this conditioning or begin to modify it."[55] She observes:

> in ascetic practice, the body, conditioned in every culture to find gratification in objects specified by the culture, becomes the ally of the religious self, a tool for breaking mechanical attraction to the objects that gratify the social self and for reorienting desire and gratification. The *same* energy that originally organized the person's pursuit of sex, power, and possessions can be removed from the socially conditioned self and relocated in the religious self.[56]

Miles insists that, contrary to popular misconceptions, the point of asceticism is not to give up objects of pleasure but rather to reorient the self toward its proper end.[57] Furthermore, while asceticism is often interpreted as being focused exclusively on the cultivation of personal holiness, Miles underscores

---

[53] Margaret Miles, *The Fullness of Life* (Philadelphia: Westminster Press, 1981), 162–63. Emphasis in original. See also Richard Valantasis, *The Making of the Self: Ancient and Modern Asceticism* (Eugene, OR: Cascade Books, 2008), 38.

[54] Miles, *Fullness of Life*, 16; eadem, *Practicing Christianity: Critical Perspective for an Embodied Spirituality* (New York: Crossroad, 1988), 94.

[55] Miles, *Fullness of Life*, 155.

[56] Miles, *Practicing Christianity*, 96. Emphasis in original. See also, Margaret Miles, *Bodies in Society: Essays on Christianity in Contemporary Culture* (Eugene, OR: Cascade Books, 2008), 7.

[57] Miles, *Practicing Christianity*, 97.

the sociopolitical significance of asceticism: "ascetic practices can dissolve the daily comforts and habits that keep human beings insulated, unfeeling, and unaware of political and social injustice."[58] Thus, far from being a privatized and apolitical activity, asceticism, according to Miles, constitutes an indispensable exercise of religious and sociopolitical formation that permits individuals to perceive the world authentically.

Similarly, Talal Asad has emphasized the significance of embodied discipline as a means of transforming the self. In line with Bourdieu and Foucault, Asad acknowledges that *habitus* inscribes on the body a particular way of being in the world (a metaphysic, an ethic, etc.), but he also insists that the human person is not merely a passive site for "cultural imprints." Thus the body is an active site for the production of particular dispositions.[59] Specifically, he argues that the practices of prayer, liturgy, and the sacraments should be interpreted not in doctrinal terms but rather as techniques of the body that engender a transformation of the self. For example, Asad contends that while the sacraments are often interpreted as symbolic or metaphorical expressions, this is not their primary significance. He suggests instead that they serve to enact a "Christian program for creating in its performers, by means of regulated practice, the 'mental and moral dispositions' appropriate to Christians."[60]

This interpretation of the sacraments is consonant with Asad's broader interpretation of religious discipline in monasticism. In "On Discipline and Humility in Medieval Christian Monasticism" Asad describes the set of practices monks adopt in order to reform their desire and conform it to the standard of Jesus Christ. In particular, the entire ensemble of daily periods of manual labor, liturgical worship, *lectio divina*, and contemplation is directed to the specific end of "forming and reforming Christian dispositions."[61] These dispositions are not universal, but instead are the products of a particular type of disciplinary formation.[62] Thus, as with Foucault's analysis of the use of discipline in the modern prison system and economy, Asad points to the disciplines of Christian spirituality as "techniques of the self" that produce virtuous desire: "monastic rites governed the economy of desire . . . the central principle on which these rites were based assumed that virtuous desire had first to be created before a

---

[58] Miles, *Bodies in Society*, 7.
[59] Talal Asad, *Genealogies of Religion*, 76.
[60] Ibid., 79.
[61] Ibid., 131.
[62] Ibid., 134.

virtuous choice could be made. It stands, therefore, in contrast to our modern assumption that choices are *sui generis* and self-justifying."[63]

Asad's analysis of the importance of discipline in the production of Christian selves is linked to the contemporary retrieval of classical Christian accounts of spirituality (John Cassian, Evagrius Ponticus, Gregory of Nyssa, Augustine of Hippo, and Bernard of Clairvaux) as a therapy of desire.[64] For example, Daniel Bell Jr. engages in a retrieval of the Cistercian monasticism of Bernard of Clairvaux as a means of reclaiming the Christian tradition "as a fully material (social, political, economic) formation that constitutes nothing less than a therapy of desire."[65] Bell finds Bernard's monastic spirituality significant because of its focus on the liberation of desire from sin through ascetic practice and the reorientation of that desire toward its proper end in God. Bell contrasts Bernard's Augustinian approach to desire with the discipline of the market and its techniques for capturing desire and directing its flow toward profit, accumulation, and consumption. In response to this situation in which the market constitutes the most pervasive form of discipline, Bell argues that Christian spirituality must be reclaimed as nothing short of an alternative way of life "that reforms or shapes desire in ways that counter the capitalist discipline of desire."[66] For Bell this means that Christianity must again become a formative *askesis* "whose practices—such as baptism, catechesis, Eucharist, discipline, prayer, and discipleship—do not merely mediate 'ideas' and 'values' but rather transform the material circumstances of Christian (and, more generally, human) existence."[67]

Broadly stated, Christian asceticism is an important vehicle through which individuals can be trained in a distinctively Christian vision of reality. As Sarah Coakley writes: "while institutions may 'discipline' us (for good or ill), we also

---

[63] Ibid., 126.

[64] For uses of Augustine's theology of desire in contemporary theology see William Cavanaugh, *Being Consumed: Economics and Christian Desire* (Grand Rapids: Eerdmans, 2008); Daniel Bell, Jr., *Economy of Desire: Christianity and Capitalism in a Postmodern World* (Grand Rapids: Baker Academic, 2012); Vincent Miller, *Consuming Religion* (New York: Continuum, 2004). On Evagrius and John Cassian in relation to Girard see Kevin Mongrain, "Theologians of Spiritual Transformation: A Proposal for Reading René Girard Through the Lenses of Hans Urs von Balthasar and John Cassian," *Modern Theology* 28 (2012): 81–111; Brian Robinette, "Deceit, Desire, and the Desert: René Girard's Mimetic Theory in Conversation with Early Monastic Practice," 130–44 in *Violence, Transformation, and the Sacred: "They Shall Be Called Children of God,"* ed. Margaret Pfeil and Tobias L. Winright (Maryknoll, NY: Orbis Books, 2012).

[65] Daniel Bell, *Liberation Theology after the End of History: The Refusal to Cease Suffering* (New York: Routledge, 2001), 86.

[66] Ibid.

[67] Ibid.

have the 'power' to discipline ourselves."[68] The ascetical practices of the Christian tradition permit individuals to begin the process through which cultural discipline can be resisted and the self can be laid bare before the discipline of God's grace. The forms these spiritual exercises take should be plural and open to innovation. For instance, commitment to regular ascetical practice could take form in terms of individual spiritual exercises or participation in an intentional community. Examples of intentional communities abound in contemporary Christian practice, from Latin American base communities and the new monasticism to Catholic Worker houses of hospitality and local parish communities. In a sense, the form is not what is vital. What is important is that Christians submit themselves to some form of counter-discipline in order to resist the distorted character of cultural discipline.

Spiritual Exercises

As noted in our discussion of Foucault, Pierre Hadot has done more than any recent scholar to reconnect philosophical and theological discourse with spiritual exercises. Hadot contends that spiritual exercises constitute an *askesis* or therapy of desire.[69] In ancient philosophy this therapy of desire represented the means through which an individual began to see the world with new eyes. Hadot observes: "to work at seeing the world as though one were seeing it for the first time is to get rid of the conventional and routine vision we have of things, to discover a brute, naïve vision of reality, to take note of the splendor of the world, which habitually escapes us."[70] In a point that is particularly significant for our purposes, Hadot argues that these elements of ancient *askesis* became central to the ascetical literature of the Christian tradition, observing: "ancient spiritual exercises were preserved and transmitted by an entire current of ancient Christian thought."[71]

---

[68] Coakley, *Powers and Submissions*, xviii.

[69] On *askesis* of desire see Hadot, *Philosophy as a Way of Life*, 83, and idem, *What is Ancient Philosophy* (Cambridge, MA: Belknap Press, 2002), 117. This emphasis on the transformation of desire in ancient philosophy is present in Martha Nussbaum's *Therapy of Desire*. Nussbaum argues that the aim of the philosophical life is to deliver the self from "the tyranny of custom and social convention, creating a community of beings who can take charge of their own life story and their thought." Martha Nussbaum, *The Therapy of Desire: Theory and Practice in Hellenistic Ethics* (Princeton, NJ: Princeton University Press, 1994), 5.

[70] Hadot, *The Present Alone is Our Happiness*, 173.

[71] Hadot, *Philosophy as a Way of Life*, 127. In particular Hadot points to the Spiritual Exercises of Saint Ignatius as the most significant modern interpretation of the ancient spiritual exercises. Ibid., 82.

This section will broaden the discussion by examining the spiritual exercises capable of cultivating in Christians a sacramental-prophetic vision of reality. The argument is that spiritual exercises encourage a form of self-emptying attention that permits individuals to be honest with reality and to respond to what is often obstructed from vision in contemporary culture: God, creation, and the suffering of others. In this section the focus is on the way in which embodied spiritual exercises are oriented toward the *kenotic* or self-emptying transformation of the self before God. Furthermore, the presentation will focus on the way in which this transformation results in the elevation of the senses to the task of spiritual perception of the world. Sarah Coakley observes of the spiritual senses: "the basic idea is that our life is set on a course of transformation and purification. We are given a sensual life, an imaginative life, an affective life, a noetic life, and each of these features of selfhood has to pass through transformation and purification en route to the vision of God. So of course that affects the mind, the sense, and the imagination."[72] The claim made here is that it is necessary to transform the senses—particularly the sense of vision—in order to encounter the presence of God in the beauty of creation (sacramental vision) and the hiddenness of God in the suffering of the innocent (prophetic vision).

While these exercises will be examined more concretely in chapters four and six in relation to sacramental and prophetic spiritualities, in what follows I will describe liturgical worship, the remembrance of suffering (*memoria passionis*), embodied encounter, and contemplative prayer as significant spiritual exercises for the current situation. There are, of course, other traditional spiritual exercises such as fasting, voluntary poverty, and solitude that could also be of some importance, but here I will focus on four spiritual exercises that are directed toward the cultivation of a sacramental-prophetic spirituality.

(1) Liturgy has served as a central form of pedagogical formation in the history of the Christian tradition.[73] For a variety of reasons its status as a practice of Christian formation is in decline at present. The dissolution of distinctive Christian subcultures has contributed to this decline, but perhaps more critical than this has been the proliferation of cultural liturgies that employ their own

---

[72] Sarah Coakley, "Prayer as Divine Propulsion," in *The Other Journal: An Intersection of Theology and Culture* (December 20, 2012), at http://theotherjournal.com/2012/12/20/prayer-as-divine-propulsion-an-interview-with-sarah-coakley.

[73] David Fagerberg, *On Liturgical Asceticism* (Washington, DC: Catholic University of America Press, 2013), 1; Stanley Hauerwas and David Wells, "How the Church Managed Before There Was Ethics," 39–51, in *The Blackwell Companion to Christian Ethics*, ed. Stanley Hauerwas and David Wells (Malden, MA: Wiley Blackwell, 2011).

distinctive sets of rituals as a means of producing particular types of selves.[74] For instance, William Cavanaugh has described the manner in which the modern nation-state uses a variety of "secular liturgies" to discipline individuals into nationalist commitments. The United States uses patriotic symbols, rituals, and ceremonies to engender in its citizens something of a religious devotion to the nation-state—the recitation of the Pledge of Allegiance every morning in classrooms across America, the performance of the national anthem at sporting events, and the celebration of elaborate ceremonies that commemorate Independence Day on the fourth of July. For Cavanaugh it is evident that these "liturgies" are religious in character and obstruct the capacity of Christians to be formed in the distinctive ethos of the Christian church. According to Cavanaugh "there is a longing in nationalist ritual that bespeaks a desire for communion that is at the heart of Christian liturgy. Patriotic liturgies have succeeded in imagining communities because Christian liturgies have failed to do so in a fully public way."[75] Analogously, James K. A. Smith suggests that consumerism constitutes a potent pedagogy of desire that forms individuals in a way that is nothing short of liturgical. According to Smith: "the rituals and practices of the mall" serve to "shape our imaginations and how we orient ourselves in the world. Embedded in them is a common set of assumptions about the shape of human flourishing, which becomes an implicit *telos*, or goal, of our own desires and actions."[76] The argument made by Cavanaugh and Smith is not that individuals have ceased to be liturgical, but that they have directed their devotion away from the church and toward either the nation-state or the market—or both.

This description of the broader cultural situation serves to sharpen the focus on the retrieval of liturgy as a form of asceticism that resists the habituation of individuals into the cultural liturgies of the nation-state and the market. M. Therese Lysaught has argued that liturgy is intended "to train us out of the habits of our dominant culture."[77] For Lysaught the liturgy calls Christians out of the world and invites them to participate in the body of Christ as "citizens of the kingdom of God."[78] Liturgy is the practice by which God transforms the imagination and desire of individuals through the senses of sight (images and

---

[74] James K. A. Smith, *Desiring the Kingdom: Worship, Worldview, and Cultural Formation* (Grand Rapids: Baker Academic, 2009), 24.

[75] William Cavanaugh, *Migrations of the Holy: God, the State, and the Political Meaning of the Church* (Grand Rapids: Eerdmans, 2011), 122.

[76] Smith, *Desiring the Kingdom*, 24.

[77] M. Therese Lysaught, "Love and Liturgy," 24–41, in *Gathered for the Journey: Moral Theology in Catholic Perspective*, ed. David Matzko McCarthy and M. Therese Lysaught (Grand Rapids: Eerdmans, 2007), at 34.

[78] Lysaught, "Love and Liturgy," 31.

icons), touch (the sign of peace), sound (music), taste (bread and wine), and smell (incense).[79] In particular, liturgy performs a set of tactical operations on the human body as a means of transforming the senses and opening them to spiritual perception. Lysaught focuses on the way bodily training engenders a transformed vision of reality because she argues, as with Murdoch and Hauerwas, that it is "by learning to see the world in a new way we are trained to act in a new way."[80] Lysaught argues that when Christians enter the space of the church and worship God they "begin to see the world, see 'reality,' in a new way. We begin to see that we live in a world not of scarce resources but of abundant gifts. We begin to see that justice means not strictly 'to each person her due' but rather a 'preferential option for the poor.'"[81]

This approach to liturgy as a means of training Christians in an authentic vision of reality is an instructive hermeneutic for understanding the significance of liturgical practice and each individual sacrament. For instance, Paul Wadell writes that the Eucharist is itself a spiritual discipline that trains Christians in a moral vision "as the ritual activity through which a people's vision is cleansed and healed. More strongly put, through worshiping together in Eucharist we should gradually take on God's view of things."[82] As will be evident in the fourth and sixth chapters, this interpretation of the Eucharist is central to the cultivation of both a sacramental and prophetic vision of reality, but even more basically this interpretation points to the fact that liturgical worship and the reception of the sacraments represent a type of spiritual formation or *askesis* that serves to reeducate desire and transform the senses.[83]

(2) The Eucharist has been an area of emphasis not only for those who focus on liturgical *askesis* but also for theologians who have considered *memoria passionis* as a contemporary spiritual exercise. Johann Baptist Metz has argued that the eucharistic ritual memorializes the history of suffering by remembering the

---

[79] M. Therese Lysaught, "Witnessing Christ in Their Bodies: Martyrs and Ascetics as Doxological Disciples," *Annual of the Society of Christian Ethics* 20 (2000): 239–62, at 257.

[80] Lysaught, "Love and Liturgy," 33.

[81] Ibid., 32.

[82] Paul Wadell, "What Do All Those Masses Do For Us? Reflections on the Christian Moral Life and the Eucharist," 153–69, in *Living No Longer for Ourselves: Liturgy and Justice in the Nineties*, ed. Kathleen Hughes and Mark R. Francis (Collegeville, MN: Liturgical Press, 1991), at 163.

[83] See Sarah Coakley, "Beyond 'Belief': Liturgy and the Cognitive Apprehension of God," 131–45, in *The Vocation of Theology Today: A Festschrift for David Ford*, ed. Tom Greggs, Simeon Zahl, and Rachel Muers (Eugene, OR: Wipf and Stock, 2013). On liturgical asceticism see Fagerberg, *On Liturgical Asceticism*.

suffering of Jesus of Nazareth on the cross.[84] Indeed, Jesus says to his disciples: "this is my body, which is given for you. Do this in memory of me" (Luke 22:19). For Metz this remembrance of Jesus' crucifixion represents the primordial example of a dangerous memory of suffering in the Christian tradition. Dangerous memories are fragments from the past that are subversive to the present order and disrupt any sense of complacency and apathy before the suffering of others. Metz describes the significance of dangerous memories in this way:

> there is another way to remember: dangerous memories, memories that challenge. These are memories in which earlier experiences flare up and unleash new dangerous insights for the present. For brief moments they illuminate, harshly and piercingly, the problematic character of things we made our peace with a long time ago and the banality of what we take to be "realism." They break through the canon of the ruling plausibility structures and take on a virtually subversive character. Memories of this sort are like dangerous and uncalculable visitations from the past. They are memories that one has to take into account, memories that have a future content, so to speak.[85]

Metz has focused his own theological reflections on the Shoah as a dangerous memory that interrupts all complacent spiritualities that proceed as if the extermination of six million Jewish people never happened. For Metz the task is to remember these victims and permit their memories to interrupt our lives and sensitize us to the way in which this type of unthinkable suffering continues unabated, day after day.

Each culture has its own history of suffering and oppression: chattel slavery in the United States, the Gulag in Soviet Russia, the Shoah in Europe, the Killing Fields in Cambodia, El Mozote in El Salvador, and on and on. The task of remembering these various histories is critical because there is an important connection between the remembrance of these histories of suffering—in liturgical worship, in song (the spirituals), and prayers of mourning and lamentation—and the cultivation of a particular way of perceiving the world in the present. Metz views *memoria passionis* as the precondition for the development of a new way of seeing the world that he describes as a mysticism of open eyes. For Metz this mysticism of open eyes "requires a willingness to change one's perspective, that change of perspective to which the biblical traditions and especially the stories about Jesus have invited humankind—namely, to see ourselves always with the eyes of others,

---

[84] On this point see Bruce T. Morrill, *Anamnesis as Dangerous Memory: Political and Liturgical Theology in Dialogue* (Collegeville, MN: Liturgical Press, 2000).

[85] Johann Baptist Metz, *Faith in History and Society*, 105.

particularly the suffering and threatened others."[86] Although there are a number of means of training Christians in this form of mysticism, Metz views *memoria passionis* as the exercise most suited to the cultivation of a prophetic, open-eyed spirituality in which God is encountered in the suffering of the other.

(3) The memory of past suffering sensitizes individuals to the violations of human dignity in the present and teaches them to look at the world from the view of the victims. In recent philosophy and theology there has been a renewed interest in the significance of embodied encounter as an important exercise of moral and spiritual formation that educates individuals in a Christian vision of reality. As with the other spiritual exercises discussed in this section, this form of encounter accents the way in which the body mediates meaning more powerfully than concepts. As the former superior general of the Jesuits, Peter-Hans Kolvenbach, has observed:

> solidarity is learned through "contact" rather than through "concepts," as the Holy Father said recently at an Italian university conference. When the heart is touched by direct experience, the mind may be challenged to change. Personal involvement with innocent suffering, with the injustice others suffer, is the catalyst for solidarity, which then gives rise to intellectual inquiry and moral reflection.[87]

Edward Schillebeeckx has described this visceral encounter with the other as a negative contrast experience that discloses the fact that the way things are is not the way they should be. For Schillebeeckx, when an individual encounters a situation of racism, sexism, poverty, or injustice the proper response is "no, it can't go on like this; we won't stand for it any longer!"[88] He observes: "these contrast-experiences show that the moral imperative is first discovered in its immediate, concrete, *inner* meaning, before it can be made the object of a science and then reduced to a generally valid principle."[89] For Kolvenbach and Schillebeeckx the embodied encounter with the other takes place at a level that

[86] Johann Baptist Metz, "Frieden im Geist der Compassion," *Süddeutsche Zeitung* 225 (28 September 2004): 17; also available in *Arbeitshilfen 187: "Lass dich nicht vom Bösen besiegen, sondern besiege das Böse durch das Gute! (Röm 12,21)—Welttag des Friedens 2005 (1. Januar 2005)* (Bonn: Sekretariat der Deutschen Bischofskonferenz, 2005).

[87] Peter-Hans Kolvenbach, "The Service of Faith and the Promotion of Justice in American Jesuit Higher Education," 144–62, in *A Jesuit Education Reader*, ed. George W. Traub (Chicago, IL: Loyola Press, 2008), at 155.

[88] Edward Schillebeeckx, *God: The Future of Man*, trans. N. D. Smith (New York: Sheed & Ward, 1968), 136.

[89] Ibid., 155.

is prior to and more basic than the articulation of a formal theory of morality that delineates the nature and scope of responsibility for others.

Along with Kolvenbach and Schillebeeckx, von Balthasar also insists on the centrality of the embodied encounter with the other and elaborates its significance in terms of the development of the spiritual senses. For him it is in and through the embodied encounter with the human other that the life of faith is affirmed at its most basic level because the image of the human person is the supreme manifestation of God in the world.[90] Von Balthasar argues that in the encounter with the other "faith compels me to see, to respect, and to anticipate in action the supremely real image which the triune God has of you."[91] This act of seeing the other from God's perspective is one way in which the spiritual senses can be developed. According to von Balthasar: "in his love for his neighbor, the Christian definitively receives his Christian senses, which of course are none 'other' than his bodily senses, but these senses in so far as they have been formed according to the form of Christ."[92] He adds, however, that it is relatively unimportant whether the form of Christ is made explicit through the encounter with the other. The critical point is that this embodied encounter with the other is a spiritual exercise by which an individual learns to perceive God's presence in the world.

In their analyses of the significance of embodiment Kolvenbach, Schille-beeckx, and von Balthasar all emphasize the prophetic dimension of the encounter with the suffering of another human being, but there has also been a focused effort recently to underscore the spiritual significance of embodied exposure to the natural world. Instead of foregrounding the negative contrast experience of the prophetic encounter, thinkers like Iris Murdoch have described the moral and spiritual significance of the positive encounter with the beauty of the natural world. For instance, she follows Plato in claiming that beauty is "perhaps the most obvious thing in our surroundings which is an occasion for 'unselfing'" because it "teaches us how real things can be looked at and loved without being seized and used."[93] Murdoch describes an example of this aesthetic unselfing in her encounter with the natural world:

> I am looking out of my window in an anxious and resentful state of mind, oblivious of my surroundings, brooding perhaps on some damage done to my prestige. Then suddenly I observe a hovering kestrel. In a moment everything is altered. The brooding self with its hurt vanity has disappeared.

[90] Hans Urs von Balthasar, *The Glory of the Lord: A Theological Aesthetics.* Vol. 1. *Seeing the Form,* trans. Erasmo Leva-Merikakis (San Francisco: Ignatius Press, 1982), 423.

[91] Ibid.

[92] Ibid., 424.

[93] Iris Murdoch, *The Sovereignty of Good* (New York: Routledge, 1970), 65.

There is nothing now but kestrel. And when I return to thinking of the other matter it seems less important.[94]

For Murdoch an encounter with the natural world yields an authentic vision of reality because contemplation of nature leads to a situation in which "selfish concerns vanish, nothing exists except the things which are seen. Beauty is that which attracts this particular sort of unselfish attention."[95]

An aesthetic experience of nature constitutes for Murdoch a spiritual exercise that opens the self to the non-instrumental value of the natural world.[96] According to her "the appreciation of beauty in art or nature is not only (for all its difficulties) the easiest available spiritual exercise; it is also a completely adequate entry into (and not just analogy of) the good life, since it is the checking of selfishness in the interest of seeing the real."[97] This feature of encounter with the natural world described by Murdoch will be the focus of the fourth chapter of this book and will be examined in relation to the writings of Henry David Thoreau, R. S. Thomas, Annie Dillard, and Wendell Berry.[98]

(4) Finally, contemplative prayer represents an important spiritual exercise capable of training individuals in a sacramental-prophetic vision of the world. Perhaps more than other spiritual exercises, contemplative prayer is often judged to be a waste of time and is marginalized as irrelevant in the face of social crises that demand urgent action. The question often raised in relation to contemplative prayer is whether an individual should spend time in silent prayer waiting for God when she could use this time more effectively to work toward social change by volunteering at a soup kitchen or petitioning government to change its environmental policies. This view is inadequate, however, because one of the most important spiritual tasks is the formation of persons capable of truthfully seeing and responding to the world.[99]

As with the other spiritual exercises, contemplative prayer is an embodied spiritual practice. The development of proper posture and attention to the body is a critical area of focus in much of the literature on contemplative prayer.[100] This focus on the body represents one of the ways in which a sense of stillness,

---

[94] Ibid., 84.

[95] Ibid., 65.

[96] Ibid., 63.

[97] Ibid., 64–65.

[98] See, e.g., Steven Chase, *Nature as Spiritual Practice* (Grand Rapids: Eerdmans, 2011).

[99] See Thomas Merton, *Contemplation in a World of Action* (Notre Dame, IN: University of Notre Dame Press, 1999), 160–61, and Coakley, *Powers and Submissions*, xvii.

[100] Kallistos Ware, "'My Helper and My Enemy': The Body in Greek Christianity," 90–110 in *Religion and the Body*, ed. Sarah Coakley (New York: Cambridge University Press, 1997).

wakefulness, and attention is cultivated. Indeed, authors as varied as Evagrius Ponticus, Gregory Palamas, St. John of the Cross, Simone Weil, and Thomas Merton suggest that one of the primary fruits of contemplative prayer is a deepened sense of awareness.[101] The early monastic tradition viewed the cultivation of attention (*prosoche*), vigilance (*nepsis*), and stillness (*hesychia*) as central to the life of contemplation.[102] The cultivation of this faculty of attention in contemplative prayer has the twofold effect of stripping the self of its attachments and creating the space for "the self's transformation and expansion into God."[103]

In the classical tradition this "expansion into God" is linked to the transformation of the senses, particularly the sense of vision. The link between contemplation and vision is more basic than the connection between vision and liturgy, *memoria passionis*, or embodied encounter because the connection is etymological. The Greek root of the Latin *contemplatio* is *theoria*. *Theoria* derives from *thea*, which means "to look at" or "to be aware of." In the Christian tradition contemplation is most basically understood as a particular type of seeing that leads to the vision of God (*visio Dei*).[104] Dorothee Soelle frames this classical description of the contemplative *visio Dei* in a mystical-prophetic idiom when she observes that mysticism is concerned not so much with "a new vision of God but a different relationship to the world—one that has borrowed the eyes of God."[105] Although Soelle does not invoke this tradition, her description of *visio Dei* is consistent with the emphasis placed on the development of the spiritual senses in the Christian tradition. Von Balthasar contends that there is an important connection between the act of renunciation endemic to contemplative prayer and God's transformation of the senses.[106] According to him, "to be a recipient of revelation means more and more the act of renunciation which gives God the space in which to become incarnate . . . only in this way is the sphere of the 'spiritual senses' given its proper place."[107] In contemplative prayer the purgative dark night involves the death of the senses, but this death

---

[101] Evagrius Ponticus, "On Prayer," in *Philokalia: The Complete Text*, vol. 1, trans. and ed. G. E. H. Palmer, Philip Sherrard, and Kallistos Ware (London: Faber and Faber, 1983), 71; Simone Weil, *Waiting for God*, trans. Emma Craufurd (New York: Perennial Classics, 2001).

[102] Douglas E. Christie, *The Blue Sapphire of the Mind: Notes for a Contemplative Ecology* (New York: Oxford University Press, 2013), 142.

[103] Coakley, *Powers and Submissions*, 36.

[104] Christie, *Blue Sapphire of the Mind*, 6.

[105] Dorothee Soelle, *The Silent Cry: Mysticism and Resistance*, trans. Barbara and Martin Rumscheidt (Minneapolis: Fortress Press, 2001), 293.

[106] See the discussion in *The Spiritual Senses: Perceiving God in Western Christianity*, ed. Paul L. Gavrilyuk and Sarah Coakley (New York: Cambridge University Press, 2011).

[107] Von Balthasar, *The Glory of the Lord*, 418.

also entails a rebirth by which the senses are transformed and raised to the task of perceiving the spiritual in the material. Von Balthasar observes: "our senses, together with images and thoughts, must die with Christ and descend to the underworld in order then to rise unto the Father in an unspeakable manner which is both sensory and suprasensory."[108]

Conclusion

While spiritual exercises have often been interpreted as private religious activities focused exclusively on the task of deepening one's relationship to God, this chapter has argued that they are more than that. Spiritual exercises also constitute an important form of resistance to broader cultural, economic, and political forces. This view is broadly consistent with the claims made by figures like Foucault and Michel de Certeau. For instance, de Certeau argues that "if it is true that the grid of 'discipline' is everywhere becoming clearer and more extensive, it is all the more urgent to discover how an entire society resists being reduced to it."[109] In his reflections on these practices of resistance de Certeau draws the distinction between strategies and tactics. Strategies represent the exercise of power by those with the institutional base and clout to effect change at a macro level. By way of contrast, tactics represent those activities of resistance undertaken by the weak and powerless in a culture; these operate at a local, micro level. De Certeau argues that tactics form a daily *bricolage* in which minute acts permit the individual to resist the control of a disciplinary society. For him tactical practices are a mode of resistance to dominant systems that creates spaces of "anti-discipline" outside the power of cultural discipline. In a sense the four spiritual exercises described above represent Christian tactics of resistance to the discipline of broader culture; through them, individuals submit themselves to the counter-discipline of the grace of God.

Influenced by Foucault, Félix Guattari, and Gilles Deleuze, a number of political theorists have made the link between these "tactics of the self" and "micropolitics" as a means of rethinking political action beyond an exclusive focus on the macropolitical institutional reform and governmental action.[110] According to Jane Bennett, the "bodily disciplines through which ethical sensibilities and social relations are formed and reformed are *themselves* political

---

[108] Ibid., 425.

[109] Michel de Certeau, *The Practice of Everyday Life*, trans. Steven Rendall (Berkeley: University of California Press, 1984), xiv.

[110] William Connolly, *Neuropolitics* (Minneapolis: University of Minnesota Press, 2002), 92, 3.

and constitute a whole (unexplored) field of 'micropolitics' without which any principle or policy risks being just a bunch of words."[111] In this regard the micropolitical is concerned to transform emotions, aesthetic judgments, perception, and dispositions as a means of changing larger political and social structures.[112] William Connolly observes: "even though micropolitics works at the level of detail, desire, feeling, perception, and sensibility, that does not mean it is 'any less coextensive with the entire social field'" than politics as it is traditionally conceived in macropolitical terms.[113] Indeed, for Connolly, "micropolitics operates below the threshold of large legislative acts and executive initiatives, even as it ranges widely and sets conditions of possibility for these more visible actions. Transforming micropolitical locations modifies what is deemed possible at the macropolitical level."[114]

While environmental degradation and global poverty are crises far too large and complex to support the view that spiritual exercises or micropolitical action alone could adequately confront them, at the same time it is important to emphasize that social transformation at the macropolitical level will not take place without a shift in personal, local, and micropolitical perception of the world. It is in this sense that Christian spirituality has the capacity to enter into the sociopolitical field as a formation of subjects at the micropolitical level.

[111] Jane Bennett, *Vibrant Matter: A Political Ecology of Things* (Durham, NC: Duke University Press, 2010), xii. Emphasis in original.

[112] Jane Bennett, *Thoreau's Nature: Ethics, Politics, and the Wild* (Thousand Oaks, CA: Sage Publications, 1994), xxii.

[113] William Connolly, *Why I Am Not a Secularist* (Minneapolis: University of Minnesota Press, 1999), 149.

[114] Connolly, *Neuropolitics*, 20, 1.

Chapter 3

The Environmental Crisis

Introduction

On April 20, 2010, a gas bubble exploded at an oil rig, named "Deepwater Horizon," in the Gulf of Mexico. It killed eleven workers and left a gaping hole in the ocean floor. Oil poured out of that hole into the Gulf of Mexico for nearly three months, until July 15, 2010. It has been estimated that over two million gallons of oil spilled into the Gulf over that three-month period. It was the worst offshore oil spill in the history of the Americas. The immediate aftermath of the spill was horrifying, with countless images of brown pelicans, gulls, and other seabirds caked in a dark sludge, unable to lift their wings, and dead turtles floating on top of brown pools of oil. Furthermore, in the years following the spill there have been widespread reports of mutations among the marine life: "shrimp with tumors on their heads; fish that lack eyes or are missing flaps over their gills; fish oozing with sores; crabs with holes in their shells; crabs that are missing claws and spikes."[1]

In short, the Gulf Oil Spill is a perfect example of what we refer to when we talk about an environmental catastrophe. While this catastrophe has forced us to confront the very real and negative effect of fossil fuels on the environment, these accidents represent only one dimension of the environmental crisis. The more worrisome feature is this: each day that the modern economy functions as planned is a day that deepens the environmental crisis. Thus even in the absence of any major accident or environmental incident, the use of fossil fuels to drive the economy leads directly to a steady increase of the amount of carbon

---

[1] "BP Oil Spill," *Yahoo News*, 19 April 2012, http://news.yahoo.com/bp-oil-spill-horribly -mutated-creatures-living-gulf-<180100880.html.

dioxide (CO_2) in the atmosphere. Bill McKibben observes that, over the period of the Gulf Oil Spill,

> if you add up all the carbon being burned in all the cars and factories and power plants, we had the equivalent of at least 5,000 Deepwater Horizons pouring carbon into the atmosphere, every minute of every day in every corner of the world. You couldn't see it—CO_2 is invisible. But that doesn't mean it's any less of an emergency.[2]

According to McKibben, "the pollution you can see, like the spill in the Gulf, is the least of our problems. . . . It's not when BP makes an outlandish mistake; it's when BP and Exxon and the rest of the fossil fuel industry carry out their daily business. It's not when things turn black; it's when they turn hot."[3] Thus environmental catastrophe (e.g., the BP oil spill) is not the exception to the rule, but the rule itself. This makes for a dangerous situation in which all we have to do to spoil the earth for future generations is to continue to live the way we live now.[4]

In this chapter I will describe the crisis of environmental degradation from three interrelated perspectives. The first section of the chapter will analyze the symptoms, immediate causes, and long-term consequences of climate change. The second section will examine the economic causes of the crisis. In this section I will also analyze Martin Heidegger's reflections on the technological character of modern culture and the instrumental ethos that stands at the root of this crisis. The final section of the chapter will examine the reflections of Benedict XVI and Norman Wirzba on the environmental crisis as a theological crisis. These two thinkers contend that the environmental crisis is rooted in humans' forgetfulness of God. Constructively, the argument of this chapter is that the environmental crisis is rooted in an ethos that is committed to limitless economic growth, the perception of the natural world as raw material or a commodity for human use, and forgetfulness of the relationship between God and creation.

---

[2] Bill McKibben, "The Real Environmental Disaster," *The Daily Beast*, 10 July 2010, http://www.thedailybeast.com/articles/2010/07/20/bp-oil-spill-global-warming-and -environmental-action.html. Alarmingly, McKibben points out that the drilling hole would have supplied only four days' worth of the oil necessary to run the economy of the United States. Bill McKibben, *Eaarth: Making a Life on a Tough New Planet* (New York: Times Books, 2010), 213.

[3] Bill McKibben, "Beyond Oil: Activism and Politics," *OnEarth Magazine*, 23 August 2010, http://www.onearth.org/article/beyond-oil-activism-and-politics.

[4] James Gustave Speth, *A Bridge at the Edge of the World: Capitalism, The Environment, and Crossing from Crisis to Sustainability* (New Haven: Yale University Press, 2008), x.

The Environmental Crisis

In 1962 Rachel Carson wrote *The Silent Spring* as a response to her experience of the negative effects of modern technology on the natural world. In particular, Carson described how the widespread use of pesticides to kill insects had annihilated the bird population around her home in Silver Spring, Maryland. This created what Carson termed the "silent spring," in which the detrimental effects of pesticides had silenced the birds. More than fifty years after the publication of *The Silent Spring*, the environmental crisis has only intensified and human destruction of the natural world has become more evident. For example, currently more than half of the world's original forests and wetlands have been destroyed.[5] The arctic has 40 percent less ice than it had in the late 1960s and could disappear altogether by the end of this decade. Some scientists have predicted that arctic ice could vanish by the summer of 2015.[6] As a result of the melting of ice caps, sustained drought in certain regions, and the overuse of freshwater sources, the world faces a dramatic freshwater crisis in the imminent future. Furthermore, there has been a massive decline in biodiversity in recent years, with species disappearing at a rate a thousand times faster than normal. The earth has not experienced this type of dramatic rate of species extinction in more than sixty-five million years—since the time the dinosaurs went extinct.[7]

These concrete manifestations of environmental degradation are linked to a much broader and deeper crisis that threatens the very possibility of a sustainable future: climate change. An overwhelming body of scientific literature indicates that the climate of the planet is being transformed as a result of human activity and that the effects of this change constitute a clear and present danger to the biosphere itself.[8] This section will examine climate change as a danger demanding an immediate and dramatic response that includes economic, political, and cultural changes.

Anthropogenic climate change is a phenomenon characterized by an unhealthy increase in the levels of carbon dioxide (CO_2) in the atmosphere as a result of human activity. While a certain level of CO_2 is necessary in order to preserve a level of warmth on the planet that makes it hospitable to life, there is also a tipping point at which an excessive amount of CO_2 in the atmosphere

[5] Peter Dauvergne, *Shadows of Consumption: Consequences for the Global Environment* (Cambridge, MA: MIT Press, 2008), 19.

[6] http://www.guardian.co.uk/environment/earth-insight/2013/may/02/white-house-arctic-ice-death-spiral.

[7] Speth, *Bridge at the Edge of the World*, 1.

[8] Richard Miller, "'Global Suicide Pact': Why Don't We Take Climate Change Seriously?" *Commonweal*, 23 March 2012, 12–15.

warms the planet beyond its capacity to continue to sustain that life. CO_2 and other greenhouse gases trap the heat of the sun, much as the glass exterior of a greenhouse serves to trap heat inside. Past a certain point these greenhouse gases begin to contribute to the phenomenon known as global warming or climate change. The amount of CO_2 in the atmosphere has increased rapidly since the Industrial Revolution, from 275 parts per million (ppm) in the 1700s to 400 ppm in 2013. Four hundred ppm represents a dramatic aberration from the stable number that has made the earth hospitable to life for hundreds of thousands of years. Scientists maintain that the current level of CO_2 in the atmosphere is the highest in approximately three million years.[9]

If fossil fuels continue to be burned at the present rate, the amount of CO_2 in the atmosphere will rise at increasingly dangerous rates. Climatologists project that by 2030 the amount of CO_2 in the atmosphere will jump to approximately 450ppm, by 2050 it will increase to 550ppm, and by 2100 it is estimated that this number will grow to anywhere from 700ppm to 860ppm. The current amount of CO_2 in the atmosphere (400ppm) has resulted in a 1.5 degree Fahrenheit increase in global temperatures.[10] According to the 2007 Intergovernmental Panel on Climate Change, depending on what actions are taken in the interim to reduce CO_2 emissions, the increase in temperature as a result of the continued increase in CO_2 will be anywhere from 2 to 11.5 degrees Fahrenheit by 2100. The best estimates suggest that this number most likely will fall in the range of 3.1 to 7.2 degrees Fahrenheit.[11]

The relatively small amount of warming we have already experienced has resulted in a dramatic increase in extreme weather events in recent years. Although there is no way to establish a direct causal relationship between any particular storm and climate change, the trend lines point unambiguously to the fact that the rapid increase in extreme weather events coincides directly with the increase in the amount of CO_2 in the atmosphere. For instance, in the last thirty years there have been four times as many weather-related disasters as in the first seventy-five years of the twentieth century.[12] In the United States alone we have experienced a diverse sampling of extreme weather events, from

---

[9] Justin Gills, "Carbon Dioxide Passes Long-Feared Milestone," *The New York Times*, 10 May 2013, http://www.nytimes.com/2013/05/11/science/earth/carbon-dioxide-level-passes -long-feared-milestone.html?smid=tw-share&_r=0.

[10] McKibben, *Eaarth*, 3.

[11] "Intergovernmental Panel on Climate Change: Fourth Assessment Report: Climate Change Science," http://www.ucsusa.org/global_warming/science_and_impacts/science /findings-of-the-ipcc-fourth-2.html.

[12] McKibben, *Eaarth*, 9.

punishing hurricanes (most recently Hurricane Sandy) and massive flooding (Vermont in 2011, Colorado in 2013) to prolonged drought conditions (the Midwest in 2012). To put it simply, we have arrived at a point at which we are beginning to experience what climatologists and scientists up to this point have only projected as the possible consequence of the steady increase in the amount of CO_2 in the atmosphere.

If this has been the result of a mere 1.5-degree increase in temperature, what would be the consequence of a continued rise in CO_2 in the atmosphere and the related increase in global temperatures? In *Six Degrees*, Mark Lynas describes the effect on the planet as the temperature gradually increases, rising one degree Celsius (1.8 degrees Fahrenheit) to six degrees Celsius (10.8 degrees Fahrenheit).[13] Lynn portrays a movement toward an entirely new world that emerges with each successive rise in temperature. The short-term effects of an increase in temperature of two to six degrees Fahrenheit would cause the extinction of nearly one-third of all living species. Drought would become a permanent feature of tropical and subtropical zones in Africa, Asia, and Latin America and would result in the dislocation of millions of people. The International Organization for Migration estimates that by 2050 there will be between 200 million and 1 billion migrants as a direct result of climate change. This will result in resource conflicts, political destabilization, and massive unrest in the affected populations. The long-term effects as earth approaches an increase of seven to eleven degrees Fahrenheit would be positively apocalyptic. Impending in those conditions are situations in which entire cities such as Boston, New York, London, Mumbai, and Shanghai are submerged as a result of rising sea levels. Sustained droughts, the expansion of desertlike conditions, and massive water shortages would make much of the world's land surface inhospitable to the growth of crops. This in turn would cause food shortages, the intensification of massive migration, and resource conflict as large segments of the world population are forced to fight to secure the basic necessities of life.

Climate change creates a situation in which the world faces not only a destructive assault on the biosphere itself but also a serious threat to its own future. Although developed nations have contributed disproportionately to the current amount of CO_2 in the atmosphere, it is the poorest countries in the world that will suffer the most devastating effects of climate change. Developed countries comprise approximately 25 percent of the world's population but have produced almost 75 percent of the cumulative CO_2 emissions and 60 percent of the current

---

[13] Mark Lynas, *Six Degrees: Our Future on a Hotter Planet* (Washington, DC: National Geographic, 2008).

CO_2 emissions.[14] The United States has been the most egregious offender in terms of its overall contribution to the increase, representing approximately 25 percent of the total CO_2 emissions since the Industrial Revolution.[15] This number is particularly notable when it is compared to countries with much larger populations such as China (9 percent) and India (2.7 percent). As James G. Speth points out, "the United States emits roughly the same amount of greenhouse gases as 2.6 billion people living in 150 developing nations."[16] It has been estimated that if the world population of 7 billion drew on natural resources at the same rate as the United States, the earth would be able to support only 1.4 billion people.[17] The United States population is 315 million, that of China 1.34 billion, and that of India 1.24 billion. China has recently eclipsed the United States in its annual CO_2 emissions. If India and China continue to develop their economies along the same path the United States has followed, the effect on the planet will be catastrophic. Bill McKibben writes: "if the Chinese, say, ever owned cars at the same rate as Americans, the number of vehicles on the planet would go from 800 million to almost 2 billion; if they ate as much meat as we do, they would require two-thirds of the planet's grain harvest."[18]

These statistics indicate that the growth fetish that stands at the foundation of the modern economy is unsustainable. The planet cannot support the level of affluence the United States and other developed countries have come to expect as the product of a fossil-fuel-based economy. This represents an urgent problem in and of itself. But, as noted above, this situation raises an important ethical dilemma as well. The commitment to economic growth without restraint has created a situation in which the most vulnerable and poorest populations in the world will be the first to experience the ravages of natural disasters, famine, and the water and food shortages caused by the material excesses of the developed world.[19] The bitter irony of this situation is that the populations that have emitted the least amount of CO_2 will be those most affected by climate change.[20] Furthermore, while affluent countries have the resources necessary to

---

[14] Speth, *Bridge at the Edge of the World*, 28.

[15] Ibid.

[16] Ibid.

[17] Fred Magdoff and John Bellamy Foster, *What Every Environmentalist Needs to Know About Capitalism: A Citizen's Guide to Capitalism and the Environment* (New York: Monthly Review Press, 2011), 28.

[18] McKibben, *Eaarth*, 48.

[19] Lynas, *Six Degrees*, 263ff.

[20] For impoverished families in the world that spend 50 to 80 percent of their income on food the scarcity caused by climate change and the increase in prices as a result of this scarcity will be devastating. Abigail Jones, Vinca LaFleur, and Nigel Purvis, "Double Jeopardy:

build the infrastructure to protect them from the dangers of climate change, poorer populations will be exposed without protection to the devastating effects of drought, flooding, and extreme weather. These effects are already being felt in impoverished countries and will only get worse as the world continues to warm in coming decades. According to Speth, "the World Health Organization estimated in 2004 the loss of 150,000 lives each year due to climate change. Its most recent report projects that loss of life caused by climate change could double by 2030, due largely to diarrhea-related disease, malaria, and malnutrition. Most of the casualties would fall in the developing world."[21]

How do we prevent this from happening, or at the very least attempt to mitigate the negative effects of this rise in temperature resulting from the increase of CO_2 in the atmosphere? Scientists suggest that 350ppm of CO_2 is a rate that is safe for a hospitable and sustainable climate for the future.[22] Alarmingly, however, even if we took all the government pledges made in Copenhagen in 2009 to reduce carbon emissions we would arrive at a number slightly above 725ppm by 2100. Indeed, even if all of the conditional proposals, policies under debate, and unofficial government statements were implemented it is unlikely that these actions could prevent the amount of CO_2 in the atmosphere from reaching 600ppm.[23] In view of this data it is clear that the environmental crisis is urgent and demands creative technological and economic as well as political and religious solutions. Incremental policy proposals that attempt to appease all sides of the debate—including those who deny anthropogenic climate change—represent a grossly inadequate response to the situation. This is not a standard political issue in which compromise is possible. As McKibben observes, climate change "is a negotiation between human beings on the one hand and physics and chemistry on the other. Which is a tough negotiation, because physics and chemistry don't compromise. They've already laid out their nonnegotiable bottom line: above 350ppm the planet doesn't work."[24]

What the Climate Crisis Means for the Poor," 10–33 in *Climate Change and Global Poverty: A Billion Lives in the Balance*, ed. Lael Brainard, Abigail Jones, and Nigel Purvis (Washington, DC: Brookings Institution, 2009), 13.

[21] Speth, *Bridge at the Edge of the World*, 24.

[22] This is the number suggested by James Hansen, the former NASA climatologist. See his "Target Carbon Dioxide: Where Should Humanity Aim?" 140–71 in idem, *Storms of My Grandchildren: The Truth about the Coming Climate Catastrophe and Our Last Chance to Save Humanity* (New York: Bloomsbury, 2009).

[23] McKibben, *Eaarth*, 20.

[24] Ibid., 81.

In this section I have described the environmental crisis in its most basic scientific terms. In some sense, however, the avalanche of statistics and numbers fails to represent adequately the destruction humans have inflicted on the environment. In search for a proper metaphor that expresses the depth and scope of the devastation, McKibben turns to the Bible, observing: "we're hard at work transforming it—hard at work sabotaging its biology, draining its diversity, affecting every other kind of life that we were born creating. We're running Genesis backward, de-creating."[25] While McKibben turns to the first book of the Bible to describe the destructive character of the environmental crisis, one could very well turn to the Bible's last book—Revelation—as a textual precedent for what is happening in the present. That is to say that the environmental crisis is quite literally apocalyptic. It is not God, however, who is creating a new heaven and new earth, as in the book of Revelation (Rev 21:1). Instead, this is a human-caused apocalypse, with all the horror associated with that idea. As McKibben puts it: "the planet on which our civilization evolved no longer exists. The stability that produced that civilization has vanished; epic changes have begun . . . the earth that we knew—the only earth that we ever knew—is done."[26]

Economic-Technological Culture

This section will examine two features of modern culture that have contributed to the environmental crisis: the economy and technology.[27] Climate change is the immediate consequence of the industrial revolution and the rise of the modern economy. The economic changes of the industrial revolution have benefited humanity in important ways, but the material benefits gained through industrialization have also led directly to the environmental crisis. At a deeper level we will examine the market ethos that shapes the way moderns perceive the world and leads to a situation in which the world is reduced to raw material to be used for the limited purposes of economic and technological development.

The modern economy is the most basic cause of environmental degradation. Indeed, climate change represents the most dangerous instance of the systemic failure of the free-market economy. As Paul Ekins observes, "the sacrifice of the

---

[25] Ibid., 25.

[26] Ibid., 27.

[27] On the economic dimension see A. Rodney Dobell, "Environmental Degradation and the Religion of the Market," 229–50, in *Population, Consumption, and the Environment: Religious and Secular Responses*, ed. Harold Coward (Albany, NY: SUNY Press, 1995); Laurel Kearns, "Religion and Ecology in the Context of Globalization," 305–35, in *Religion, Globalization, and Culture*, ed. Peter Beyer and Lori Beaman (Leiden: Brill, 2007).

environment to economic growth" has been "a feature of economic development at least since the birth of industrialism."[28] This claim can be demonstrated in historical terms. The dramatic increase in CO_2 ppm in the atmosphere from the 1700s to the present coincides with the rise of the modern economy and its dependence on fossil fuels for its dramatic growth over the past several hundred years.[29] McKibben describes Thomas Newcomen's discovery of coal as a source of energy for the steam engine in 1712 as the event that revolutionized the modern economy. Coal would soon be followed by oil and gas as stable, cheap sources of energy. McKibben observes: "one barrel of oil yields as much energy as twenty-five thousand hours of human labor—more than a decade of human labor per barrel."[30] The discovery in the early 1700s of these fossil fuels as forms of energy previously trapped below the earth's surface for millions of years created conditions ripe for a dramatic explosion in the growth of the economy over the last three hundred years. And while segments of the world's population have benefited enormously from the use of fossil fuels, the process of burning these fuels as a cheap, efficient form of energy has caused the rapid growth in CO_2 emissions in the atmosphere. Specifically, as noted in the previous section, since the discovery of fossil fuels as a potent form of energy the amount of CO_2 in the atmosphere has increased from 275ppm in 1712 to 400ppm in 2014.[31]

There exists, therefore, a direct connection between the practices of the modern economy and the degradation of the environment. Wendell Berry bluntly summarizes the assessment of much of the environmental movement when he observes: "among people who wish to preserve things other than money . . . there is a growing perception that the global 'free market' economy is inherently an enemy to the natural world."[32] This view has led a number of environmental thinkers to suggest that in order to slow the rise of CO_2 emissions it is necessary to transform the modern economy. Speth observes: "the damages are already huge and are on a path to be ruinous in the future. So, a fundamental question facing societies today—perhaps *the* fundamental question—is how can

---

[28] Paul Ekins, *Economic Growth and Environmental Sustainability: The Prospects for Green Growth* (New York: Routledge, 2000), 317.

[29] Bill McKibben, *Deep Economy: The Wealth of Communities and the Durable Future* (New York: Times Books, 2007); Speth, *Bridge at the Edge of the World*; Magdoff and Bellamy Foster, *What Every Environmentalist Needs to Know about Capitalism*; Tim Jackson, *Prosperity without Growth: Economics for a Finite Planet* (Sterling, VA: Earthscan, 2009); Dauvergne, *Shadows of Consumption*.

[30] McKibben, *Eaarth*, 27.

[31] Ibid., 20.

[32] Wendell Berry, *The Art of the Commonplace: Agrarian Essays of Wendell Berry* (Washington, DC: Counterpoint, 2002), 256.

the operating instructions for the modern world economy be changed so that economic activity both protects and restores the natural world?"[33] There are three interrelated reasons why the modern economy is criticized from an environmental perspective: it prioritizes profits for private corporations over the common good of the public (privatization); it prioritizes prosperity in the present over the sustainability of the future (contemporocentrism); it prioritizes narrow human economic interests over the flourishing of the biosphere (anthropocentrism).

First, one of the basic features of the modern economy that is problematic from an environmental perspective is the phenomenon known as externality. Externality is the process by which private corporations pass the cost of their business operation on to the public. Speth argues that "today's corporations have been called 'externalizing machines,' so committed are they to keeping the real costs of their activities external to (that is, off) their books."[34] For instance, if a business produces enormous amounts of air pollution it does not calculate the cost of the cleanup or the illnesses that will result from this pollution into its costs of operation. Instead, it makes the cleanup and the medical costs external to its bottom line by passing these costs off to the local community, the state, or the federal government. Another concrete example would be the use of coal in the United States. Coal is the cheapest form of energy available. Gas is almost twice as expensive as coal, and oil is over five times as costly. Thus, from the narrow perspective of economic logic, coal is the most cost-efficient fossil fuel. However, this data does not represent the total cost of the production and use of coal to create usable energy. Coal mining has immediate and devastating effects on the land (strip mining, the destruction of mountains and valleys) and on human health (lung disease). Furthermore, it is virtually impossible to calculate the cost "of the mercury pollution on our lakes and the ocean—the cost of the contamination of fish and humans by that mercury, the greater acidity of the oceans, runoff from the waste coal storage, the global warming effects of the carbon dioxide released into the atmosphere and methane released during mining, and so on."[35] Externality—of which CO_2 is the most significant instance—is the most obvious example of the prioritization of the interests of the private sphere over the public good. This is particularly true when what counts as the public good is expanded to include the biosphere itself as well as a sustainable future for subsequent generations.

---

[33] Speth, *Bridge at the Edge of the World*, 6–7. Emphasis in original.

[34] Ibid., 60.

[35] Magdoff and Bellamy Foster, *What Every Environmentalist Needs to Know About Capitalism*, 40.

It is in relation to this point that the second problematic feature of the modern economy becomes evident: the tendency to prioritize the present over the future.[36] Wendell Berry observes:

> a corporation, essentially, is a pile of money to which a number of persons have sold their moral allegiance. As such, unlike a person, a corporation does not age. It does not arrive, as most persons finally do, at a realization of the shortness and smallness of human lives; it does not come to see the future as the lifetimes of the children and grandchildren of anybody in particular. It can experience no personal hope or remorse, no change of heart. It cannot humble itself. It goes about its business as if it were immortal, with the single purpose of becoming a bigger pile of money.[37]

The economy devalues future generations because they do not contribute to the market goals of growth and profit in the present. This is a particularly important issue in relation to CO_2 emissions because the transformation of the climate that occurs as a result of an increase of CO_2 in the atmosphere is irreversible for over a thousand years.[38] Furthermore, this type of externality is connected not only to future generations but also to those who are excluded from the fossil-fuel-based economy and will be most vulnerable to its effects. Thus the poor become the externality of the lifestyles of those who live in the affluent world.

Finally, Speth contends that anthropocentrism stands at the root of the modern economy and modern culture. According to him this "view of the world—that nature belongs to us rather than we to nature—is powerful and persuasive, and it has led to much mischief."[39] The problems that arise from anthropocentrism will be treated in the discussion of Martin Heidegger, Benedict XVI, and Norman Wirzba. But we may offer a provisional definition: anthropocentrism is a worldview that sustains a culture in which the materialistic interests of human beings are prioritized over other values, including the sustainability of the broader biotic community. Indeed, it is precisely because ethical responsibilities and duties have been restricted to the narrow purview of human self-interest that an environmental crisis exists in the first place.

---

[36] Speth, *Bridge at the Edge of the World*, 61.

[37] Berry, *Art of the Commonplace*, 255.

[38] Susan Solomon, Gian-Kasper Plattner, et al., "Irreversible Climate Change Due to Carbon Dioxide Emissions," *PNAS* 106 (2009): 1704–9.

[39] James Gustave Speth, *Red Sky at Morning: America and the Crisis of the Global Environment* (New Haven: Yale University Press, 2004), 138.

In view of these features of the modern economy Speth concludes that "most environmental deterioration is a result of systemic failures of the capitalism that we have today and that long-term solutions must seek transformative change in the key features of this contemporary capitalism."[40] In terms of immediate, short-term policy solutions a number of steps can be taken to respond to the negative effects of the modern economy on the environment.

First, government must intervene to regulate industry in order to limit externality, reduce pollution and CO_2 emissions, and provide incentives for the development of a greener economy. The task of government is to limit the power of corporations and businesses and to preserve the common good.[41] The problem is that more often than not political power has served to support the expansion of an unrestrained and unregulated economy into every aspect of life. According to Speth:

> in the United States today, the government in Washington is hobbled, corrupted by money, and typically at the service of economic interests, focused on the short-time horizons of election cycles, and poorly guided by an anemic environmental politics, a poorly informed public, and a pathetic level of discourse on the environment.[42]

Thus we live in a situation in which the market fails to protect the environment and government fails to limit the negative effect the market has on the environment.[43] This task of governmental regulation has been obstructed by a climate skepticism funded by the private industries and corporations that benefit from a political climate of deregulation. The success of these climate skepticism efforts is all the more remarkable in view of the fact that 98 percent of the scientific community supports the position that human activities have changed the climate.[44] In face of the success of this financially backed misinformation campaign, the only recourse environmentalists have is to attempt to reshape public perception of the issue of climate change through micropolitics. This form of environmental

---

[40] Speth, *Bridge at the Edge of the World*, 9.

[41] See Adrian Parr, *The Wrath of Capital: Neoliberalism and Climate Change Politics* (New York: Columbia University Press, 2013).

[42] Speth, *Bridge at the Edge of the World*, 63.

[43] Ibid., 52.

[44] Pallab Ghosh, "Study Examines Scientists' 'Climate Credibility,'" *BBC News*, 22 June 2010, http://www.bbc.co.uk/news/10370955. Notwithstanding this fact, as Naomi Klein observes, "a 2007 Harris poll found that 71 percent of Americans believed that the continued burning of fossil fuels would cause the climate to change. By 2009 the figure had dropped to 51 percent. In June 2011 the number of Americans who agreed was down to 44 percent—well under half the population." Naomi Klein, "Capitalism vs. the Climate," *The Nation*, 28 November 2011.

organization is of particular importance because, as Jane Bennett argues, "there will be no greening of the economy . . . without human dispositions, moods, and cultural ensembles hospitable to these effects."[45]

Second, there is widespread consensus among environmentalists that the growth fetish of capitalism is the foundation of the environmental crisis. For this reason McKibben, Speth, and others argue that it is necessary to initiate a move toward an economy that no longer views growth and expansion as its exclusive goals.[46] The commitment to endless growth assumes that we live in a world in which resources are infinite. But the world is finite. The past several decades have made it increasingly evident that the world is incapable of absorbing the unlimited and unrestrained use of its resources by human beings. From this angle the environmental reasons for shifting to a post-growth economy are self-evident. But there are also arguments made from the perspective of questions about human flourishing. McKibben and Speth, for instance, both point to the fact that recent studies in the social sciences demonstrate that there is no direct correlation between happiness and affluence.[47] These studies suggest that there is little evidence that, after one has achieved a basic level of income, a further increase results in a positive effect on overall individual happiness. McKibben observes that "in general, researchers report that money consistently buys happiness right up to about $10,000 per capita income, and that after that point the correlation disappears."[48] In this sense the data suggests that moving toward a post-growth economy makes solid sense from both an environmental perspective and a holistic understanding of human flourishing. Religious thinkers like Benedict XVI have made this same point by arguing that more developed countries should reduce consumption and adopt "more sober lifestyles" as a concrete response to the environmental crisis and practice lifestyles more consistent with Gospel values.[49] It is true that the adoption of these lifestyles will involve some

---

[45] Jane Bennett, *Vibrant Matter: A Political Ecology of Things* (Durham: Duke University Press, 2010), xii.

[46] Bill McKibben, "A Foreword by Bill McKibben," in *Prosperity without Growth*, xiii. More broadly see McKibben, *Deep Economy*; Speth, *Bridge at the Edge of the World*; Tim Jackson, *Prosperity without Growth: Economics for a Finite Planet* (Washington, DC: Earthscan, 2009); Herman Daly, *Beyond Growth: The Economics of Sustainable Development* (Boston: Beacon Press, 1996); Peter Victor, *Managing Without Growth: Slower by Design, Not Disaster* (Northampton, MA: Edward Elgar, 2008).

[47] McKibben, *Deep Economy*, 35–38, and Speth, *Bridge at the Edge of the World*, 126–46.

[48] McKibben, *Deep Economy*, 41. Original italics removed.

[49] Benedict XVI, "If You Want to Cultivate Peace, Protect Creation," 1 January 2010, http://www.vatican.va/holy_father/benedict_xvi/messages/peace/documents/hf_ben-xvi_mes_20091208_xliii-world-day-peace_en.html.

sacrifice and will be, as Wendell Berry writes, "harder, more laborious, poorer in luxuries and gadgets." But he adds that this type of lifestyle will also be "richer in meaning and more abundant in real pleasure."[50]

Finally, environmentalists have advocated not only for moving toward a post-growth scenario but for a turn toward a more local economy as a means of resisting the destructive features of the global economy. Because multinational corporations find themselves accountable only to the imperatives of profit and economic growth and because governments have failed or are unwilling to limit the negative effects these corporations have on the environment, the turn to the local economy is a concrete means by which individuals can regulate economic life.[51] This move toward the local economy is characterized by an attempt to cultivate spaces in which responsible forms of consumer exchange can take place, forms that limit the distance between producers and consumers and thereby establish a more direct relationship between buyer and seller.[52] Although the modern economy presents individuals with a dizzying array of consumer choices, what it does not provide is an answer to basic questions like: Where did this product come from? What chemicals were used to produce it? What were the ecological costs of producing and transporting this item from one location to another?[53] These types of questions can be answered at the local level—and the individuals who answer them can be held accountable—in a manner that is simply unimaginable within the framework of the global economy.

Because the modern economy has contributed decisively to the environmental crisis, it follows that any adequate response to that crisis must involve a transformation of the modern economy and the way it functions. However, this approach represents only one strategy for confronting the crisis. Many environmental thinkers have argued that this single strategy is insufficient because the economic logic that has damaged the environment is only an expression of the deeper values of a culture. They believe that, consequently, the standard approach to environmental problems in which the problem (e.g., climate change) is described and then public policy or a technical solution (e.g., cap and trade)

---

[50] Berry, *Art of the Commonplace*, 87.

[51] McKibben argues: "building a local economy will mean . . . ceasing to worship markets as infallible and consciously setting limits on their scope. We will need to downplay efficiency and pay attention to other goals. We will have to make the biggest changes to our daily habits in generations—and the biggest change, as well, to our worldview, our sense of what constitutes progress." McKibben, *Deep Economy*, 2.

[52] Berry, *Art of the Commonplace*, 259.

[53] Ibid.

is offered is not working. For these thinkers, contesting the destructive character of the modern economy requires striking at the deeper root of the problem.

In *The Death of Environmentalism*, Michael Shellenberger and Ted Nordhaus argue that environmentalists have failed to articulate "a vision of the future commensurate with the magnitude of the crisis. Instead they are promoting technical policy fixes like pollution controls and higher vehicle mileage standards—proposals that provide neither the popular inspirations nor the political alliances the community needs to deal with the problem."[54] In a similar vein, Thomas Berry has written:

> There is a certain futility in the efforts being made—truly sincere, dedicated, and intelligent efforts—to remedy our environmental devastation simply by activating renewable sources of energy and by reducing the deleterious impact of the industrial world. The difficulty is that the natural world is seen primarily for human use, not as a mode of sacred presence primarily to be communed with in wonder, beauty and intimacy. In our present attitude the natural world remains a commodity to be bought and sold, not a sacred reality to be venerated. The deep psychic shift needed to withdraw us from the fascination of the industrial world and the deceptive gifts that it gives us is too difficult for simply the avoidance of its difficulties or the attractions of its benefits. Eventually, only our sense of the sacred will save us.[55]

These thinkers all agree that something deeper is necessary to confront the crisis we now face, whether it be a "big vision" (Shellenberger and Nordhaus), a "sense of the sacred" (Berry), or what Brian Treanor describes as "a shift in the cultural imagination."[56] In the rest of this section I will follow this suggestion and turn from the economic causes of environmental degradation to an analysis of the technological culture that supports the practices of the modern economy. In particular I will approach the root cause of the environmental crisis from a different angle by analyzing the philosophical writings of Martin Heidegger on the instrumental ethos of modern culture.[57]

[54] Michael Shellenberger and Ted Nordhaus, *The Death of Environmentalism: Global Warming Politics in a Post-Environmental World* (New York: Nathan Cummings Foundation, 2004), 6–7.

[55] Thomas Berry, "Foreword," 13–20, in *Thomas Merton: When the Trees Say Nothing: Writings on Nature,* ed. Kathleen Deignan (Notre Dame, IN: Sorin Books, 2003), at 18–19.

[56] See Brian Treanor, "Turn Around and Step Forward: Ideology and Utopia in the Environmental Movement," *Environmental Philosophy* 7 (2010): 27–46, at 34. Original italics removed.

[57] The link between Heidegger's reflections on technology and the ecological crisis has been made by a number of authors. See esp. Michael Zimmerman, *Heidegger's Confrontation*

In his later philosophy Heidegger engaged in a probing analysis of the fundamental ontology at the roots of modern culture.[58] He described technology as the most basic dimension of modern ontology (broadly, what we have described as the cultural imaginary). Heidegger's use of the term "technology" has little to do with the tools, instruments, or machines that perform a set of complex tasks. Instead, modern technology describes a pervasive sensibility that reduces everything in the world to the values of efficiency and expediency.[59] For Heidegger, modern technology is the ethos of a culture and is nothing less than a way of construing the world.[60] Specifically, he describes technological culture as the particular way of seeing that dominates modernity and "holds complete dominion over all the phenomena that distinguish the age."[61] Thus Heidegger maintains that technological culture shapes the way things are seen as raw material for human use.

For Heidegger modern technology is characterized by an "enframing" (*Gestell*) of reality in which entities have been reduced to mere resources for human industry. Because enframing reveals the world as raw material ("standing-reserve" or *Bestand*) for human projects, the fundamental posture humans adopt vis-à-vis the world is one of aggressive instrumentalization. Heidegger observes: "the revealing that rules in modern technology is a challenging [*Herausfordern*], which puts to nature the unreasonable demand that it supply energy that can be extracted and stored as such . . . a tract of land is challenged into the putting

---

with *Modernity: Technology, Politics, and Art* (Bloomington: Indiana University Press, 1990); idem, *Contesting the Earth's Future: Radical Ecology and Postmodernity* (Berkeley: University of California Press, 1994); Bruce Foltz, *Inhabiting the Earth: Heidegger, Environmental Ethics, and the Metaphysics of Nature* (Amherst, NY: Humanity Books, 1995); Ruth Irwin, *Heidegger, Politics and Climate Change: Risking It All*; and *Heidegger and the Earth: Essays in Environmental Philosophy*, ed. Ladelle McWhorter and Gail Stenstad (Toronto: University of Toronto Press, 2009).

[58] This discussion of Heidegger is drawn from Matthew T. Eggemeier, "A Sacramental Vision: Environmental Degradation and the Aesthetics of Creation," *Modern Theology* 29 (2013): 338–60.

[59] On technology as a way of seeing, see Don Ihde, *Instrumental Realism: The Interface between Philosophy of Science and Philosophy of Technology* (Bloomington: Indiana University Press, 1991), 55–58, and David Michael Levin, *The Philosopher's Gaze: Modernity in the Shadows of Enlightenment* (Berkeley: University of California Press, 1999), 116–69.

[60] According to Heidegger the essence of technology "is nothing technological, nothing of the order of the machine. It is the way in which the real reveals itself as standing-reserve." Heidegger, *The Question Concerning Technology, and Other Essays*, trans. William Lovitt (New York: Harper & Row, 1977), 23.

[61] Ibid., 115.

out of coal and ore. The earth now reveals itself as a coal mining district, the soil as a mineral deposit."[62] Long before contemporary debates over the energy crisis and its environmental impact, Heidegger had described the potential ecological implications of this technological approach to reality and its reduction of the earth to a mere resource for human energy needs. According to Heidegger, "the world now appears as an object open to the attacks of calculative thought . . . nature becomes a gigantic gasoline station, an energy source for modern technology and industry."[63] He renders critical judgment on this approach to the world and the practices it engenders, observing: "the devastation of the earth and the annihilation of the human essence that goes with it" is "evil [*das Böse*]."[64]

From a Heideggerian perspective there exists a clear connection between technological culture and the contemporary environmental crisis. The link is made evident in Heidegger's philosophy in three interrelated ways. First, he is highly critical of the anthropocentrism of technological culture that leads the human subject to determine the value of a thing based on its capacity to make human projects more efficient, economical, and profitable. Within this technological frame things in the world are viewed as inherently valueless apart from their capacity to increase efficiency and economic productivity.[65] In this regard the modern technological vision of the world is not only nihilistic but also deeply destructive, because it reduces everything in the world to a mere resource to be exploited by the gaze of instrumental thought. Practically, this means that moderns feel free to disrupt, disturb, and destroy the natural world in the attempt to make human projects more efficient and profitable.

Second, modern technology blocks any understanding of reality that differs from the instrumental understanding of the world as a resource awaiting optimization.[66] Heidegger views this situation as extremely dangerous because this technological mode of perception marginalizes other ways of perceiving the world that exceed the values of efficiency and economic productivity. He worries that the capacity to perceive the world as beautiful or holy is obscured by technological culture because it eviscerates the contemplative posture necessary to view things in this way.

---

[62] Ibid., 14.

[63] Martin Heidegger, *Discourse on Thinking*, trans. John M. Anderson and E. Hans Freund (New York: Harper & Row, 1966), 50.

[64] Martin Heidegger, *Country Path Conversations*, trans. Bret W. Davis (Bloomington: Indiana University Press, 2010), 133.

[65] Heidegger, *The Question Concerning Technology*, 17.

[66] Ibid., 27.

Finally, when things in creation are reduced to replaceable commodities, human beings lose a felt sense of the particularity of things and their significance within their natural environment. Heidegger maintains that within technological culture "everything becomes equal and indifferent in consequence of the uniformly calculated availability of the whole earth."[67] In contrast to technological culture, in which indifference to the particularity of places and things is the norm, Heidegger argues that the task in the present is to learn to dwell "on what lies close . . . on this patch of home ground."[68]

Overall, Heidegger's fundamental problem with technology is not with the use of specific instruments or tools but rather with the way technological culture forms persons to perceive all of reality as bereft of objective significance and as mere stuff to be manipulated for human purposes. The modern constriction of reality to raw material for human use supports the view that the destruction of the earth for the expansion of human projects constitutes a legitimate use of human power. In response to this problem mere technical fixes will do little to alleviate the current crisis. Instead, Heidegger argues that nothing short of an alternative way of seeing is needed to resist the nightmare of a thoroughly instrumentalized world.

Heidegger specifically focuses on the revelation of the beautiful in the work of art and the remembrance of the gods as ways of disclosing reality that permits the emergence of a new relationship to the world.[69] The encounter with the beautiful in a work of art serves to open up a new approach to reality that surpasses the disclosure of the world as "raw material" in technological culture. In his analysis of Heidegger's approach to art, Iain Thomson observes: "Heidegger calls an artwork's manifestation of the truth of being 'beauty' and thus understands beauty in a post-aesthetic way, ultimately, as the revelation of a new understanding of being."[70] Although he never describes the beautiful as a transcendental of Being (as the medievals did), Heidegger's analysis of the status of

---

[67] Martin Heidegger, *On the Way to Language*, trans. Peter D. Herz (New York: Harper and Row, 1971), 105. Quoted in Mark Wrathall, *Heidegger and Unconcealment: Truth, Language, and History* (New York: Cambridge University Press, 2011), 202.

[68] Heidegger, *Discourse on Thinking*, 47. See also Wrathall, *Heidegger and Unconcealment*, 201.

[69] See Martin Heidegger, *Nietzsche*, vol. 1, *The Will to Power as Art*, trans. David Farrell Krell (San Francisco: Harper & Row, 1979), 196; idem, *The Question Concerning Technology*, 34 and 35; idem, "The Origin of the Work of Art," 15–86 in his *Poetry, Language, Thought*, trans. Albert Hofstadter (New York: Harper & Row, 1971; Perennial ed. 2001), 79.

[70] Iain D. Thomson, *Heidegger, Art, Postmodernity* (New York: Cambridge University Press, 2011), 63n39.

the beautiful is redolent of this understanding.[71] Indeed, he describes the work of art as possessing "the saving power" because it discloses the world as beautiful and reveals an alternative vision of reality that exceeds the instrumental character of technological culture.[72]

In addition to focusing on the disclosive power of the work of art, Heidegger also points to the importance of recovering a sense of the holy as an antidote to the detrimental features of technological culture. For complex reasons that need not sidetrack us here he rejected Christianity as a potential resource for resisting technological culture. Instead, he looked toward a mythical retrieval of the gods as a means of disclosing a new vision of the world. For Heidegger the gods serve a soteriological function by casting a light on the holiness of things and permitting them to show themselves to human beings as significant and worthy of reverence.[73] Mark Wrathall argues that in Heidegger's later philosophy the gods constitute those realities that make things in the world significant, independent of their capacity to serve a utilitarian function for human beings.[74] The gods are those "focal practices that give us a place, determining what is important to us, and what counts as unimportant or trivial" and thereby provide human beings with "a way of being attuned to objects as having a transcendental importance or weightiness."[75] Heidegger's quasi-religious discourse on the gods represents an attempt to remythologize a world desacralized by the leveling gaze of modern technology.

A renewed sense of the beautiful and the holy serves to support an alternative way of being in the world that Heidegger characterizes as a contemplative letting-be and a poetic form of dwelling. In contrast to the dangerous practices of technological culture in which the earth is imperiled by the energy needs of humanity, Heidegger maintains that "mortals dwell in that they save the earth"; saving the earth "consists in not exploiting it, not mastering it, and not subjugating it."[76] He argues that to dwell is to cultivate a disposition of contemplative wonder before the world and to care for and preserve the things of the world.

---

[71] See Karsten Harries, *Art Matters: A Critical Commentary on Heidegger's "The Origin of the Work of Art"* (New York: Springer, 2009), 188–90.

[72] Heidegger, *The Question Concerning Technology*, 35.

[73] Heidegger famously announced in an interview with *Der Spiegel*: "only a god can save us." Martin Heidegger, "Only a God Can Save Us: *Der Spiegel's* Interview with Martin Heidegger," trans. John Caputo, 91–116, in *The Heidegger Controversy: A Critical Reader* (Cambridge, MA: MIT Press, 1993), at 107.

[74] Wrathall, *Heidegger and Unconcealment*, 199.

[75] Ibid., 197 and 199.

[76] Heidegger, *Poetry, Language, Thought*, 150.

While there are dimensions of Heidegger's analysis that are problematic from a Christian perspective, the central point he makes is important: technological culture has taken hold of the modern world in such a way that it has transformed the way moderns perceive the world. From Heidegger's perspective mere technical fixes represent an inadequate response to the nature of the current crisis. Instead, nothing short of a transformation of perception (or ontology) is needed if we are to face this crisis adequately. As we turn to the theological analyses of Benedict XVI and Norman Wirzba we find a similar emphasis on the importance of analyzing the deeper roots of the crisis of environmental degradation as a means of responding to it.

A Culture of Creation

Heidegger contended that the cultivation of a contemplative and aesthetic comportment toward the world is the most adequate means of resisting the instrumental ethos of modern technological culture. This section examines the writings of Benedict XVI and Norman Wirzba who argue, much as Heidegger did, that the root of the environmental crisis goes much deeper than current public policy debates suggest. The arguments made by Benedict XVI and Wirzba are similar to Heidegger's insofar as these thinkers agree that the modern era is characterized by a widespread shift in perception in which the world has been reduced to mere raw material for human use. They depart from Heidegger, however, by attributing this shift in perception to a forgetfulness of God.[77]

In a variety of public speeches during his pontificate, Benedict XVI reflected on the environmental crisis and examined its root causes.[78] His conviction is that the forgetfulness of God stands at the root of a variety of contemporary moral, social, and political crises, not least among them the environmental crisis. When God is erased from the world as its ultimate horizon, other realities begin to inhabit the space of ultimacy formerly occupied by God. Benedict maintains that a crude form of anthropocentrism dominates Western culture and supports

---

[77] On this point see also Elizabeth Johnson, "Losing and Finding Creation in the Christian Tradition," 3–21, in *Christianity and Ecology: Seeking the Well-Being of Earth and Humans*, ed. Dieter T. Hessel and Rosemary Radford Ruether (Cambridge, MA: Harvard University Press, 2000); eadem, *Women, Earth, and Creator Spirit* (New York: Paulist Press, 1993).

[78] There are two collections that gather together Benedict XVI's various statements on the environment: Benedict XVI, *The Environment*, ed. Jacquelyn Lindsey (Huntington, IN: Our Sunday Visitor, 2012), and Woodeene Koenig-Bricker, *Ten Commandments for the Environment: Pope Benedict XVI Speaks Out for Creation and Justice* (Notre Dame, IN: Ave Maria Press, 2009).

a reductionist vision of the world based on the values of materialism and self-interest. He observes: "the brutal consumption of Creation begins where God is not, where matter is henceforth only material for us, where we ourselves are the ultimate demand, where the whole is merely our property and we consume it for ourselves alone. And the wasting of creation begins when we no longer recognize any need superior to our own, but see only ourselves."[79] Because he views the elimination of God as the transcendent horizon of human existence as the root cause of environmental degradation, Benedict asserts that the proper antidote to this crisis must be rooted in the remembrance of God and the attempt to reestablish a relationship with the world as creation. He writes:

> I believe, therefore, that true and effective measures against the waste and destruction of Creation can only be realized and developed, understood and lived, when Creation is considered as beginning with God; when life is considered on the basis of God and has its major dimensions in responsibility before God; life that one day will be given by God in its fullness and never taken away.[80]

While his response to the environmental crisis is multifaceted and involves a call for concrete political solutions, a transformation of the economic order, and the adoption of simpler lifestyles, Benedict argues that a real and substantive response to the crisis will happen only when humanity begins to rediscover "in Creation the face of the Creator."[81]

Like Benedict XVI, Norman Wirzba argues that the root causes of environmental degradation are linked to the widespread forgetfulness of creation in contemporary culture. Wirzba, however, engages in a more extensive historical analysis of the transformation of modern culture that has created the conditions ripe for the degradation of the environment. Specifically, he argues that the environmental crisis is a crisis of culture. For him, contemporary culture fails to see the world as intrinsically significant and reduces it to mere material for human use and consumption. According to Wirzba: "put philosophically, our perception of the 'being' of the world, its essence, or what we understand to be its character has, in the modern period, taken a turn that is clearly at odds with

---

[79] Benedict XVI, Meeting of the Holy Father Benedict XVI with the Clergy of the Diocese of Blozano-Bressanone, http://www.vatican.va/holy_father/benedict_xvi/speeches/2008/august/documents/hf_ben-xvi_spe_20080806_clero-bressanone_en.html.

[80] Ibid.

[81] Benedict XVI, "World Youth Day Interview," http://ncronline.org/news/wyd-transcript-benedict-xvi-press-conference.

scriptural views."[82] Framing the issue in theological terms, he argues that the culture of modernity has produced a situation in which the conditions necessary to experience the world as creation have disappeared.[83]

Wirzba argues that this erosion has been caused by a number of interrelated developments. First, the development of modern science gave rise to an approach to the natural world in which it was viewed exclusively in mechanistic terms without reference to divine intention. Figures like Bacon and Galileo acknowledged the reality of God, but only as a deistic entity that had no active role in the universe. Wirzba contends that this led to a situation in which the significance of the God who was "once understood to be the source and goal of the world, created a hole that would be filled by human beings now positioned themselves as the center or source of meaning and value."[84] From this vacuum emerged a form of anthropocentrism that had unburdened itself from the view that there is a divine intention for the world. The result is that human beings began to see the natural world as an arena in which to pursue their own narrow interests, independent of any transcendent horizon. Wirzba observes:

> the sense of the world as creation, as ordered in terms of a divine plan, is largely gone. The sense of humans as microcosms of creation, as containing within themselves the responsibility to bring creation to its perfection in God, is eclipsed by the autonomous self who, with the aid of scientific technique, transforms the world according to a human plan.[85]

The end result is that the world is subjected to human manipulation, domination, and exploitation in the name of scientific and technological progress. Furthermore, truth is reduced to what is pragmatic, with the result that any sense of wonder and reverence is purged from the world. As Wirzba observes: "when value is determined by a pragmatic human calculus, thought and action are no longer captivated by wonder, amazement, respect, or admiration."[86]

Second, modern technology inscribes on the body patterns of perception that produce specific ways of relating to the world. This is connected to the loss of contact with the natural world in modern society, but it goes much deeper and touches on the very way in which the world is perceived in modernity.[87] According to Wirzba the dominance of technology creates a situation in which

---

[82] Norman Wirzba, *The Paradise of God: Renewing Religion in an Ecological Age* (New York: Oxford University Press, 2003), 62.

[83] Ibid., 61–62.

[84] Ibid., 68.

[85] Ibid., 70.

[86] Ibid.

[87] Ibid., 72.

we do not engage reality on its own terms, but rather as packaged or framed by someone else and in terms set by the limits of the medium . . . we have become spectators of a world of someone else's invention and control, particularly when we realize how many hours are spent weekly in front of a television or computer screen.[88]

He sees media as a poor substitute for the type of sustained engagement with the world that was at one time an inescapable feature of life. In particular, Wirzba, like Heidegger, maintains that technological culture flattens our perception of the world so that it is viewed only as raw material available for human use. According to him we see the world as a mere resource for economic activity and aesthetic pleasure and thereby diminish our capacity to practice the form of "deep perception" that "see[s] in things the hand of God."[89]

Both of these transitions in modernity have created a situation in which human beings have become insulated from any substantial, sustained encounter with the natural world. This, in turn, has severely eroded the sense of interdependence between humanity and the rest of creation.

These features of modern culture have contributed in important ways to the current environmental crisis. But, as noted above, the broadest and deepest source of that crisis is the elimination of God from the world. For Wirzba this situation is complicated, because the banishment is not motivated by a militant atheism or a widespread collapse of belief in God. It is, instead, characterized by a sense that God is superfluous or not relevant to everyday life in the modern world. Wirzba observes: "[t]hough we may claim that God exists, it does not matter, since the patterns of our day-to-day lives, as well as the goals of our culture, proceed on terms set by economic demands and without reference to God."[90]

The current situation is not one in which individuals have ceased to believe in God. On the contrary, belief in God continues largely unabated, but that belief has ceased to shape the lives of individuals in any substantive way.

Talal Asad has explored this paradox and framed it in economic terms by asking: "How does it happen that in modern capitalist society Christians and non-Christians, believers and non-believers, live more or less the same life?"[91] Wirzba describes the implications of this situation in which the values of the market have eclipsed religious values:

---

[88] Ibid., 79.

[89] Ibid., 80–81.

[90] Ibid., 90.

[91] Talal Asad, "Thinking about Religion, Belief, and Politics," 36–57, in *The Cambridge Companion to Religious Studies*, ed. Robert Orsi (New York: Cambridge University Press, 2012), at 49.

economies cease to be driven and constrained by a transcendent vision of justice and the good. Work ceases to be a vocation, but instead becomes a task for the procurement of money, which now becomes the universally acclaimed "good." How far this new economic way of thinking departed from traditional understanding can be seen in the fact that the virtue of the free-market economy, indeed its necessary precondition—the drive for personal wealth—was considered a vice in almost every spiritual tradition that preceded it.[92]

Because economic logic has eclipsed any alternative system of values, we have also lost any sense that there exist values that exceed the scope of narrow self-interest. The dominance of this anthropocentric horizon manifests itself in concrete ways and broadly shapes the ethos of modernity. Wirzba observes:

given the autonomous, market-driven, and technological character of our age, it is safe to say that God is absent. God has been banished by us in the drive to fashion a world according to our own liking or, failing that, the liking of corporate, global, and economic forces. In this divine banishment, it is not surprising that the nature of the divine power as being-for-another should be entirely lost on us. We cannot be the caretakers of creation because the divine model for such care has been systematically denied or repressed by the dominant cultural trends of the last several centuries.[93]

The fact that the loss of a sense of responsibility for creation coincides with the elimination of God as the *telos* of human existence is not a coincidence. Indeed, for Wirzba these two movements are directly related and have created a context in which self-interested economic values have eclipsed the religious value of being-for-another as the ethos that dominates the contemporary cultural landscape.

The antidote Wirzba offers to this situation is similar to that proposed by Benedict XVI in that both thinkers identify the root cause of the environmental crisis in terms of the elimination of God from the world. For Wirzba the materialist assumptions of modern culture have created a situation in which "the world has little purpose other than the instrumental purposes humans ascribe to it."[94] As a result, he argues that it is necessary to restore a horizon of meaning that exceeds the instrumental and economic logic of modern culture. Wirzba contends that this horizon is granted by God as the Creator who has endowed

---

[92] Wirzba, *The Paradise of God*, 69.
[93] Ibid., 92.
[94] Ibid., 62.

creation with an intrinsic significance worthy of respect and reverence. For him the remembrance of God involves the recognition not only that creation possesses an intrinsic significance but also that God has called humanity into a relationship of responsibility with creation. According to Wirzba

> the teaching of creation, besides being a teaching of how the world began, is about the characterization of human identity and vocation within the world. In it we see who we are and what we are to become. A developed account of creation will thus invariably alert us to the value and character of what is, and, in doing so, inform us about the nature of our interdependence with the creator and the creation and our responsibility for this interdependence.[95]

Conclusion

In this chapter I have moved from a description of the basic facts of the environmental crisis and its tangible symptoms to an examination of its deeper economic and technological causes. While advocating for political and economic reform is an important way of responding to the environmental crisis, merely tinkering with institutional reform is insufficient because it fails to strike at the deeper root of the problem. In particular, Benedict XVI and Norman Wirzba point to the fact that at the root cause of these economic and technological dimensions of the crisis is a pervasive anthropocentrism that can only be confronted through the focused remembrance of God. As will be argued in the next chapter, one of the primary ways to remember God is by cultivating an aesthetic-sacramental perception of creation because, as Benedict XVI has said, "the beauty of creation is one of the sources where we can truly touch God's beauty, we can see that the Creator exists and is good."[96]

---

[95] Ibid., 13.

[96] Benedict XVI, Interview: Pastoral Visit to Loreto 9/1/2007, http://www.vatican .va/holy_father/benedict_xvi/speeches/2007/september/documents/hf_ben-xvi_spe _20070901_veglia-loreto_en.html.

Chapter 4

Sacramental Vision

Introduction

The previous chapter described the crisis of environmental degradation and examined the economic, technological, and theological roots of this crisis. In the face of the radical changes that are necessary to prevent environmental catastrophes in the future, the situation appears bleak. The pessimistic tone of the previous chapter, however, will give way here to a more positive and constructive theological vision of care for creation. Representative of this shift is the claim made by the poet Mary Oliver that her approach to the environmental crisis is not to describe the catastrophes that await the world if human beings do not change their behavior. Rather, Oliver invites people to look at the world differently:

> I am not very hopeful about the Earth remaining as it was when I was child. It's already greatly changed. But I think when we lose the connection with the natural world, we tend to forget that we're animals, that we need the Earth. And that can be devastating. Wendell Berry is a wonderful poet, and he talks about the coming devastation a great deal. I just happen to think that you catch more flies with honey than with vinegar. So I try do more of the "Have you noticed this wonderful thing? Do you remember this?"[1]

Oliver's wager is that when we enjoy and appreciate the beauty of the natural world we will begin to defend it against the forces of degradation.[2] Consistent

---

[1] Mary Oliver, "Interview with Maria Shriver," http://www.oprah.com/entertainment /Maria-Shriver-Interviews-Poet-Mary-Oliver/3.

[2] In "Among Wind and Time," Oliver writes: "in order to want to save the world we must learn to love it—and in order to love it we must become familiar with it again. That is

with this approach, this chapter will focus on the significance of theological aesthetics as a means of cultivating a contemplative-sacramental perception of creation.

This chapter has three main sections. The first describes the contribution of theological aesthetics to constructing a Christian response to the environmental crisis by examining the work of Hans Urs von Balthasar. In particular it will be argued that the emphasis von Balthasar places on the task of perception (*aisthesis*) of the splendor of the world as a manifestation of the glory of God establishes a sacramental vision of creation that serves as an important alternative to economic-technological culture. This section will also link von Balthasar's theological aesthetics with the land ethic of Aldo Leopold in order to make explicit the connection between theological aesthetics and environmental ethics. The second section analyzes spiritual exercises that have the capacity to cultivate this contemplative-sacramental mysticism and train individuals in an aesthetic vision of creation: liturgy and the sacraments, mourning (*penthos*), immersion in the natural world, and contemplative prayer. The third section examines the lives and writings of two individuals who witness in different ways to the sacramentality of creation in an age of environmental degradation: Annie Dillard and Wendell Berry.

Theological Aesthetics

The previous chapter argued that one of the primary causes of the environmental crisis is the distorted perception of the world that is dominant in the modern era. In different ways Martin Heidegger, Benedict XVI, and Norman Wirzba all made the argument that economic-technological culture has transformed the way moderns perceive the world. Consequently, an adequate response to the crisis of environmental degradation must take root in a transformed way of perceiving the world. The focus on both perception (*aisthesis*) and beauty in theological aesthetics makes that field an important resource to explore for the development of a Christian response to the environmental crisis.

For Hans Urs von Balthasar the task of theological aesthetics is to cultivate the imaginative capacity to perceive the beauty of creation as a manifestation of the glory of God.[3] He argues, however, that the modern period is a time in which

---

where my work begins, and why I keep walking, and looking." Mary Oliver, "Among Wind and Time," *Sierra* (Nov–Dec 1991): 33–34.

[3] Hans Urs von Balthasar, *The Glory of the Lord*, vol. 1, *Seeing the Form*, trans. Erasmo Leiva-Merikakis, ed. Joseph Fessio and John Riches (San Francisco: Ignatius Press, 1982), Foreword, 9–12. A version of this section on von Balthasar's theological aesthetics was published in

it has become difficult to perceive the glory of God in creation because we live in the midst of what he describes as a "technical civilization."[4] In his diagnosis of the loss of a sense of glory in modern culture von Balthasar draws from Romano Guardini's theology (as well as Heidegger's philosophy). Guardini's reflections on technology spanned his entire career from his early thoughts on the dissolution of local culture under the power of modern technology in *Letters from Lake Como* (1927)[5] to his later apocalyptic discussion of the technological orientation of the modern era in *The End of the Modern World* (1950).[6] In *Letters from Lake Como*, Guardini contended that in the modern era the organic, contemplative knowledge characteristic of previous epochs has given way to an instrumental form of knowledge focused on exerting human control over nature.[7] In response to this situation Guardini calls for the recovery of a contemplative-liturgical attitude that will reawaken moderns to a vision of reality that has been displaced within technological culture.[8]

Von Balthasar follows Guardini's criticism of technological culture and argues that the contemporary situation is one of "extreme danger" in which the human spirit has been reduced to "an instrument of human power for the mastery of the world and as such has already outgrown man's remaining control, thus enslaving him: the person has become a thing."[9] In his discussion of Guardini's thought von Balthasar specifically suggests that the dominance of this technological approach to the world is rooted in a distorted vision. He observes:

> seeing has become a matter of observing and verifying to which is afterwards added the activity of an abstract intellect as it orders and elaborates what is perceived . . . the life formed in accordance with nature's great images,

---

Matthew T. Eggemeier, "A Sacramental Vision: Environmental Degradation and the Aesthetics of Creation," *Modern Theology* 29 (2013): 338–60.

[4] Hans Urs von Balthasar, *Test Everything: Hold Fast to What Is Good; An Interview with Hans Urs von Balthasar* (San Francisco: Ignatius Press, 1989), 49.

[5] Romano Guardini, *Letters from Lake Como: Explorations in Technology and the Human Race*, trans. Geoffrey W. Bromiley (Grand Rapids: Eerdmans, 1994).

[6] Romano Guardini, *The End of the Modern World* (Wilmington, DE: ISI Books, 1998), 117–18.

[7] Guardini, *Letters from Lake Como*.

[8] Guardini, *End of the Modern World*, 214. See also idem, *The Spirit of the Liturgy* (New York: Crossroad, 1998).

[9] Hans Urs von Balthasar, *Romano Guardini: Reform from the Source*, trans. Albert K. Wimmer and D. C. Schindler (San Francisco: Ignatius Press, 2010), 16.

with the natural symbols which shape existence, is becoming more and more alien and insubstantial for man because of technology.[10]

More deeply, von Balthasar describes the modern cultural situation as characterized by nothing short of "a fateful loss of sight" in which "the light of Being no longer shines over the world."[11] As a result, he contends, the fundamental task of Christians in the present is to preserve the glory of creation in an age that has become blind to any vision of reality that exceeds the limited forms of perception dominant in technological culture. Von Balthasar writes:

> the Christians of today, living in a night which is deeper than that of the later Middle Ages, are given the task of performing the act of affirming Being, unperturbed by the darkness and the distortion, in a way that is vicarious and representative for all humanity: an act which is at first theological, but which contains within itself the whole dimension of the metaphysical act of the affirmation of Being.[12]

The tone adopted here by von Balthasar is similar to Heidegger's proclamations on the "world's night" in which he describes modernity as a time when the light of Being has ceased to shine in the world.[13] Von Balthasar responds to this crisis by attempting to restore a premodern way of seeing that has been covered over by the technological culture of modernity; he insists that the Christian tradition alone is capable of preserving the glory of creation in the modern era,[14] writing that "the decision falls uniquely—and the history of the modern period has no clearer result—for or against the Glory of Being, and history has fashioned the Either-Or so simply that it has become a decision between Christianity and nihilism."[15]

For von Balthasar this either-or amounts to a decision between the nihilism of technological culture (as described broadly by Heidegger) or the Christian vision of reality grounded in the view that there exists an intrinsic relationship

---

[10] Von Balthasar, *The Glory of the Lord: Seeing the Form*, 389–90.

[11] Hans Urs von Balthasar, *The Glory of the Lord. A Theological Aesthetics*, vol. 5, *The Realm of Metaphysics in the Modern Age*, trans. Oliver Davies, Andrew Louth, Brian McNeil, John Saward, and Rowan Williams, ed. Brian McNeil and John Riches (San Francisco, CA: Ignatius Press, 1991), 624.

[12] Ibid., 648. See also *Glory of the Lord: Seeing the Form*, 18–19.

[13] Heidegger, *Poetry, Language, Thought*, 91.

[14] Von Balthasar, *The Glory of the Lord: Seeing the Form*, 24; idem, *The Glory of the Lord: The Realm of Metaphysics in the Modern Age*, 656.

[15] Von Balthasar, *The Glory of the Lord: The Realm of Metaphysics in the Modern Age*, 249.

between God and the world.[16] This view of the relationship between Creator and creation (the analogy of being) serves as the basis for the development of the so-called aesthetic analogy between the beauty of creation and the glory of God. Von Balthasar finds an important precedent for this aesthetic analogy in his retrieval of patristic and medieval theologians who viewed "the beautiful as one of the transcendental attributes of Being" because "they possessed a theology of creation which, likewise unhesitatingly, attributed creation's aesthetic values *eminenter* to the creating principle itself."[17] For von Balthasar, however, the most important warrant for the analogy of being is Jesus Christ, who is "the *analogia entis* in concrete form."[18] He observes: "God's Incarnation perfects the whole ontology and aesthetics of created Being. The Incarnation uses created Being at a new depth as a language and as a means of expression for the divine Being and essence."[19] The Incarnation expresses in a concentrated form the sacramental vision of the Christian tradition in which creation represents the very medium through which God is revealed.

An important implication of von Balthasar's defense of this Christian aesthetic of creation is the need to preserve a vision of creation in which everything that exists is significant by virtue of the fact that God created it. This point is of particular importance when viewed in relation to Heidegger's concern that in technological culture things in the world have become meaningless apart from their utilitarian function. But where Heidegger attempts to restore a sense of the sacred by retrieving the significance of the work of art and revitalizing the significance of the gods, von Balthasar contests the nihilism of technological culture and its reduction of entities to resources through an aesthetic defense of the sacramentality of creation. According to him:

> the infinite Creator has equipped it [created being] with the grace of participation in the inexhaustibility of its origin. It bears in itself a wealth that cannot be consumed like a finite sum of money. You are never finished with any being, be it the tiniest gnat or the most inconspicuous stone. It has a secret [*geheime*] opening, through which never-failing replenishments of sense and significance ceaselessly flow to it from eternity.[20]

---

[16] Ibid., 548–49. See also Hans Urs von Balthasar, *The Theology of Karl Barth*, trans. Edward Oakes (San Francisco: Ignatius Press, 1992).

[17] Von Balthasar, *The Glory of the Lord: Seeing the Form*, 38.

[18] On Platonism see Hans Urs von Balthasar, "The Fathers, the Scholastics, and Ourselves," *Communio* 24 (1997): 347–96, at 373.

[19] Von Balthasar, *The Glory of the Lord: Seeing the Form*, 29.

[20] Hans Urs von Balthasar, *Theo-Logic: Truth of the World*, trans. Adrian J. Walker (San Francisco: Ignatius Press, 2000), 107.

For von Balthasar a Christian vision of reality is committed to the view that each worldly being possesses a transcendent significance beyond its mere immanent utility.[21] Thus, in his view, it is God's transcendent glory manifest in the beauty of creation that alone guarantees the intrinsic significance of all things as sacramental manifestations of God.

But only by faith [handwritten marginalia]

In order to contest the distorted instrumental vision of the world that dominates technological culture, von Balthasar retrieves from the Christian tradition alternative pictures of the world that present an aesthetic-sacramental vision of reality to moderns. His project of retrieval represents a concerted effort to enlarge the sense of what is true, good, and beautiful. In particular, in two volumes of his seven-volume theological aesthetics, *Clerical Styles* and *Lay Styles*, von Balthasar analyzes twelve thinkers from the theological tradition who described distinctively Christian "pictures of the world."[22] He emphasizes the aesthetic quality of the theological, mystical, and poetic works of these thinkers whose lives and writings witness to the glory of God present in all creation. In these two volumes von Balthasar describes the pictures of the world in the writings of Christians from Irenaeus, Augustine, and Dionysius the Areopagite to John of the Cross, Gerard Manley Hopkins, and Charles Peguy. A number of these thinkers are relevant for our present purposes—particularly Hopkins, with his profoundly sacramental poetry—but rather than analyzing von Balthasar's interpretation of these individuals, this chapter will examine some contemporary writers (Annie Dillard and Wendell Berry) who witness to an aesthetic-sacramental perception of the natural world. But first we turn to von Balthasar's analysis of the development of the spiritual senses as a means of cultivating this vision of reality.

In the first volume of *The Glory of the Lord*, von Balthasar echoes Hopkins's famous line in "As Kingfishers Catch Fire" that "Christ plays in ten thousand places" when he argues that for the human person the "sensory environment, in which he lives and with which he is apparently wholly familiar, is through and through determined by the central image and event of Christ, so that, by a thousand open and hidden paths, his wholly real and corporeal sense-experiences bring him into contact with that central point."[23] This quotation is representative of von Balthasar's insistence that a properly aesthetic interpretation of the Christian tradition is one that affirms that God can be perceived in and through human senses.[24] Indeed,

---

[21] Ibid., 59.

[22] Von Balthasar, *The Glory of the Lord*, vol. 2: *Studies in Theological Style: Clerical Styles*, trans. Andrew Louth et al. (San Francisco: Ignatius Press, 1984), 13.

[23] Von Balthasar, *The Glory of the Lord: Seeing the Form*, 419–20.

[24] On von Balthasar on the spiritual senses see Mark McInroy's intriguing discussion in *Perceiving Splendor: The "Doctrine of the Spiritual Senses" in Hans Urs von Balthasar's Theological*

he argues that because the sensible form mediates God's presence to the human person, the spiritual act of perceiving the form becomes the central task of Christian existence.

Von Balthasar's emphasis on the spiritual significance of the form and the intimate connection between the sensible and the transcendent is one implication of the incarnational logic of the Christian tradition, in which human flesh is the vehicle through which God is revealed to the world. Accordingly, the spirituality von Balthasar privileges as a response to the incarnation and the sacramental worldview it generates is committed to the work of "finding God in all things."[25]

But, as noted above, von Balthasar argues that the modern era is an inhospitable time for seeing the form insofar as technological culture discloses things as mere resources bereft of transcendent significance. The result is that moderns have become virtually blind to the spiritual depth of creation and perceive it only as raw material for maximizing the efficiency of human projects. In response to the destructive effects of this technological culture von Balthasar points to the need to return to a form of asceticism that preserves an alternative vision of the world.[26] To this end he argues that spiritual exercises serve as important preparatory activities, cultivating a basic receptivity to God's grace.[27] He focuses particularly on the *kenotic* element of ascetical practice, which "simply means making room for God; it is a preparation for contemplation, for God to 'increase' and the self to 'decrease.'"[28] For von Balthasar the experience of "non-experience" in the desert of prayer is one of the central practices in the Christian tradition, in which the self is decreased and thereby prepared for God's transformation. Whether this ascetical disposition is described by von Balthasar as an Eckhartian "letting be" (*Gelassenheit*) or Ignatian "indifference" (*indiferencia*), the central point is that a posture of prayerful receptivity is a religious discipline that elevates the senses to the task of perceiving the spiritual form in creation.[29]

Aesthetics. Dissertation, Harvard Divinity School (Ann Arbor: ProQuest/UMI, 2009), no. AAT 3356448, and Stephen Fields, "Balthasar and Rahner on the Spiritual Senses," *Theological Studies* 57 (1996): 224–41.

[25] Hans Urs von Balthasar, *Explorations in Theology*, vol. 1, *The Word Made Flesh* (San Francisco: Ignatius Press, 1989), 177. See also idem, "The Fathers, the Scholastics, and Ourselves," 395.

[26] Von Balthasar, *Test Everything*, 50.

[27] Von Balthasar, *The Glory of the Lord: Seeing the Form*, 418.

[28] Hans Urs von Balthasar, *Two Sisters in the Spirit: Thérèse of Lisieux and Elizabeth of the Trinity*, trans. Donald Nichols, Anne Englund Nash, and Dennis Martin (San Francisco: Ignatius Press, 1992), 302. See also idem, "The Fathers, the Scholastics, and Ourselves," 395.

[29] On letting be in relation to God's revelation see von Balthasar, *My Work: In Retrospect* (San Francisco: Ignatius Press, 1993), 81. On von Balthasar's interpretation of letting be

Following Romano Guardini, von Balthasar applies this analysis of the ascetic transformation of the senses to the sense of sight, observing that "seeing is anything but passive; rather, it betokens a determined effort to offer a space, to make oneself available to that which can be perceived as truth."[30] The truth to be perceived is that "creation as a whole has become a monstrance of God's real presence."[31] Von Balthasar writes: "in Christianity God appears to man right in the midst of worldly reality. The centre of this act of encounter must, therefore, lie where the profane human senses . . . become 'spiritual.'"[32] The Christian tradition affirms that God can be perceived by the senses of sight, touch, sound, smell, and taste. Indeed, God is present in creation as a gift, but the perception of this gift is possible only for the person whose perception has been purified through spiritual exercises. In this sense von Balthasar rightly emphasizes the role a renewed commitment to ascetical practices can play in elevating the senses to the spiritual task of perceiving the suprasensory in the sensory.[33]

In an essay entitled "The Sacrament of Creation," Michael and Kenneth Himes argue that a Christian response to the ecological crisis should be rooted in a retrieval of a sacramental vision of the world. According to the Himeses this vision of the world should be understood as "a Christian aesthetic that needs cultivation. The whole of Catholic praxis is training in sacramental vision."[34] In concluding this essay the authors quote a line from Gerard Manley Hopkins's "Hurrahing in Harvest": "'These things, these things were here, and but the beholder/Wanting.'" They then reflect: "At present, 'beholders' are desperately wanted."[35] Although von Balthasar never raises the crisis of environmental

---

(*Gelassenheit*) see Werner Löser, SJ, "The Ignatian Exercises in the Work of Hans Urs von Balthasar," 103–20, in *Hans Urs von Balthasar: His Life and Work*, ed. David L. Schindler (San Francisco: Ignatius Press, 1992), and Cyril O'Regan, "Von Balthasar's Valorization and Critique of Heidegger's Genealogy of Modernity," 123–58, in *Christian Spirituality and the Culture of Modernity: The Thought of Louis Dupré*, ed. Peter J. Casarella and George P. Schner (Grand Rapids: Eerdmans, 1998).

[30] Balthasar, *Romano Guardini: Reform from the Source* 22. See also idem, 24; *The Glory of the Lord: Seeing the Form*, 24; *The Glory of the Lord: A Theological Aesthetics*, vol. 6, *The Old Covenant*, trans. Brian McNeil and Erasmo Leva-Merikakis (San Francisco: Ignatius Press, 1982), 85.

[31] Von Balthasar, *The Glory of the Lord: Seeing the Form*, 420.

[32] Ibid., 365.

[33] Ibid., 425.

[34] Michael and Kenneth Himes, "The Sacrament of Creation: Toward an Environmental Theology," 270–83, in *Readings in Ecology and Feminist Theology*, ed. Mary Heather MacKinnon and Moni McIntyre (Kansas City: Sheed & Ward, 1995), at 277.

[35] Ibid.

degradation to the level of a fundamental problem in his theology, the response of the Himeses to the ecological crisis is consistent with the whole of his theology as a focused attempt to retrieve an aesthetic-sacramental experience of creation for the Christian life. In this sense von Balthasar's retrieval of the significance of theological aesthetics and the spiritual senses represents an important resource for articulating a Christian response to the environmental crisis.

In order to make this connection between theological aesthetics and environmental ethics more explicit, I will conclude this section by turning to the environmental writings of Aldo Leopold. As one of the most important American writers in the environmental movement, Leopold is most famous for his description of the land ethic in *A Sand County Almanac*. While the land ethic is rightly viewed as a landmark statement on the proper relationship between human beings and the natural world, what is far less frequently commented on is the link Leopold draws between the cultivation of the land aesthetic and the practice of a land ethic.[36] Leopold's basic argument is that "we can be ethical only in relation to something we can see, feel, understand, love."[37]

In *A Sand County Almanac*, Leopold expressed concern with the fact that the prevailing way of relating to the world was dominated by an economic logic that views the land as a mere unit to be used and consumed for the development needs and profit motives of human beings. He wrote: "there is as yet no ethic dealing with man's relation to land and to animals and plants which grow upon it . . . the land-relation is still strictly economic, entailing privileges but not obligations."[38] For Leopold every ethic commits itself to a sense of community and extends obligations and duties only toward those who belong to this community. The innovation of the land ethic is that it "enlarges the boundaries of the community to include soils, waters, plants, and animals, or collectively: the land."[39] Thus, in response to the environmental crisis Leopold maintains that it is necessary to expand the sense of community beyond its anthropocentric strictures so that humanity can recognize that its duties and obligations extend

---

[36] Indeed, Leopold's reflections on the connection between these two realities stemmed from his concern that progress in the material and economic realm is erasing the very possibility of a profound experience of the natural world. He wrote: "like winds and sunsets, wild things were taken for granted until progress began to do away with them. Now we face the question whether a still higher 'standard of living' is worth its cost in things natural, wild, and free. For us of the minority, the opportunity to see geese is more important than television." Leopold, *A Sand County Almanac* (New York: Ballantine Books, 1990), 21.

[37] Ibid., 179.

[38] Ibid., 168.

[39] Ibid., 171.

to the natural world. The land ethic straightforwardly proposes that "a thing is right when it tends to preserve the integrity, stability, and beauty of the biotic community. It is wrong when it tends otherwise."[40]

Leopold engaged in an important environmental task by articulating the theoretical grounds of an ethic that includes the welfare of the biosphere itself in its deliberations. But for him the critical issue is how, in fact, this ethic can be cultivated in a cultural climate in which an instrumental and economic relationship with the land is dominant. While Leopold acknowledges that the prevailing disposition toward the natural world is dominated by the idea "that the human relation to the land is only economic," he adds, "it is, or should be, esthetic as well."[41] Leopold maintains that it is at the aesthetic level that a relationship with the natural world can be cultivated that supports the land ethic and resists the prevailing instrumental commitments of culture. He writes: "it is inconceivable to me that an ethical relation to the land can exist without love, respect, and admiration for land, and a high regard for its value. By value, I of course mean something far broader than mere economic value."[42]

Leopold never set forth a formal theory of the land aesthetic. Instead, he produced a series of descriptions of his own aesthetic experiences in the natural world. Leopold claimed that an aesthetic relation to the land develops over time and takes place through one particular organ. He wrote: "our ability to perceive quality in nature begins, as in art, with the pretty. It expands through successive stages of the beautiful to the values yet uncaptured by language."[43] Leopold observes that the tendency is to be attracted first to the "pretty," in terms of manicured landscapes and the more refined "sites" of beauty displayed in the natural parks (the Grand Canyon, Yosemite, etc.). He suggests, however, that individuals gradually learn to have an aesthetic experience of the mundane rather than the spectacular. According to Leopold:

> the taste for country displays the same diversity in aesthetic competence among individuals as the taste for opera. . . . There are those who are willing to be herded in droves through "scenic" places: who find mountains grand if they be proper mountains with waterfalls, cliffs, and lakes. To such the Kansas plains are tedious.[44]

[40] Ibid., 189.

[41] Aldo Leopold, *The River of the Mother of God: And Other Essays by Aldo Leopold*, ed. Susan Flader and J. Baird Callicott (Madison: University of Wisconsin Press, 1991), 337.

[42] Leopold, *A Sand County Almanac*, 21.

[43] Ibid., 160.

[44] Aldo Leopold, *Round River*, ed. Luna B. Leopold (New York: Oxford University Press, 1993), 33.

For Leopold, of course, a deeper experience of the Kansas plains is available to those who devote themselves to a place: "in country, as in people, a plain exterior often conceals hidden riches, to perceive which requires much living in and with."[45]

This progression is important because it is critical that we come to see not only the Grand Canyon and Yosemite as worthy of preservation but also more mundane and less exalted landscapes. Indeed, the land ethic is concerned to defend the entire biotic community from human exploitation and not simply those places that are deemed "pretty" by the prevailing standards of a culture.

In *It All Turns on Affection*, Wendell Berry maintains that Leopold's life is evidence of the truthfulness of this argument. Berry observes: "I don't hesitate to say that damage or destruction of the land-community is morally wrong, just as Leopold did not hesitate to say so when he was composing his essay, 'The Land Ethic,' in 1947." Berry then describes the way affection for the natural world (the land aesthetic, in Leopold's terminology) was the motivating source for Leopold's own concrete application of the land ethic to a small piece of land in Wisconsin. Berry observes:

> the primary motive for good care and good use is always going to be affection, because affection involves us entirely. And here Leopold himself set the example. In 1935 he bought an exhausted Wisconsin farm and, with his family, began its restoration. To do this was morally right, of course, but the motive was affection. Leopold was an ecologist. He felt, we may be sure, an informed sorrow for the place in its ruin. He imagined it as it had been, as it was, and as it might be. And a profound, delighted affection radiates from every sentence he wrote about it.[46]

Leopold's life therefore constitutes an important witness to the inseparability of an environmental aesthetic from a concrete environmental ethic.[47] This con-

---

[45] Ibid.

[46] Wendell Berry, *It All Turns on Affection: The Jefferson Lecture & Other Essays* (Berkeley: Counterpoint, 2012), 32–33.

[47] See the introduction to *The River of the Mother of God*, 14. More broadly on this relationship see J. Baird Callicott, "Leopold's Land Aesthetic," 105–18, in *Nature, Aesthetics, and Environmentalism: From Beauty to Duty*, ed. Allen Carlson and Sheila Lintott (New York: Columbia University Press, 2008); idem, "The Land Aesthetic," *Environmental Review* 7/4 (Winter 1983): 345–58; J. Baird Callicott, *In Defense of the Land Ethic: Essays in Environmental Philosophy* (Albany: SUNY Press, 1989), and Joni L. Kinsey, "Through Successive Stages of the Beautiful," 279–83, in *The Essential Aldo Leopold: Quotations and Commentaries* (Madison: University of Wisconsin Press, 1999).

nection is all the more urgent in a time when our collective perception of the world has been shaped by the instrumental values of economic-technological culture. Indeed, Heidegger, von Balthasar, Benedict XVI, and Wirzba all argue that at the root of the environmental crisis lies the fact that any sense that the world is significant beyond anthropocentric, economic, and utilitarian values has been eliminated from the horizon of modern culture.

Leopold's focus on the aesthetic is instructive for a theological approach to the environmental crisis because it underscores the link between the perception of the natural world's beauty and the development of a land ethic that attempts to preserve the biosphere. Theological aesthetics could supplement Leopold's naturalist aesthetics by emphasizing that the encounter with worldly beauty is an encounter with divine glory. Furthermore, the aesthetic analogy of being supports a sacramental vision of reality that views even the tiniest and most insignificant gnat as worthy of reverence as a creature of God.

Contemplative-Sacramental Mysticism

We have already touched on the issue of which spiritual exercises or practices are available to cultivate this aesthetic-sacramental vision of reality. In his theological aesthetics Hans Urs von Balthasar privileges the contemplative and liturgical dimensions of Christian life as spiritual exercises that form persons in this aesthetic-sacramental perception of creation. In a different way, Aldo Leopold emphasizes the centrality of the sustained embodied encounter with the natural world as a means of developing an aesthetic perception of the natural world. This section will analyze these and other spiritual exercises that possess the capacity to train individuals in this aesthetic-sacramental vision. Specifically, it will examine four practices of contemplative-sacramental mysticism: liturgy and the sacraments, mourning, the embodied encounter with the natural world, and contemplative prayer.

(1) In his philosophy, Albert Borgmann has offered a provocative analysis of the way that technology affects modern culture. He also has advocated for a return to the resources of the Christian tradition as a means of resisting its influence: "making room for Christianity is in fact the most promising response to technology."[48] Following Heidegger, Borgmann contends that the technological relation with the world is a virtually omnipresent feature of modern life that trains individuals to view things as commodities.

---

[48] Albert Borgmann, *Power Failure: Christianity in a Culture of Technology* (Grand Rapids: Brazos Press, 2003), 8.

From a Christian perspective this is a worrisome development because technological culture forms the imagination in a way that obstructs the perception of the sacraments. Indeed, he sees a culture of commodification as "deeply inhospitable to grace and sacrament" because "by transforming the very notion of what is reality it has likely clouded the very reality of the sacraments."[49] Borgmann claims that because technological culture affects individuals at the level of perception it blocks their capacity to perceive the world as sacramental. He contends, therefore, to perceive the world as it is—that is, sacramentally—it is necessary to engage in ascetic practices that liberate us "from the indolence and shallowness of technology" and open "to us the festive engagement with life."[50] He observes:

> since technology as a way of life is so pervasive, so well entrenched, and so concealed in its quotidianity, Christians must meet the rule of technology with a deliberate and regular counterpractice . . . here we must consider again the ancient senses of theology, the senses that extend from reflection to prayer. We must also recover the ascetic tradition of practice and discipline and ask how the ascesis of being still and solitary in meditation is related to the practice of being communally engaged in the breaking of the bread.[51]

Because God's presence in the world often goes unnoticed as a result of broader cultural forces that obstruct individuals' perception of this presence in creation, the sacraments are those events by which Christians remember and celebrate God's presence in creation.[52] Michael Himes observes: "The whole Catholic sacramental life is a training to be beholders. Catholic liturgy is a life-long pedagogy to bring us to see what is there, to behold what is always present, in the conviction that if we truly see and fully appreciate what is there, whether we use the language or not, we will be encountering grace."[53] In this sense liturgical worship is a communal event that trains individuals to encounter the grace of God in the individual sacraments.

But, as with other spiritual exercises, liturgical worship also transforms the senses so that God's presence is perceived not only within the confines of the

---

[49] Ibid., 126.

[50] Ibid., 94. More broadly on the issue of the relationship between the culture of commodities and the sacramental imagination, see Vincent J. Miller, *Consuming Religion: Christian Faith and Practice in a Consumer Culture* (New York: Continuum, 2004), 188–92.

[51] Ibid., 94.

[52] Michael Himes, "'Finding God in All Things': A Sacramental Worldview and Its Effects," 91–105, in *As Leaven in the World: Catholic Perspectives on Faith, Vocation, and the Intellectual Life*, ed. Thomas Landy (Franklin, WI: Sheed and Water, 2001), 99.

[53] Ibid., 100.

church but throughout all of creation. Indeed, the sacraments express the fact that all that exists possesses the capacity to reveal God—water (baptism), oil (anointing of the sick), bread and wine (Eucharist). In relation to the Eucharist, John Habgood observes: "what happens to water, bread, and wine when they are used as vehicles of God's grace is no isolated miracle. All matter shares this potential."[54] Sacraments serve both to reveal and to transform. They are carriers of meaning in that they disclose a distinctive way of imagining the world. But, as emphasized in the second chapter, sacraments also constitute embodied rituals that train individuals to conform their perception to the disclosure of God's presence in creation.[55] Thus liturgical action should be a form of *askesis* that affects individuals at a level deeper than conscious awareness. The images from Scripture, the words preached in a homily, the various embodied gestures and ritual action in liturgy should serve to instill in the participants a sacramental form of perception that sees God in all of creation.

(2) As discussed in the second chapter, the remembrance of suffering is a critical dimension of an authentic Christian spirituality. In environmental discourse, this remembrance takes the form of mourning.[56] Mourning is a critical environmental practice, therefore, because, like *memoria passionis*, it alerts us not only to what has been lost in the past but also to what continues to be damaged or destroyed in the present. For example, Aldo Leopold has applied the work of mourning to the environmental crisis, observing: "One of the penalties of an ecological education is that one lives alone in a world of wounds."[57] For Leopold, there exists an important connection between an intimate knowledge of the natural world and the possibility of mourning its destruction. As he puts it: "We only grieve for what we know."[58] Together with Leopold, Terry Tempest Williams has argued that the process of mourning presupposes an intimate knowledge of the natural world (what Wendell Berry terms "local memories").[59] She observes:

---

[54] John Habgood, "A Sacramental Approach to Environmental Issues," http://www.religion-online.org/showarticle.asp?title=2320.

[55] On the link between liturgy and ecology, see also Margaret Pfiel, "Liturgy and Ethics: The Liturgical Asceticism of Energy Conservation," *Journal of the Society of Christian Ethics* 27/2 (Fall/Winter 2007): 127–49.

[56] This section is particularly indebted to the work of Douglas Burton-Christie on mourning in American nature writing and Christian monasticism in "The Gift of Tears: Loss, Mourning, and the Work of Ecological Restoration," *Worldviews: Global Religion, Culture, and Ecology* 15 (2011): 29–46, and *The Blue Sapphire of the Mind: Notes for a Contemplative Ecology* (New York: Oxford University Press, 2013).

[57] Leopold, *Round River*, 165.

[58] Leopold, *A Sand County Almanac*, 86.

[59] Wendell Berry, *Citizenship Papers* (Washington, DC: Shoemaker & Hoard, 2003), 89.

> . . . if we don't know pronghorn antelope, if we don't know blacktail jack rabbit, if we don't know sage, pinyon, juniper, then I think we are living a life without specificity . . . . I remember a phone call from a friend of mine who lives along the MacKenzie River. She said, "This is the first year in 20 that the chinook salmon have not returned." This woman knows the names of things. This woman is committed to a place. And she sounded the alarm.[60]

For Tempest Williams it is this practice of learning the names of things in the natural world that leads us to begin to "extend our sense of community, our idea of community, to include all life forms—plants, animals, rocks, rivers *and* human beings."[61] It is from this expansion of what constitutes community that a "politics of place emerges where we are deeply accountable to our communities, to our neighborhoods, to our home."[62]

The work of mourning also represents an important spiritual practice that occupies a central place in the history of Christian spirituality. *Penthos*, or the "gift of tears," was an important spiritual act in the ancient monastic tradition and was grounded in Jesus' beatitude: "Blessed are those who mourn, for they shall be comforted" (Matt 5:4). In the world of ancient monasticism tears not only expressed serious compunction and sorrow about one's life and sins but also represented the act that liberated the monk from sinful patterns of behavior. Tears represented a concrete, external expression of the fact that the monk was reckoning with his past life and genuine in his desire to follow the path of conversion toward a new life.[63] In this sense the work of mourning is not only an important environmental practice (Leopold, Tempest Williams) but also a "restorative spiritual practice" (Christie) that permits us to see the world with new eyes and to acknowledge that we live in a world of wounds.[64]

The Canadian poet Tim Lilburn has turned to the ancient monastic practice of *penthos* as an important spiritual exercise in an age of environmental degradation. For Lilburn *penthos* is a purgative practice that can engender a return to a "right relationship" with all things. He suggests that the "gift of tears" is "in a primitive sense, political, a social labor; [tears] are, says Gregory

---

[60] Terry Tempest Williams, *A Voice in the Wilderness: Conversations with Terry Tempest Williams* (Logan: Utah State University Press, 2006), 52–53.

[61] Ibid., 52.

[62] Ibid.

[63] See Burton-Christie, "The Gift of Tears," 33–37.

[64] Ibid., 30, and idem, *The Blue Sapphire of the Mind*, 85–86.

of Nazianzen, 'the purification of the world.'"[65] Lilburn directs the experience of *penthos* toward the destructive relationship with the land in North America, writing that we should be moved to "compunction, to apology, tears, sorrow" for "all of these imperialisms that we've engaged in. This foolish sense that we were and are entitled in an unlimited way."[66] He deems *penthos* an activity that not only cultivates an awareness of failure, loss, and alienation but also opens the possibility of plotting a return to a nonexploitative relationship with the natural world.[67]

Lilburn specifically links *penthos* with *kenosis* or the work of "unselfing," and observes of this ancient monastic practice: "the monk is poured into waiting, watching and tears, the *ascesis* contemplative knowing calls forth, the thinning of the self, the building and focusing of desire."[68] In this regard Lilburn writes that contemplative practice, of which *penthos* is an integral part, is a "therapeutics for the soul" that opens the possibility of "a return to nature, an *apokatastasis*, not just of the individual, but of the human world and the cosmos itself."[69] He argues that this return to the world is cosmic in scope, and to signify this he invokes the Christian teaching on universal salvation (*apokatastasis*). Lilburn redirects the tradition of *apokatastasis* beyond what he describes as its narrowly anthropocentric concerns and suggests that the work of contemplation and mourning are a means of developing a "broad politics, an *apokatastasis* of all things, a pandemic return home, nonpartisan, nonanthropocentric, embracing human communities, yet reaching beyond their narrowly understood concerns."[70]

(3) The second chapter examined Iris Murdoch's description of the significance of the encounter with the beauty of the natural world as a spiritual exercise that opens the self to a more authentic relation with the world. Henry David Thoreau and R. S. Thomas provide interesting examples of the way in which immersion in the natural world becomes spiritually significant, particularly as it takes form in the discipline of walking in the environs of Walden Pond and bird-watching on the cliffs of the Welsh countryside.

[65] Tim Lilburn, *Living in the World As If It Were Home* (Dunvegan, ON: Cormorant, 2002), 66.

[66] Tim Lilburn, "Listening with Courtesy: A Conversation with Tim Lilburn." Interview by Darryl Whetter in *Studies in Canadian Literature* 22 (1997): 135–44, at 142.

[67] Lilburn, *Living in the World*, 64.

[68] Ibid., 12.

[69] Ibid., 10.

[70] Ibid., 7.

One of the most important spiritual metaphors in Thoreau's writings is wakefulness. For him, moral and spiritual reform is throwing off sleep.[71] Thoreau observes: "The millions are awake enough for physical labor; but only one in a million is awake enough for effective intellectual exertion, only one in a hundred millions to a poetic or divine life. To be awake is to be alive. I have never yet met a man who was quite awake."[72]

Thoreau has a number of strategies for cultivating this sense of wakefulness, but none is more important than the discipline of walking. And for him there are proper and improper ways to walk: "I believe there is a subtle magnetism in Nature, if we unconsciously yield to it, will direct us aright. It is not indifferent to us which way we walk, there is a right way."[73] For Thoreau the proper way to walk is to do it "so gently as to hear the finest sounds—the faculties being in repose—your mind must not perspire."[74] Thoreau chooses the term "saunter" to describe this approach to walking. Sauntering has nothing to do with physical exertion. Instead, it is more akin to a spiritual exercise. According to Thoreau, sauntering is a word that "is beautifully derived 'from idle people who roved about the country, in the Middle Ages, and asked charity, under pretence of going á la Sainte Terre' to the Holy Land."[75] For him, sauntering is a form of spiritual pilgrimage à la Sainte Terre. The holy land, however, is not a place at all but rather the process of attending to the spiritual depth present in the natural world. Thoreau practiced this form of walking daily and deemed it so critical that he insisted his spiritual health could not be preserved "unless I spend four hours a day at least,—and it is commonly more than that,—sauntering through the woods and over the hills and fields, absolutely free from all worldly engagements."[76]

To be out of one's senses or to be inattentive to one's surroundings is an experience of spiritual alienation, for Thoreau, because the sensuous life is the authentic life. And for him, walking represented the means by which he returned to his senses. Thoreau observes: "it sometimes happens . . . that the thought of some work will run in my head, and I am not where my body is,—I am out

---

[71] Henry David Thoreau, *Walden: Or Life in the Woods and Other Writings* (New York: Bantam Dell, 2004).

[72] Ibid., 181.

[73] Henry David Thoreau, "Walking" (1862), 62–80, in *Civil Disobedience and Other Essays* (Dover, 1993), at 68.

[74] Henry David Thoreau, *The Heart of Thoreau's Journals*, ed. Odell Shepard (New York: Dover Publications, 1961), 51.

[75] Thoreau, "Walking," 62.

[76] Ibid., 63.

of my senses. In my walks I would fain return to my senses."[77] In this return to the senses is representative of a return to an authentic perception. Significantly, however, he maintains that the senses need "not to be spiritualized, but *naturalized*, on the soil of the earth."[78] In this regard the immersion of the senses in the concrete things of the earth such as dirt, soil, and leaves represented the condition for the possibility of elevating the senses to the task of divine sensation. Thus for him it is not by detaching oneself from earthly things that one has a spiritual experience, but rather through a sensuous immersion in these things. According to Thoreau,

> we need pray for no higher heaven than the pure senses can furnish, a *purely* sensuous life. Our present senses are but the rudiments of what they are destined to become. We are comparatively deaf and dumb and blind, and without smell or taste or feeling. Every generation makes the discovery, that its divine vigor has been dissipated, and each sense and faculty misapplied and debauched. The ears were made, not for such trivial uses as men are wont to suppose, but to hear celestial sounds. The eyes were not made for such grovelling uses as they are now put to and worn out by, but to behold beauty now invisible. May we not *see* God?[79]

The key to Thoreau's corpus is his concern to cultivate the capacity to perceive the transcendent in the ordinary and to see the divine in the mundane things of the earth. His goal was to fully immerse himself in the "natural life" and by doing so to catch a glimpse of the supernatural life because, for him, "we need to be earth-born as well as heaven-born."[80]

In the writings and poetry of the Welsh theologian and priest R. S. Thomas we find a more distinctively Christian interpretation of the spiritual significance of immersion in the natural world. In the tradition of Gerard Manley Hopkins's poetry, Thomas refers to himself as a nature mystic, describing his daily experience of watching the sea on the Welsh coast:

> at moments such as these, every problem concerning the purpose of life, death and morality disappears, and man feels in touch with existence, pure and simple. For a moment he is one with the creation, participating in the

---

[77] Ibid., 65.

[78] Henry David Thoreau, *A Week on the Concord and Merrimack Rivers* (New York: Penguin Books, 1985), 304. Emphasis in original.

[79] Ibid., 307. Emphasis in original.

[80] Ibid., 305.

genius of life, as every creature in time has done over millions of years. My name for such a rare, but not alien, experience, is nature-mysticism.[81]

This nature-mysticism might be more accurately described as a sacramental or analogical mysticism because for Thomas "it is the world 'created' that is the word. Nature isn't my God. I'm not in love with things and scenes for themselves. They are the creation."[82] Thomas's mysticism is not a pantheistic form that collapses the difference between God and the world. Rather, it is one grounded in the analogy of being, in which the natural world becomes the medium through which God is revealed. Thomas confirms this when he invokes Aquinas's central epistemological axiom to describe his encounter with God in creation, referring to himself in the third person: "Thomas Aquinas believed that God revealed Himself according to the creature's ability to receive Him. If he did this to R. S., he chose to do so through the medium of the world of nature."[83]

Like Thoreau, for whom a daily, solitary walk in the wilderness was the means of cultivating the experience of wakefulness to the traces of the divine in the world, Thomas engaged in the discipline of bird-watching on the Welsh coastline as a means of waiting for God. In "Sea-watching" he describes this experience of waiting:

> Grey waters, vast
> > as an area of prayer
> that one enters. Daily
> > over a period of years
> I have let the eye rest on them.
> Was I waiting for something?

Initially the poet responds to this question by suggesting he was waiting for nothing. But he then turns to describe his encounter with a rare bird that functions in the poem as a metaphor for God, writing:

---

[81] R. S. Thomas, *Autobiographies*, trans. Jason Walford Davies (London: Weidenfeld & Nicolson, 1997), 122. More broadly see Christopher Morgan, *R. S. Thomas: Identity, Environment, Deity* (Manchester: Manchester University Press, 2010); William V. Davis, *R. S. Thomas: Poetry and Theology* (Waco: Baylor University Press, 2007). Daniel Westover, "A God of Grass and Pen: R. S. Thomas and the Romantic Imagination," *North American Journal of Welsh Studies* 3 (Summer 2003): 18–38; Mark Jarman, "Praying and Bird Watching: The Life of R. S. Thomas," *The Hudson Review* 60/1 (Spring 2007): 169–75; Barry Sloan, "The Discipline of Watching and Waiting: R. S. Thomas, Poetry, and Prayer," *Religion & Literature* 34/2 (2002): 29–49.

[82] Quoted in Morgan, *R. S. Thomas: Identity, Environment, Deity*, 55.

[83] R. S. Thomas, *Autobiographies*, 106.

Ah, but a rare bird is
rare. It is when one is not looking,
at times one is not there
  that it comes.
You must wear eyes out,
as others their knees.

For Thomas, bird-watching becomes a metaphor for the dialectic between the experience of the absence and presence of God. He encountered not only a rare bird through this practice of watching and waiting at the sea, but also God. Accordingly, in the concluding lines to "Sea-watching," Thomas suggests that it becomes impossible to distinguish "my watching from praying."[84] He elaborates on this relationship between prayer and bird-watching when he describes his experience of watching the seabirds that migrate through the Llyn Peninsula from August to October:

> thinking of these migrations, looking at the stars at night and bearing in mind the millions of small bodies on their way to a country they had never seen before, RS would marvel at how miraculous the creation was. And spending an hour or two looking over the sea hoping to see a migratory bird, he came to see the similarity between this and praying. He had to watch patiently for a long time for fear of losing the rare bird, because he did not know when it would come by. It is exactly the same with the relationship between man and God that is known in prayer. Great patience is called for, because no-one knows when God will choose to reveal Himself.[85]

For Thomas, immersion in the natural world was his own contemplative discipline of waiting for God. This exercise was so central to his life that it enabled him to continue to believe in God. He observes: "going into the quiet and beauty of the moorland was like entering a more beautiful church than any he had ever seen. And looking on the morning dew in the sun was like listening to the heavenly choir singing glory to God. He was doubtful whether, in an industrial town, he could have worshipped and continued to believe. That is, the country side was indispensable to his faith."[86]

 (4) Finally, we turn to contemplation as a spiritual exercise capable of cultivating a sacramental form of mysticism. Following R. S. Thomas's reflections on

---

[84] R. S. Thomas, "Sea-Watching," *Collected Poems: 1945–1990* (London: Phoenix, 2000), 306.

[85] Thomas, *Autobiographies*, 100.

[86] Ibid., 84.

bird-watching, Rowan Williams suggests that there exist important similarities between bird-watching, prayer, and an awake or open-eyed spirituality. He writes:

> I've always rather liked that image of prayer as bird-watching. You sit very still because something is liable to burst into view, and sometimes of course it means a long day sitting in the rain with nothing very much happening, and I suspect that most of us know that a lot of our experience of prayer is precisely that. But the odd occasions when you do see what T. S. Eliot called "the kingfisher's wing flashing light to light" make it all worthwhile. And I think that living in expectancy—living in awareness, your eyes sufficiently open and your mind sufficiently both slack and attentive to see that when it happens—has a great deal to do with discipleship, indeed with discipleship as the gospels present it to us. Interesting (isn't it?) that in the gospels the disciples don't just listen, they're expected to look as well.[87]

For Williams prayer involves the cultivation of awareness, attention, and openness to what lies outside the self. The parallel he draws between the experience of the natural world and the experience of the divine is present in American naturalist writing as well as in the monastic literature of the Desert Fathers and Mothers.[88] Thomas Merton is an interesting example of the way the threads of the American naturalist tradition and Christian contemplative traditions converge in their focus on the cultivation of a form of contemplative attention to the natural world.

Like Thoreau before him, Merton criticized the technological character of contemporary culture insofar as it blinds individuals to the spiritual significance of creation.[89] Merton's issue with technology was not with gadgets or instruments but rather that "[t]echnology has its own ethic of expediency and efficiency. What can be done efficiently *must* be done in the most efficient way."[90] Merton

---

[87] Rowan Williams, "Being Disciples," http://www.fulcrum-anglican.org.uk/events/2007/williams.cfm?doc=209. Thomas makes this point in his *Autobiographies*, 100. On the contemplative dimension of Thomas's poetry see Sloan, "The Discipline of Watching and Waiting," 29–49.

[88] Douglas Burton-Christie, "Mapping the Sacred Landscape: Spirituality and the Contemporary Literature of Nature," *Horizons* 21 (1994): 22–47; Belden Lane, *The Solace of Fierce Landscapes: Exploring Desert and Mountain Spirituality* (New York: Oxford University Press, 2007).

[89] Thomas Merton, *Thomas Merton, Spiritual Master: The Essential Writings*, ed. Lawrence Cunningham (New York: Paulist, 1992), 391.

[90] Thomas Merton, *Conjectures of a Guilty Bystander* (Garden City, NY: Doubleday, 1966), 70. Emphasis in original.

saw this technological ethos as creating a culture that alienates individuals from creation and dulls their faculties of perception. He argued:

> technology alienates those who depend on it and live by it. It deadens their human qualities and their moral perceptiveness. Gradually, everything becomes centered on the most efficient use of machines and techniques of production, and the style of life, the culture, the tempo and the manner of existence responds more and more to the needs of the technological process itself.[91]

Similar to von Balthasar, Merton concluded that the current situation is one in which the modern person "has lost his 'sight' and is blundering around aimlessly in the midst of the wonderful works of God."[92]

Consequently, Merton argued that the most fundamental responsibility of Christians within technological culture is "toward creation and God's will for his creation."[93] He presupposes the Christian teaching that God's presence has been offered in creation to every person at each moment of his or her life. In *New Seeds of Contemplation*, Merton observed that each and every moment of existence "brings with it germs of spiritual vitality that come to rest imperceptibly in the minds and wills of men." The problem, for Merton, is that the majority of these seeds perish because humanity is "not prepared to receive them: for such seeds as these cannot spring up anywhere except in the good soil of freedom, spontaneity, and love."[94]

In his writings Merton focused his attention on contemplation as the antidote needed to awaken moderns from their slumber and open them to the possibility of a spiritual perception of creation.[95] Merton argued that contemplation cultivates a sense of wonder before creation because contemplation itself is "life itself, fully awake, fully active, fully aware that it is alive. It is spiritual wonder.

---

[91] Thomas Merton, "Answers to Hernan Lavin Cerda: On War, Technology, and the Individual," *The Merton Annual* 2 (1989): 3–12, at 6. Quoted in Philip M. Thompson, *Between Science and Religion: The Engagement of Catholic Intellectuals with Science and Technology in the Twentieth Century* (Lanham, MD: Lexington Books, 2009), 118.

[92] Thomas Merton, *Witness to Freedom: The Letters of Thomas Merton in a Time of Crisis* (New York: Farrar, Straus & Giroux, 1994), 71.

[93] *Spiritual Master*, 211.

[94] Thomas Merton, *New Seeds of Contemplation* (New York: New Directions, 1972), 14.

[95] The significance of attention in Merton's vision is analyzed in Robert Waldron, *Thomas Merton: Master of Attention: An Exploration of Prayer* (New York: Paulist, 2008), and Monica Weis, *The Environmental Vision of Thomas Merton* (Lexington, KY: University of Kentucky Press, 2011).

It is spontaneous awe at the sacredness of life, of being. It is gratitude for life."[96] In this sense he rejected the view of contemplative prayer as a disembodied, immaterial, spiritual experience that moves an individual beyond the created world. Instead, Merton maintained that contemplative prayer is the practice that permits individuals to see the world from the perspective of the divine. He wrote:

> we do not detach ourselves from things in order to attach ourselves to God, but rather we become detached from ourselves in order to see and use all things in and for God. . . . there is no evil in anything created by God, nor can anything of His become an obstacle to our union with Him. The obstacle is in our "self," that is to say in the tenacious need to maintain our separate, external, egoistic will.[97]

Merton explicitly elaborated this relationship between contemplation and a sacramental perception of creation in terms of the classical threefold path of spiritual progress as described by Evagrius Ponticus and Maximus the Confessor. For Evagrius the contemplative life follows the threefold path of development of ascetic discipline (*praktikē*) and purification of the soul (*kartharsis*), the contemplation of God in the things of the world (*theoria physikē*), and union with God (*theologikē*). Merton focused on the second stage, observing: "*Theoria physikē* is the intuition of divine things in and through the reflection of God in nature and in the symbols of revelation. It presupposes a complete purification of heart by a long ascetic preparation . . . . When the eye is clear and 'single' (that is to say disinterested—having only 'one intention'), then it can see things as they are."[98] Consistent with the reflections of Evagrius Ponticus and the Christian mystical tradition more broadly, Merton insisted that this form of natural contemplation involves labor, preparation, and a form of asceticism that makes it possible for grace to transform the self's perceptual faculties. Furthermore, he wrote that this "natural contemplation" is "a contemplation which man seeks and prepares by his own initiative but which, by a gift of God, is completed in mystical intuition."[99] At this stage of the contemplative life, Merton observed, contemplation leads to a simple and direct perception of things so that the contemplative is capable of seeing "straight into the nature of things as they are."[100]

---

[96] *New Seeds of Contemplation*, 1.

[97] Ibid., 21.

[98] Thomas Merton *The Inner Experience: Notes on Contemplation*, ed. William Shannon (New York: Harper Collins, 2004), 67; see also Thomas Merton, *Ascent to Truth: A Study of St. John of the Cross* (New York: Burns & Oates, 1994), 21.

[99] *Inner Experience*, 68.

[100] Ibid.

Sacramental Witness

This section will address two forms of sacramental witness in the lives and writings of Annie Dillard and Wendell Berry. Dillard and Berry are important examples of different ways of cultivating an ethical relationship to the natural world in an age of environmental degradation. Dillard's writings witness to a self-emptying form of contemplative attention to the natural world that contains important environmental implications when viewed from the perspective of the link between aesthetics and ethics. Berry, on the other hand, while emphasizing the importance of recovering an aesthetic appreciation (or affection) for the natural world, also focuses his attention on the political and economic commitments needed to confront this crisis.

In *The Environmental Imagination*, Lawrence Buell identifies the "aesthetics of relinquishment" as one of the fundamental themes in American nature literature.[101] For Buell the aesthetics of relinquishment involves collapsing the distance between the subject and object and dissolving "the illusion of mental and even bodily apartness from one's environment."[102] He writes that this relinquishment entails a movement from egocentrism to ecocentrism.[103] In American nature writing this relinquishment is often described in optical metaphors, as with Henry David Thoreau's call for the cultivation of a "sauntering of the eye" and Ralph Waldo Emerson's famous description of the humbling of the ego before the natural world in which he becomes "a transparent eyeball; I am nothing; I see all."[104]

Around the turn of the twentieth century John Burroughs penned two important essays on the relationship between selfless attention to the natural world and the capacity to see things, entitled "Sharp Eyes" (1879) and "The Art of Seeing Things" (1909). In "The Art of Seeing Things" Burroughs contended that in contrast to the skill set involved in detached science, which can be acquired through study, the art of seeing things "comes by practice or inspiration"

---

[101] The discussion of Dillard is part of a broader argument made in Matthew T. Eggemeier, "Ecology and Vision: Contemplation as Environmental Practice," *Worldviews* 18 (2014): 54–76.

[102] Lawrence Buell, *The Environmental Imagination: Thoreau, Nature Writing, and the Formation of American Culture* (Cambridge, MA: Harvard University Press, 1996), 144.

[103] Ibid., 384.

[104] Henry David Thoreau, *The Heart of Thoreau's Journals*, ed. Odell Shepard (Mineola, NY: Dover Publications, 1961), 99; Ralph Waldo Emerson, *Nature and Selected Essays*, ed. Larzer Ziff (New York: Penguin Books, 2003), 39.

and involves "the art of keeping your eyes and ears open."[105] He wrote specifically about how this art is achieved: "Power of attention and a mind sensitive to outward objects, in these lies the secret of seeing things" as well as in direct "proportion to the love and desire behind it."[106]

While one can detect the religious sensibility of transcendentalism in the writings of Thoreau, Emerson, and even Burroughs, the role of attention in the act of seeing things has been described in explicitly Christian terms in Annie Dillard's writings, as something that resembles or, in some cases, is identical to prayer. In this sense she applies to the natural world the observation made by Simone Weil that "attention, taken to its highest degree, is the same thing as prayer . . . [A]bsolutely unmixed attention is prayer."[107] For Weil a genuine act of attention also entails the disappearance of the "I" before the object to which it attends.[108] Dillard, therefore, brings Buell's aesthetics of relinquishment into conversation with the Christian spirituality of *kenosis* in describing her own contemplative perception of the natural world.

Annie Dillard was born on April 30, 1945, in Pittsburgh, Pennsylvania. She attended Hollins College in Virginia and received a BA and an MA in 1968. In a decision that is of some significance in view of her subsequent work, Dillard wrote her master's thesis on the role played by the concrete location of Walden Pond in the dialectic between heaven and earth in Thoreau's *Walden*. She is the author of more than ten books of essays, poetry, and fiction, all of which focus in some way on her experience of the natural world. Her first publication, in 1974, was a volume of poetry entitled *Tickets for a Prayer Wheel*; it was followed only months later by the publication of *Pilgrim at Tinker Creek*, a series of essays that chronicle Dillard's experience of spending a year in solitude in the hills of the Blue Ridge Mountains of Virginia. Similar to *Walden*, *Pilgrim at Tinker Creek* is characterized by a wide-ranging exploration of her surroundings and consists of scientific observations, reflections on the spiritual life, and mystical experiences of union with the natural world.

Raised a Presbyterian, Dillard converted to Catholicism in 1988. Although she has rarely engaged in any sustained analysis of the theological traditions of Christianity, she has occasionally reflected on her experience of sacrament and worship in the church as a means of describing her immersion in the

[105] John Burroughs, *The Art of Seeing Things: Essays*, ed. Charlotte Zoë Walker (Syracuse, NY: Syracuse University Press, 2001), 3, 8.

[106] Ibid., 8, 14.

[107] Simone Weil, *Gravity and Grace*, trans. Emma Crawford and Mario von der Ruhr (London and New York: Routledge, 2002), 117.

[108] Ibid., 171–72.

natural world. For instance, in "An Expedition to the Pole," she observes that if Christians had even the foggiest idea of what was going on in the church on Sunday morning they would wear crash helmets and the ushers would issue life preservers.[109] Dillard describes her experience of the natural world in a similar way and contends that the contemplative sensibility needed to perceive God in church is similar to that needed to see God in the mystery of the natural world. She observes:

> we don't know what's going on here. . . . Our life is a faint tracing on the surface of mystery, like the idle, curved tunnels of leaf miners on the face of a leaf. We must somehow take a wider view, look at the whole landscape, really see it, and describe what's going on here. Then we can at least wail the right question into the swaddling band of darkness, or, if it comes to that, choir the proper praise.[110]

This quotation is representative of Dillard's focus on the spiritual significance of seeing the world. In a manner consistent with Emerson, Thoreau, and Burroughs, she observes of her pilgrimage into the natural world: "It's all a matter of keeping my eyes open."[111]

In particular, in the second chapter of *Pilgrim at Tinker Creek*, entitled "Seeing," she analyzes two modalities of seeing: seeing as "verbalization" and seeing as "letting go." Dillard describes seeing as verbalization in active, assertive terms: "When I see this way I analyze and pry. I hurl over logs and roll away stones."[112] Seeing as verbalization constitutes a willful form of seeing that lurches toward nature, aggressively inspecting and analyzing it. Dillard contrasts this instrumental approach to the world with a form of seeing that resembles the Emersonian transparent eyeball, observing that this way of seeing "involves a letting go. When I see in this way I sway transfixed and emptied."[113] For her, seeing in this way involves letting go of the "running description of the present," a letting-go that opens the self to an encounter with what is given.[114]

At the end of "Seeing," Dillard describes the experience of being emptied and standing transparent before a cedar tree in her backyard. She writes that she perceived the cedar tree as "charged and transfigured, each cell buzzing with flame. I stood on the grass with lights in it, grass that was wholly fire,

---

[109] Annie Dillard, *Teaching a Stone to Talk* (New York: Harper Perennial, 1988), 52.
[110] Annie Dillard, *Pilgrim at Tinker Creek* (New York: Harper Perennial, 2007), 10–11.
[111] Ibid., 19.
[112] Ibid., 33.
[113] Ibid.
[114] Ibid.

utterly focused and utterly dreamed. It was less like seeing than like being for the first time seen, knocked back breathless by a powerful glance."[115] She recalls that during this experience, with "rising exultation," she proclaimed: "this is it, this is it; praise the lord; praise the land."[116] This encounter involves an experience of the aesthetics of relinquishment in which intentionality is reversed and the self no longer has the experience of seeing, but rather of being seen by an object. Furthermore, it is an example of the way in which a contemplative attentiveness to the present moment is a central means of being attuned to the graced character of the world. Dillard describes its significance: "experiencing the present purely is being emptied and hollow; you catch grace as a man fills his cup under a waterfall."[117]

Dillard recognizes that there is little she can do to produce this way of seeing beyond committing to the discipline of waiting in silence before the world. She writes: "I can't go out and try to see this way. I'll fail, I'll go mad. All I can do is try to gag the commentator, to hush the noise of useless interior babble that keeps me from seeing. . . . The effort is really a discipline requiring a lifetime of dedicated struggle; it marks the literature of saints and monks of every order East and West, under every rule and no rule, discalced and shod."[118] Thus she keeps vigil in order to still the ego and diminish the self so that she can encounter the world as it is. According to Dillard, "the death of the self of which the great writers speak is no violent act. It is merely the joining of the great rock heart of the earth in its roll. It is merely the slow cessation of the will's sprints and the intellect's chatter: it is waiting like a hollow bell with stilled tongue. *Fuge, tace, quiesce.* The waiting itself is the thing."[119] Her invocation of monks, saints, and the maxim of the Desert Fathers to flee, be silent, keep still, and wait is not accidental, and at times she explicitly links the act of attending to the natural world to the encounter with God. Dillard maintains that looking at the world with attention is itself a form of prayer. She goes so far as to suggest that it is permissible to address the world in prayer: "at a certain point you say to the woods, to the sea, to the mountains, the world, now I am ready. Now I will stop and be wholly attentive. You empty yourself and wait, listening . . . you take a step in the right direction to pray to this silence, and even to address the prayer to 'World.' Distinctions blur. Quit your tents. Pray without ceasing."[120]

---

[115] Ibid., 36.
[116] Ibid., 82.
[117] Ibid.
[118] Ibid., 34–35.
[119] Ibid., 265.
[120] *Teaching a Stone to Talk*, 89–90, 94.

In this way quiet attention before creation becomes, for Dillard, one important way to respond to St. Paul's directive to pray without ceasing (1 Thess 5:17). The doxological quality in Dillard's writings is rooted in a profoundly sacramental view of the world that resembles Gerard Manley Hopkins's poetry in its affirmation that "God is in the thing."[121] In particular, Dillard describes her writings as an example of the *via positiva*, in which the act of attending to the goodness of creation represents a path to God.[122] Indeed, the task of learning to perceive the beauty of creation is the vocation most proper to the human person: "We are here to witness the creation and abet it. We are here to notice each thing so each thing gets noticed. Together we notice not only each mountain shadow and each stone on the beach but, especially, we notice the beautiful faces and complex natures of each other. . . . Otherwise, creation would be playing to an empty house."[123]

The writings of Annie Dillard bear witness to the most basic insight of Christian theological aesthetics, that "there seems to be such a thing as beauty, a grace wholly gratuitous."[124] This description of grace takes on a distinctively sacramental quality in her writings. She illustrates this when she describes her childhood ritual of hiding a penny on the sidewalk for a passer-by to discover as an analogy for the sacramental character of creation. Dillard describes her excitement "at the thought of the first lucky passer-by who would receive in this way, regardless of merit, a free gift from the universe."[125] The penny becomes a metaphor for the spiritual significance of each and every thing in creation as a gift from God: "The world is fairly studded and strewn with pennies cast broadside from a generous hand. But—and this is the point—who gets excited by a mere penny?"[126] The problem is that most people do not possess the capacity to see the mundane things of the world as gifts from a generous hand. The challenge Dillard poses to her readers, then, is to "cultivate a healthy poverty and simplicity, so that finding a penny will literally make your day, then, since the world is in fact planted in pennies, you have with your poverty bought a lifetime of days. It is that simple. What you see is what you get."[127]

---

[121] Annie Dillard, *Holy the Firm* (New York: Harper Perennial, 1988), 70.

[122] *Pilgrim at Tinker Creek*, 279–80.

[123] Annie Dillard in "The Meaning of Life: Reflections in Words and Pictures on Why We Are Here," ed. David Friend, *Life Magazine* (Dec. 1991), 14.

[124] *Pilgrim at Tinker Creek*, 8.

[125] Ibid., 16.

[126] Ibid., 17.

[127] Ibid.

While Dillard's nature writings have been associated with Aldo Leopold's land ethic, she distances herself from any explicit ethical concerns in her writings: "I don't write at all about ethics. . . . The kind of art I write is shockingly uncommitted—appallingly isolated from political, social, and economic affairs."[128] Thus Dillard explicitly denies that there is an environmental ethic present in her writings. Notwithstanding this disavowal, her writings constitute a series of profound meditations on the spiritual significance of seeing the natural world from a contemplative perspective, and it is this approach to the world that contains within it important—if only implicit—environmental implications.[129] As with Aldo Leopold and Mary Oliver, Annie Dillard's writings witness to the important link between aesthetics and ethics. This also represents an important feature of the writings of Wendell Berry, to which I now turn.

In Wendell Berry's writings we find a similar focus on the cultivation of a contemplative-sacramental appreciation of the natural world, but this is also linked to a sustained criticism of the technological and economic culture that has caused the environmental crisis. Berry is, furthermore, much more explicit than Dillard about the political and economic remedies needed to respond to this crisis. Berry was born in 1934 in Henry County, Kentucky. Raised a Baptist, he observes that he has always had the experience of being "an outsider to the sects and denominations."[130] Berry attended college at the University of Kentucky, where he received both a BA and an MA. After graduating in 1957 he traveled to California, New York, and Italy, only to return to Kentucky in the early 1960s. Wallace Stegner observes that Berry's decision to return to Kentucky "was a move as radical as Thoreau's retreat to Walden, and much more permanent."[131] Berry is descended from five generations of farmers, and in 1965 he bought a twelve-acre farm in Port Royal, where he still resides. His work is wide-ranging and brings together the various threads examined in both the third chapter on the environmental crisis and the present chapter on the contemplative and sacramental resources capable of responding to this crisis.

---

[128] Phillip Yancey, "A Face Aflame: An Interview with Annie Dillard," *Christianity Today* 22 (May 1978): 960.

[129] As Mary Oliver notes: "what we enjoy, we value. What we feel is making our lives rich and more meaningful, we cherish. And what we cherish, we will defend." Mary Oliver, "Foreword," xi–xv, in *Poetry Comes Up Where It Can: An Anthology*, ed. Brian Swann (Salt Lake City: University of Utah Press, 2000), at xiii.

[130] Wendell Berry, *Conversations with Wendell Berry*, ed. Morris Allen Grubbs (Jackson: University Press of Mississippi, 2007), 118.

[131] Quoted in Bernard W. Quetchenbach, *Back from the Far Field: American Nature Poetry in the Late Twentieth Century* (Charlottesville: University of Virginia Press, 2000), 123.

In terms that closely resemble Heidegger's diagnosis of modern culture as technological, Berry argues: "we have assumed increasingly over the last five hundred years that nature is merely a supply of 'raw materials,' and that we may safely possess those materials merely by taking them. This taking, as our technical means have increased, has involved always less reverence or respect, less gratitude, less local knowledge, and less skill."[132] Furthermore, he maintains that within technological culture everything is commodified and reduced to "interchangeable parts."[133] Berry views the effects of this technological ethos on modern culture as dangerous because, as a result, we have become insulated from the natural world. The lives of moderns have "become less creaturely and more engineered, less familiar and more remote from local places, pleasures and associations. Our knowledge, in short, has become increasingly statistical."[134] The virtues of reverence and gratitude that are the fruit of sustained immersion in the rhythms of the natural world have been replaced in modern culture by the industrial virtues of mastery and efficiency.

These industrial values are supported by the modern economy, which, for Berry, is a total economy in which all other cultural values have been usurped by economic values and the market itself has taken on "the standing of ultimate reality."[135] Berry's argument is consistent with the claim made in previous chapters that the emergence of the total economy orients the entire culture toward a set of values that are harmful not only to the environment but also to the human community. He focuses on competition, in particular, as the central value of the total economy that serves both to reduce human beings to the level of "rats and roaches" and to destroy the environment in the process.[136] He writes that

> competition proposes simply to lower costs at any cost, and to raise profits at any limits. It does not hesitate at the destruction of the life of a family or the life of a community. . . . The human economy is pitted without limit against nature. For in the unlimited competition of neighbor and neighbor, buyer and seller, all available means must be used; none may be spared.[137]

---

[132] Wendell Berry, *The Art of the Commonplace: The Agrarian Essays of Wendell Berry*, ed. Norman Wirzba (Washington, DC: Counterpoint, 2002), 250.

[133] Wendell Berry, *Life Is a Miracle: An Essay against Modern Superstition* (Washington, DC: Counterpoint, 2000), 41–42.

[134] Berry, *It All Turns on Affection*, 23.

[135] Ibid., 31.

[136] *The Art of the Commonplace*, 212.

[137] Ibid., 209.

While Berry views the industrial economy as the fundamental cause of the environmental crisis, he also points to the fact that individuals share a measure of responsibility for that crisis through their daily consent to this economic order, even when they do not approve of it.[138] He observes: "we have an 'environmental crisis' because we have consented to an economy in which by eating, drinking, working, resting, traveling, and enjoying ourselves we are destroying the natural, god-given world."[139]

Because the cause of the environmental crisis is cultural, Berry suggests that an antidote must likewise be found at the level of the forms of life a culture promotes. He rejects technocratic solutions, writing that it is foolish to think we could solve the environmental crisis by "tinkering with the institutional machinery." He instead argues that the changes required to confront this crisis "are fundamental changes in the way we are living."[140] Thus he argues, in a manner consistent with Leopold's defense of the land ethic, that we must develop what he terms a "healthy community." A healthy community is

> a neighborhood of humans in a place, plus the place itself: its soil, its water, its air, and all the families and tribes of the nonhuman creatures that belong to it. If the place is well preserved, if its entire membership, natural and human, is present in it, and if the human economy is in practical harmony with the nature of the place, then the community is healthy.[141]

In particular Berry believes it is necessary to return to those types of practices that connect people to the natural world and to each other in local communities. He argues that there are a number of interrelated ways of restoring this connection: the recovery of the agrarian approach to the world; the theological retrieval of the world as creation; a return to a local politics and a local economy.

First Berry suggests that to restore a way of being in the world rooted in the values of reverence and gratitude it is necessary to restore a sense of "affection" for the land and submit to the discipline of becoming an "apprentice of creation."[142] He describes his own experience of cultivating this affection for the land:

---

[138] *It All Turns on Affection*, 23.

[139] *The Art of the Commonplace*, 251.

[140] Ibid., 84.

[141] Wendell Berry, *Sex, Economy, Freedom, and Community: Eight Essays* (New York: Pantheon Books, 1993), 14.

[142] Wendell Berry, *The Long-Legged House* (New York: Harcourt Brace & World, 1969), 201. On this point see Norman Wirzba's analysis of the mystical dimension of Berry's thought in "The Dark Night of the Soil: An Agrarian Approach to the Mystical Life," 148–69, in

to live and work attentively in a diverse landscape such as this one—made up of native woodlands, pastures, croplands, ponds, and streams—is to live from one revelation to another, things unexpected, always of interest, often wonderful. After a while, you understand that there can be no end to this. The place is essentially interesting, inexhaustibly beautiful and wonderful. To know this is a defense against the incessant sales talk that is always telling you that what you have is not good enough; your life is not good enough. There aren't many right answers to that. One of them, one of the best, comes from living watchfully and carefully the life uniquely granted to you by your place: My life, thank you very much, is just fine.[143]

This is a description of what Berry describes as the agrarian mind, to which he juxtaposes the industrial-economic mind that "sees creatures as machines, minds as computers, soil fertility as chemistry."[144] The agrarian mind, for Berry, "is, at bottom, a religious mind" and "begins with love of fields and ramifies in good farming, good eating, and gratitude to God."[145]

While Berry advocates for the traditional means of cultivating the agrarian mind, such as walking (Thoreau) and watching (Thomas), he also suggests that gardening is a critical means of cultivating a sense of affection for the natural world as well as an important environmental practice in its own right. Furthermore, it is a practice that is available to virtually anyone. Berry observes: "odd as I am sure it will appear to some, I can think of no better form of personal involvement in the cure of the environment than that of gardening."[146] He lists the environmental benefits of activities such as composting and recycling waste, the production of food that does not involve the use of fossil fuels to ship it from coast to coast, and the concrete healing of a particular piece of land. Berry also describes gardening as a discipline that immerses individuals in the natural world and creates a sense of affection for the land. He argues that the person who gardens is "making vital contact with the soil and the weather on which his life depends. He will no longer look upon rain as an impediment of traffic, or upon the sun as a holiday decoration. And his sense of man's dependence on the world will have grown precise enough, one would hope, to be politically

---

Wendell Berry and Religion: Heaven's Earthly Life, ed. Joel James Shuman and L. Roger Owens (Lexington: University of Kentucky Press, 2009).

[143] http://www.dissentmagazine.org/article/nature-as-an-ally-an-interview-with-wendell -berry.

[144] *The Art of the Commonplace*, 240–41.

[145] Berry, *Citizenship Papers*, 118.

[146] *The Art of the Commonplace*, 88.

clarifying and useful."[147] At the most basic level, Berry maintains, to garden is to reestablish a relationship with the natural order and harmony of creation, from which moderns have violently abstracted themselves. The result of this abstraction, it should be noted, has been catastrophic for the natural world.

In addition to this focus on this process of cultivating an agrarian mind, Berry points to the recovery of the full meaning of the Christian doctrine of creation as an important means of resisting a culture of degradation. He trenchantly criticizes the ways Christians have misread the Bible as a means of justifying their own exploitative relationship with the natural world. Berry detects "some virtually catastrophic discrepancies between biblical instruction and Christian behavior," insofar as the "certified" Christian is as likely as the non-Christian to participate in the "murder (of) Creation."[148]

The problem, as I have repeatedly noted, is that there is a profound disconnect between belief and practice among Christians in the modern world. This disconnect is particularly evident in the way the economy has displaced the Christian tradition as the system of values that determines the ethos of modern people. Thus, if Christianity and the economy come into conflict, economic interests prevail. Berry observes that Christianity

> makes peace with a destructive economy and divorces itself from economic issues because it is economically compelled to do so . . . if it comes to a choice between the extermination of the fowls of the air and the lilies of the field and the extermination of a building fund, the organized church will—indeed, has already elected—to save the building fund.[149]

Berry views the complicity of Christians with the modern economy not only as environmentally harmful and destructive but more basically as blasphemous behavior. He writes: "our destruction of nature is not just bad stewardship, or stupid economics, or betrayal of family responsibility; it is the most horrid blasphemy. It is flinging God's gifts into His face, as if they were of no worth beyond that assigned to them by our destruction of them."[150]

Berry contrasts the blasphemous practices of modern culture and modern Christianity with the possibility of developing a culture that embodies the values of the Christian doctrine of creation. For him the doctrine of creation teaches that God created the world for God's pleasure. He writes: "that God created all things for His pleasure, and that they continue to exist because they

---

[147] Ibid., 89.

[148] Ibid., 306.

[149] Wendell Berry, *What Are People For?* (Berkeley, CA: Counterpoint, 1990), 96.

[150] *The Art of the Commonplace*, 308.

please Him, is formidable doctrine indeed, as far as possible both from the 'anthropocentric' utilitarianism that some environmentalist critics claim to find in the Bible and from the grouchy spirituality of many Christians."[151] He contends that this doctrine entails recognizing that there is an order to creation that limits the way in which the natural world can be used by human beings.[152] When properly understood, the Christian doctrine of creation undermines the view that humans are free to impose their own narrow economic values on the natural world. Indeed, the doctrine of creation reveals not only the fact that there exists an order created by God but also that responsible stewardship represents the path to deification, through which we begin to "possess the likeness to God that is spoken of in Genesis."[153]

Finally, Berry suggests that in order to develop a healthy community it is necessary to retrieve the significance of a different form of politics and economics. For him this means quite simply that politics and the economy need to be returned to the local level, where individuals can take personal responsibility for the environment. In this context he tries to reimagine the meaning of the political and the economic beyond the view of politics as statecraft and the economy as an industrial business.

Berry makes the case that the environmental problems we face are not merely political but go much deeper and touch on the very forms of life cultivated in America. He observes: our environmental problems, moreover, are not, at root, political; they are cultural . . . our country is not being destroyed by bad politics; it is being destroyed by a bad way of life. Bad politics is merely another result. To see that the problem is far more than political is to return to reality."[154] Berry's criticism of those who think of environmental problems as only political is a critique of politics as statecraft. He regards statecraft approaches to the environmental crisis as insufficient and often even a means of evading the actual problem. A problem is presented and a law or plan is constructed as a response to it. Berry dryly notes: "the result, mostly, has been the persistence of the problem."[155] Thus while we certainly need more effective environmental policies at both the state and national level, what is more urgently needed is the cultivation at the local level of a sense of gratitude, reverence, and responsibility. Berry writes:

---

[151] Ibid., 214.

[152] Wendell Berry, *Recollected Essays: 1965–1980* (San Francisco: North Point, 1981), 172.

[153] *The Art of the Commonplace*, 214.

[154] Wendell Berry, "A Few Words in Favor of Edward Abbey," 19–28 in *Earthly Words: Essays on Contemporary American Nature and Environmental Writers*, ed. John Cooley (Ann Arbor: University of Michigan Press, 1994), at 20.

[155] *The Art of the Commonplace*, 86.

we are going to have to go far beyond public protest and political action. We are going to have to rebuild the substance and the integrity of private life in this country. . . . We need better government, no doubt about it. But we also need better minds, better friendships, better marriages, better communities. We need persons and households that do not have to wait upon organizations, but can make necessary changes in themselves, on their own.[156]

For Berry the act of protesting against corporations and the government is an important environmental practice, but he emphasizes that protest alone is insufficient, because individuals who protest the environmental practices of corporations or the environmental policies of government continue to degrade the environment in their private life each day. He writes: "nearly every one of us, nearly every day of his life, is contributing directly to the ruin of this planet. A protest meeting on the issue of environmental abuse is not a convocation of accusers, it is a convocation of the guilty."[157] Of course, Berry himself has protested the government's environmental policies in both Frankfort, Kentucky, and Washington, DC. He suggests, however, that there remains the deeper possibility that one's entire life can be lived as a protest. In this regard Berry suggests that there exists "the possibility of a protest that is more complex and permanent, public in effect but private in its motive and implementation. . . . [We] can *live* in protest."[158]

Living life as a protest involves a commitment to concrete forms of resistance to the broader economic culture of degradation. Berry observes:

> if one deplores the destructiveness and wastefulness of the economy, then one is under an obligation to live as far out on the margin of the economy as one is able: to be economically independent of exploitative industries, to learn to need less, to waste less, to make things last, to give up meaningless luxuries, to understand and resist the language of salesmen and public relations experts, to see through attractive packages, to refuse to purchase fashion or glamour or prestige.[159]

Indeed, according to Berry, individuals who protest with their lives in this way are worth more than a hundred individuals who protest by insisting that corporations and government change their behavior. That corporations and government

---

[156] Ibid.
[157] Ibid., 83.
[158] Berry, *The Long-Legged House*, 87. Emphasis in original.
[159] Ibid., 87.

need to mend their ways is evident. But while we await these large-scale changes it is important that individuals take a local responsibility for the environment.[160]

This transformation is linked to Berry's call for the cultivation of a local economy in response to the environmental crisis. He believes it is possible to enjoy the fruits of the modern economy only to the extent that we commit ourselves to a willful ignorance of its consequences.[161] Provocatively, Berry compares the global economy to a one-night stand in which we willingly submit to a state of ignorance about the products we consume.[162] We neither ask nor want to know where the products we buy and the food we eat were produced, or under what conditions. Berry observes: "the global economy institutionalizes a global ignorance, in which producers and consumers cannot know or care about one another, and in which the histories of all products will be lost. In such a circumstance, the degradation of products and places, producers and consumers is inevitable."[163] Thus for him the inevitable consequence of the global, industrial economy is that the true cost of any item is directly hidden from the consumer, so that "the cost of soil erosion is not deducted from the profit on a package of beefsteak, just as the loss of forest, topsoil, and human homes on a Kentucky mountainside does not reduce the profit on a ton of coal."[164]

It is in relation to these broader patterns of degradation that Berry emphasizes the importance of returning to the local economy as a means of resisting the negative environmental effects of the industrial economy.[165] The local economy is an alternative because it creates a context in which consumers and producers share a common interest in preserving the natural world in their own local community. Berry argues: "consumers who understand their economy will not tolerate the destruction of the local soil or ecosystem or watershed as a cost of production. Only a healthy local economy can keep nature and work together in the consciousness of the community."[166] Moreover, a local economy limits the distance between producers and consumers and permits consumers to have some control over how food production affects the environment. The benefits

[160] Ibid. In the same passage he instructs: "if you are fearful of the destruction of the environment, then learn to quit being an environmental parasite. We all are, in one way or another, and the remedies are not always obvious, though they certainly will always be difficult."

[161] Wendell Berry, *What Matters? Economics for a Renewed Commonwealth* (Berkeley, CA: Counterpoint, 2010), 97.

[162] *The Art of the Commonplace*, 213, 236.

[163] Ibid., 244.

[164] Berry, *What Matters?* 72.

[165] Berry, *Conversations with Wendell Berry*, 106.

[166] *The Art of the Commonplace*, 244.

of the local economy, of course, go beyond environmental stewardship and are the basis for the cultivation of a sense of community that is simply not possible within the anonymity of the industrial food economy. Advocates for globalization might criticize this turn to the local as "protectionism"; Berry willingly accepts this as an accurate description of his position. Contrary to the nativist or isolationist connotations of protectionism, however, he contends that this turn to the local is intended to preserve and protect precisely what the global, industrial economy has destroyed—local communities and the natural world.[167]

In his writings, Berry's overarching conviction is that it is in creation that we find our home, and that the "the care of the earth is our most ancient and most worthy and, after all, our most pleasing responsibility. To cherish what remains of it, and to foster its renewal, is our only legitimate hope."[168] Berry's hope is grounded in a realistic assessment of the cultural forces that have caused the environmental crisis, but it is also a hope rooted in the conviction that we can resist the destructive elements of culture, one small act at a time. Indeed, as Berry reflects: "a lot of my work, I think, has been trying to push on beyond despair and depression, looking for the possibility that there's something somebody can do."[169]

Conclusion

This chapter has examined the significance of the recovery of a sacramental vision of creation as a Christian resource for responding to the environmental crisis. In itself this recovery is insufficient. The environmental crisis is too far-reaching to allow us to adopt the position that Christian spirituality alone can serve as an adequate response. But, as noted previously, there will be no greening of the economy until the dispositions hospitable to environmental concerns are cultivated. Thus, while one may very well view the theological aesthetics of Hans Urs von Balthasar or the nature writings of Annie Dillard as tangential to the environmental crisis, that would be to view environmental politics in far too narrow a fashion. It would also mean failing to see that in a very real way the response to the environmental crisis turns on affection (Wendell Berry) or aesthetics (Aldo Leopold).[170] Thus the forms of life to which Dillard and Berry

---

[167] Ibid., 260.

[168] Wendell Berry, *The Unsettling of America: Culture & Agriculture* (San Francisco: Sierra Club Books, 1986), 14.

[169] Wendell Berry, "Hunting for Reasons to Hope: A Conversation with Wendell Berry," interview with Harold K. Bush, *Christianity and Literature* 56/2 (2007): 215–34, at 222.

[170] Berry, *It All Turns on Affection*, 32.

witness possess the capacity to form sensibilities and reshape perception in a manner that is significant from an environmental and spiritual perspective. Jane Bennett, for instance, points to the way in which Thoreau's writings "draw our attention to those disciplines and practices that engender a particular mood, sensibility, or existential orientation. Such affective states surely enter into political life and inflect its direction and character, even if the practices that produce them do not traditionally count as *political exercises*."[171]

Indeed, this is the entire point of micropolitics, and Christian spirituality represents an important site at which environmental micropolitical action takes place, insofar as it trains the imagination and disciplines the body to perceive creation non-instrumentally as a manifestation of the glory of God. Berry points to this when he describes the faculty of the imagination as the capacity to see clearly[172] and applies this sense of the imagination to St. Paul's teaching on the mystical body of Christ, writing of St. Paul:

> he was using a far more inclusive "we" than Christian institutions have generally thought. For me, this is the meaning of ecology. Whether we know it or not, whether we want to be or not, we are members of one another: humans (ourselves and our enemies), earthworms, whales, snakes, squirrels, trees, topsoil, flowers, weeds, germs, hills, rivers, swifts, and stones—all of "us." The work of the imagination, I feel, is to understand this.[173]

This expansion of the imagination is linked to concrete practices of environmental preservation. If, with Benedict XVI, we acknowledge that environmental sin exists, it follows that a critical task of contemporary Christian spirituality is to engage in the types of practices that resist broader forces of degradation and heal the environment one small piece at a time. For Berry, we do not have the right to ask whether our small, humble efforts will succeed. Instead, we only have the right to ask what the right thing to do is and what type of local action the earth demands if we are to continue to inhabit it.[174] Berry points to the witness of Dorothy Day and her politics of the little way as an example of the type of environmental action that is most urgently needed. For Berry

---

[171] Jane Bennett, *Thoreau's Nature: Ethics, Politics, and the Wild* (Thousand Oaks, CA: Sage, 1994), xxii. Emphasis in original.

[172] Berry observes: "'to imagine' contains the full richness of the verb 'to see.' To imagine is to see most clearly, familiarly, and understandingly with the eyes." Berry, *It All Turns on Affection*, 14.

[173] Berry, *Conversations with Wendell Berry*, 23.

[174] Wendell Berry, "Wendell Berry on His Hopes for Humanity: Interview with Bill Moyers," http://billmoyers.com/segment/wendell-berry-on-his-hopes-for-humanity/.

"the real work of planet-saving will be small, humble, and humbling," and what is needed urgently is individuals "willing to go down and down into the daunting, humbling, almost hopeless local presence of the problem—to face the great problem one small life at a time."[175] This type of local action could be practiced in different ways, from cultivating a local garden, transforming one's eating habits, and supporting Community-Supported Agriculture (CSA) to the adoption of a simpler lifestyle.[176] While these efforts are small, concrete, and local, when done properly they take on a sacramental quality. As Berry notes: "to live we must daily break the body and shed the blood of Creation. When we do this knowingly, lovingly, skillfully, reverently, it is a sacrament. When we do it ignorantly, greedily, clumsily, destructively, it is a desecration."[177]

---

[175] Berry, *Sex, Economy, Freedom & Community,* 25.

[176] On the significance of supporting CSAs as a concrete practice of environmental justice see Rebecca Todd Peters, "Supporting Community Farming," 17–28 in *Justice in a Global Economy: Strategies for Home, Community, and World,* ed. Pamela Brubaker, Rebecca Todd Peters, and Laura A. Stivers (Louisville: Westminster John Knox, 2006).

[177] *The Art of the Commonplace,* 308.

Chapter 5

Global Poverty and Consumerism

Introduction

Peter Singer's classic 1972 article, "Famine, Affluence, and Morality," attempts to establish a link between poverty and consumerism by describing the following situation: "if I am walking past a shallow pond and see a child drowning in it, I ought to wade in and pull the child out. This will mean getting my clothes muddy, but this is insignificant, while the death of the child would presumably be a very bad thing."[1] Any reasonable and moral person obviously would sacrifice her or his clothing and presumably much more in order to save the life of a child drowning in a pond. It might cost that person hundreds of dollars to replace the shoes and the suit or dress, but that is a very small price to pay to save the life of another human being. Singer argues that there is no legitimate reason why this basic moral intuition should not apply to those we do not encounter daily, but whose lives are nevertheless in danger. To put this more concretely, Singer suggests that if we take seriously the logic of the pond argument—namely, that we have an obligation to give up certain things in order to save the lives of others—it should follow that we should sacrifice some of life's luxuries in order to save the life of one of the 50,000 human beings who die every day as a result of extreme poverty.

Following the analysis of Peter Unger in *Living High and Letting Die*,[2] Singer writes that for approximately \$200 it is possible to save a child's life. This number

---

[1] Peter Singer, "Famine, Affluence, and Morality," 105–17, in *Writings on an Ethical Life* (New York: Ecco Press, 2000), 107.

[2] Peter K. Unger, *Living High and Letting Die: Our Illusion of Innocence* (New York: Oxford University Press, 1996).

should give consumers in the affluent world pause before they purchase unnecessary luxury items. Is a $500 pair of shoes necessary when a $100 pair of shoes would serve just as well? According to Unger's calculations, for the difference between a luxury item and one that fulfills basic needs, the lives of two children could be saved. These numbers become even more alarming when we analyze the way the developed world spends its money. In 2004 the New York Metropolitan Museum of Art paid $45 million dollars for a Madonna and Child painted by the Italian artist Duccio di Buoninsegna. Singer observes that since a cataract operation costs only $50 in the developing world, the price paid for that one small painting could have restored the sight of 900,000 people.[3] A soccer game in 2001 between two European teams had twenty-two starters with combined salaries of almost $700 million. Jon Sobrino notes that this number is roughly twice the nation of Chad's entire budget.[4] The 1998 UNDP *Human Development Report* released an astonishing set of statistics related to patterns of consumption in the developed world:

> Americans spend $8 billion a year on cosmetics—$2 billion more than the estimated annual total needed to provide basic education for everyone in the world. Europeans spend $11 billion a year on ice cream—$2 billion more than the estimated annual total needed to provide clean water and safe sewers for the world's population. Americans and Europeans spend $17 billion a year on pet food—$4 billion more than the estimated annual additional total needed to provide basic health and nutrition for everyone in the world.[5]

These numbers and Singer's argument point to the fact that there is a relationship between excessive consumption and extreme global poverty. It is, of course, understandable that consumers do not often perceive this relationship as direct or causal. For instance, an American who purchases an expensive pair of shoes rarely associates that act with the death of an impoverished child in the Congo. Furthermore, it is quite easy to evade any sense of responsibility for the child in the Congo because, unlike the child in Singer's pond, the poor child in the Congo has no direct contact with most Americans.[6] At a deeper

---

[3] Peter Singer, *The Life You Can Save* (New York: Random House, 2009), 149.

[4] Jon Sobrino, *No Salvation Outside the Poor* (Maryknoll, NY: Orbis Books, 2008), 47.

[5] Barbara Crossette, "Kofi Annan's Astonishing Facts," *New York Times*, 28 September 1998. See also Thomas Pogge, *World Poverty and Human Rights* (Malden, MA: Polity, 2002), 239.

[6] Singer, *The Life You Can Save*, 49, quotes Mother Teresa to the effect that "if I look at the mass I will never act. If I look at the one, I will."

level this evasion of responsibility for the global poor is aided by contemporary culture's investment in a consumer ethos that directs the time, attention, and lives of individuals toward the acquisition of commodities and subordinates all other activities to that end. This consumer formation of desire stands in marked contrast to the Christian tradition's concern to direct the lives of individuals toward the God who is manifest in the poor.[7]

This chapter examines the challenges posed by the market imaginary to the cultivation of a Christian spirituality rooted in the option for the poor. The first section describes the situation of global poverty, examines its immediate causes, and analyzes different interpretations of the nature and scope of the affluent world's responsibility for the most extreme forms of global poverty. The second analyzes how the market has come to function as a religion that directs the lives of individuals toward particular ends: wealth accumulation and conspicuous forms of consumption. Finally, I will examine how the religion of the market and the consumer ethos it produces stand in fundamental tension with the basic commitments of the Christian tradition and its attempt to place the suffering of the poor at the center of the Christian life. Thus the constructive argument made in this chapter is that market and consumer culture deforms desire and distorts human relations by making it normative for persons to devote their lives to wealth accumulation and the consumption of commodities rather than to justice for the poor and the oppressed.

The Crisis of Global Poverty

Two billion, seven hundred million people currently live below the World Bank's $2 per day poverty line or in relative poverty. More than 1.3 billion people live on less than $1.25 a day, that is, in situations of extreme or absolute poverty.[8] Nearly a third of all deaths each year stem from poverty-related causes. That

---

[7] As Pope Francis observes, "The culture of prosperity deadens us; we are thrilled if the market offers us something new to purchase. In the meantime all those lives stunted for lack of opportunity seem a mere spectacle; they fail to move us. One cause of this situation is found in our relationship with money, since we calmly accept its dominion over ourselves and our societies." *Evangelii Gaudium* 54. Available at http://www.vatican.va/holy_father/francesco/apost_exhortations /documents/papa-francesco_esortazione-ap_20131124_evangelii-gaudium_en.html.

[8] These poverty numbers are set by the World Bank and represent optimistic estimates. Setting the extreme poverty line at $1.25 serves to keep the global numbers down, but that poverty line would translate into $456 US per individual in calendar year 2010. This is an unimaginably low number in the United States. See Thomas Pogge, "Thomas Pogge on the Past, Present, and Future of Global Poverty," *Truthout,* May 2011, http://truth-out.org/news /item/792:thomas-pogge-on-the-past-present-and-future-of-global-poverty.

amounts to 50,000 deaths a day and 18 million deaths annually from poverty. In a striking image that attempts to account for the enormity of the scale of death caused by extreme poverty over the past twenty years, Thomas Pogge observes that when we total the 18 million deaths per year from poverty over just the past twenty years we have a figure that exceeds the number of people killed in all the political violence and wars in the twentieth century (200 million).[9] Pogge observes, furthermore, that if we were to build a monument to memorialize the names of those who have died from poverty in the past twenty years similar to the one commemorating the soldiers who died during the Vietnam War it would be over 540 miles long.[10] The Vietnam Memorial Wall is 493 feet long and contains 58,272 names. A wall to commemorate the deaths from poverty over the past twenty years would stretch from Detroit to Washington, DC, and bear 360 million names.

These numbers are shocking. But, as noted in the introduction, the most dehumanizing dimensions of this crisis are preventable. There are enough resources for the entire world to receive basic necessities. The problem is that, while the market economy creates enormous amounts of wealth, the wealth thus created benefits only a small group of people. The income disparity between the wealthiest and poorest countries has risen dramatically in the past two hundred years, from three to one (1820), to eleven to one (1913), to thirty-five to one (1950), to forty-four to one (1973), to seventy-four to one (1997), and recent data suggest that the current level of inequality has reached a ratio of one hundred to one.[11] The wealthiest 1 percent of the world population possesses wealth equivalent to the bottom 57 percent.[12] Roughly 85 individuals now own as much wealth as the lowest 50 percent (3.5 billion persons) of the world population.[13] The richest three people in the world possess assets that exceed the combined gross domestic product of the forty-eight least-developed countries.[14]

---

[9] Thomas Pogge, *Politics as Usual: What Lies Behind the Pro-Poor Rhetoric* (Malden, MA: Polity Press, 2010), 11.

[10] See Pogge, *World Poverty and Human Rights*, 104.

[11] See Branko Milanovic, "Global Inequality: From Class to Location, from Proletarians to Migrants," http://econ.worldbank.org/external/default/main?pagePK=64165259&piPK=64165421&theSitePK=469382&menuPK=64166093&entityID=000158349_20110929082257.

[12] Branko Milanovic, "True World Income Distribution, 1988 and 1993: First Calculation Based on Household Surveys Alone," *Economic Journal* 476 (2002): 51–92, at 50. Available at http://128.118.178.162/eps/hew/papers/0305/0305002.pdf.

[13] Laura Shin, "The 85 Richest People in the World Have as Much Wealth as the 3.5 Billion Poorest," *Forbes*. Available at: http//www.forbes.com/sites/laurashin/2014/01/23/the-85-richest-people-in-the-world-have-as-much-wealth-as-the-3-5-billion-poorest/.

[14] Crossette, "Kofi Annan's Astonishing Facts."

The situation of inequality in the United States is not substantially different from that throughout the globe. In 2005 the top 20 percent of the United States population controlled 85 percent of the wealth.[15] From 1980 to 2005, 80 percent of the income increase went to the top 1 percent of the American population. Thomas Pogge observes:

> in the 1980–2007 period, the income share of the bottom half declined from 17.68% to 12.26%. In roughly the same period (1978–2007), the income share of the top one percent rose from 8.95% to 23.50% . . . the top hundredth percent—some 14,000 tax returns—now have nearly half as much income as the bottom half (150 million) of the US population.[16]

In 1978 the average CEO in the United States made twenty-nine times as much as the average worker. By 2012 that number had exploded to 273 to one.[17] Of the thirty nations that make up the OECD (Organization for Economic Cooperation and Development), the United States ranks twenty-seventh in income inequality, ahead of only Portugal, Turkey, and Mexico.[18]

This type of inequality is problematic for a variety of reasons, but most significant among them is the fact that extreme global poverty could be eliminated through the wider distribution of resources and by providing people greater access to basic goods such as vaccines, mosquito nets, antibiotics, potable water, improved nutrition, and access to the outside world. It has been estimated that a commitment of roughly $200 to $300 billion annually would all but eliminate the most extreme forms of global poverty that kill 18 million people a year. It is even conceivable that the loss of 360 million lives over the past twenty years from poverty-related causes could have been prevented had significant action been taken decades ago. In view of this situation, the central question is: what is the scope of the affluent world's responsibility for the global poor? In what follows I will examine three responses to this question: positive duties (Peter Singer), negative duties (Thomas Pogge), and the Christian option for the poor.

Peter Singer has produced the most influential philosophical argument on the developed world's responsibility for the global poor in "Famine, Affluence,

---

[15] Gordon Douglass, "Poisonous Inequality," 75–96 in *Resistance: The New Role of Progressive Christians*, ed. John B. Cobb Jr. (Louisville: Westminster John Knox, 2008), at 80.

[16] Thomas Pogge, "Responses to the Critics," 175–250 in *Thomas Pogge and His Critics*, ed. Alison M. Jaggar (Malden, MA: Polity, 2010), at 188.

[17] Lawrence Mishel and Natalie Sabadish, "CEO Pay in 2012 Was Extraordinarily High Relative to Typical Workers and Other High Earners," http://www.epi.org/publication/ceo-pay-2012-extraordinarily-high.

[18] Timothy Noah, *The Great Divergence: America's Growing Inequality Crisis and What We Can Do About It* (New York: Bloomsbury, 2012), 4.

and Morality"[19] as well as in subsequent works, *One World: The Ethics of Global-ization*, and *The Life You Can Save*. As noted in the introduction to this chapter, Singer argues that giving up excessive pleasures in order to aid human beings who live in conditions of extreme poverty is a basic moral responsibility. Singer's argument is as follows: (1) suffering and death from a lack of food, water, and medical care are bad things; (2) if we can prevent something bad from happening without having to sacrifice anything of comparable significance, we should do so; (3) because we can prevent suffering and death from extreme poverty by giving more to aid relief organizations, we should sacrifice some luxuries in order to save the lives of others. Singer contends that this is not only the right thing to do but represents a concrete moral duty. We are doing something wrong if we fail to help. He observes: "the failure of people in the rich nations to make any significant sacrifices in order to assist people who are dying from poverty-related causes is ethically indefensible. It is not simply the absence of charity, let alone of moral saintliness: It is wrong."[20]

If Singer is correct and the affluent world does have a basic moral duty to help others by giving out of its excess, the inevitable next question is: how much should one give to the global poor? In response to this question, Singer has proposed a number of different possibilities. He notes that the average American household spends $30,000 a year on basic necessities like food and shelter. Thus, in the strictest scenario, Singer argues that any income in excess of that $30,000 should be given away to international charities like Oxfam, Against Malaria Foundation, or The Hunger Project. This means that if a household makes $50,000 in annual income it should come as close as possible to giving $20,000 of that annual income to charities devoted to aiding the global poor.[21] Elsewhere Singer is less exorbitant in his demands and proposes a general rule that 5 percent of annual income should be donated to organizations that fight global poverty.[22] This general rule can be modulated in relation to income level. His website has a calculator that proposes the following: if you earn an annual income after taxes of $40,000 US you should give 1.6 percent ($632), at $70,000 you should give 2.8 percent ($1,944), at $150,000 you should give 5.1 percent

[19] See n. 1 above.

[20] Peter Singer, "Poverty, Facts, and Political Philosophies: A Debate with Andrew Kuper," 173–81 in *Global Responsibilities: Who Must Deliver on Human Rights?* ed. Andrew Kuper (New York: Routledge, 2005), 179.

[21] Peter Singer, "The Singer Solution to World Poverty," in *Writings on an Ethical Life*, 123.

[22] Singer, *The Life You Can Save*, 160.

($7,600), at $500,000 you should give 9.7 percent ($48,450), and so on.[23] Americans are not living up to these minimal standards of giving. They give on average approximately 2 percent of their income after taxes to private organizations, but very little of this is directed toward international aid to eradicate global poverty. Americans give only .07 percent of their gross income to foreign aid: seven cents on each one hundred dollars of income.[24]

In *World Poverty and Human Rights*, Thomas Pogge acknowledges that positive duties toward the poor exist and that individuals have failed to live up to those duties. But for Pogge the problem is more basic than failure to respond to the needs of the poor in terms of the positive duties of aid and charity. Pogge contends that there are negative duties that are more fundamental than positive duties. Negative duties entail not participating in activities that harm another human being or result in her or his death. In relation to the crisis of global poverty this means that individuals in the developed world have a "negative duty not to uphold injustice, not to contribute to or profit from the unjust impoverishment of others."[25] Pogge extends this individual duty to all of society, so that negative duties also involve "moral claims on the organization of one's society."[26] Thus he argues that, insofar as individuals in the developed world benefit from a global economic order that results in massive income inequality and perpetuates deadly forms of poverty, those individuals are obliged to attempt to transform this order and to mitigate its negative consequences.

For Pogge this broad sense of duty to respond to the violation of the human rights of the world's poor is motivated by the history of colonialism, which created enormous wealth for Europe and North America and decimated Latin America, Africa, and Asia. He contends that this history continues in a different form today in the developed world's support of policies that either cause or perpetuate the suffering of the global poor.[27] Pogge argues that the institutions that set global economic policy (the World Trade Organization, the World Bank,

---

[23] http://www.thelifeyoucansave.org/ThePledge/HowMuch.aspx. If the top 10 percent of income earners in the United States followed the number suggested by Singer's calculator it would yield the astonishing sum of 471 billion dollars annually. See Tara Siegel Bernard, "Making a Difference in the Season of Giving," *The New York Times* (December 6, 2013). Available at http://www.nytimes.com/2013/12/07/your-money/making-a-difference-in-the-giving-season.html?hp&_r=0.

[24] Singer, *The Life You Can Save*, 24. More broadly on the charitable activities of Christians see Christian Smith, Michael O. Emerson, and Patricia Snell, *Passing the Plate: Why American Christians Don't Give Away More Money* (New York: Oxford University Press, 2008).

[25] Pogge, *World Poverty and Human Rights*, 197.

[26] Ibid., 64.

[27] Ibid., 125–26.

and the International Monetary Fund) promote policies that serve the interests of the economically privileged and not policies focused on poverty reduction.[28] According to Pogge "the present rules of the game favor the affluent countries by allowing them to continue protecting their markets through quotas, tariffs, anti-dumping duties, export credits, and huge subsidies to domestic producers in ways that poor countries are not permitted, or cannot afford, to match."[29] Furthermore, the structural adjustments imposed by the International Monetary Fund and World Bank have caused developing countries to neglect their own populations and focus on the type of economic activity that can repay debts to foreign countries. The result has been that for every dollar a developing country receives in aid, twenty-five dollars are being taken out of that country to repay debts to the developed world.[30] Thus the common explanation that attributes the persistence of extreme poverty to corruption, tyranny, and civil wars is inadequate insofar as it fails to recognize that policies imposed on the developing world by the affluent world create conditions inhospitable to the eradication of poverty.[31] This is not to absolve corrupt regimes of their responsibility for the conditions in their countries, but simply to point to the fact that the affluent world shares a significant measure of responsibility for the persistence of extreme poverty in the developing world.

In response to this situation Pogge contends that it is necessary for those who benefit from this economic order to make an effort to eliminate or reduce the harm done to the poor. This means that the policies of international institutions like the World Trade Organization, the World Bank, and the International Monetary Fund should be challenged and resisted. He additionally proposes a compensatory mechanism that attempts to ameliorate the most negative features of the global economic order. To compensate is not to aid others out of a sense of generosity or beneficence, but to acknowledge that individuals in the developed world have caused enormous harm to the poor through their support of international institutions and policies that serve their own interests.

---

[28] Pogge observes: "We, the affluent countries and their citizens, continue to impose a global economic order under which millions avoidably die each year from poverty-related causes. We would regard it as a grave injustice if such an economic order were imposed within a national society." Pogge, *World Poverty and Human Rights*, 115.

[29] Thomas Pogge, "Severe Poverty as a Human Rights Violation," 11–54 in *Freedom from Poverty as a Human Right: Who Owes What to the Very Poor?* ed. idem (New York: Oxford University Press, 2007), at 35.

[30] Kristin Heyer, *Kinship Across Borders: A Christian Ethic of Immigration* (Washington, DC: Georgetown University Press, 2012), 102.

[31] Pogge, *World Poverty and Human Rights*, 125–26.

The recognition of this fact means that extreme global poverty is an injustice for which individuals should be compensated. To this end Pogge proposes a natural resource dividend (or tax) on the use or sale of natural resources. The global poor own an inalienable stake in the natural resources of the world, but they rarely receive any benefit from their stake in these resources. A natural resource dividend would amount to a consumption tax, because the price of the dividend would be passed on to consumers. The proceeds of the dividend would be gathered by an international body (not a government) and distributed to those living below the international poverty line. Pogge argues that a 1 percent natural resource dividend would divert approximately $300 billion from the affluent to the global poor.[32] The wealth thus transferred would be used to meet the "basic needs of the global poor" and would be directed toward "basic education, basic health, population programs, water supply, and sanitation."[33] Thus a minor modification in the global economic order—one that would barely affect the income level of individuals in the developed world—would be sufficient to achieve a dramatic reduction in the millions of preventable deaths caused each year by extreme poverty.

In contrast to Singer, for whom we must attempt to eliminate global poverty because we have a positive duty to do so, Pogge argues that because we are complicit in the global order that contributes to the poverty of billions we have a negative duty to transform structures that continue to deny individuals the capacity to fulfill their basic human rights.[34] The duty of the developed world is not to assist the poor but to rectify injustices that the affluent have imposed on the poor.[35] In this sense the task is not simply to do more in terms of positive aid but to do less in terms of negative harm to the world's poor. For Pogge, failing to try to rectify injustices imposed on the poor by a global economic order is tantamount to supporting a government that violates the human rights of its citizens. He writes:

> we call it tragic that the basic human rights of so many remain unfulfilled, and are willing to admit that we should do more to help. But it is unthinkable to us that we are actively responsible for this catastrophe. If we were, then we, civilized and sophisticated denizens of the developed countries, would be guilty of the largest crime against humanity ever committed,

[32] Thomas Pogge, "Eradicating Systemic Poverty: A Brief For a Global Resources Dividend," *Journal of Human Development* 2 (2001): 59–77, at 67.

[33] Pogge, *World Poverty and Human Rights*, 213.

[34] Ibid., 307.

[35] Thomas Pogge, "World Poverty and Human Rights," *Ethics and International Affairs* 19 (2005): 1–7, at 2.

the death toll of which exceeds, every week, that of the 2004 tsunami, and every three years that of World War II, the concentration camps and gulags included.[36]

For Pogge the consistent failure of the developed world to create international institutions that uphold basic human rights and implement serious poverty prevention policies makes it justifiable to accuse the affluent of being "hunger's willing executioners" and "accomplices in a monumental crime against humanity."[37]

A charged rhetoric similar to that employed by Pogge has been employed by Latin American liberation theologians in their condemnation of the developed world's role in perpetuating extreme forms of poverty in Latin America. Ignacio Ellacuría and Jon Sobrino, in particular, have argued that the world's poor are a crucified people who have been put to death by the apathy and institutions of the developed world. The image of the crucified people makes evident the fact that there exist both individual and structural forms of sin that cause the death of millions of innocent human beings every year in a manner similar to the way structures of sin crucified Jesus of Nazareth. As Sobrino puts it: "to die crucified does not mean simply to die, but to be put to death; it means that there are victims and there are executioners. It means that there is a very grave sin."[38]

Because sin causes the crucifixion of the poor, that sin can be resisted by taking the crucified down from their cross. Furthermore, taking the crucified down from their cross is the means by which persons in the developed world encounter God: "since God desires their salvation and liberation and makes an option for them, our option for their salvation and liberation is an expression of our deification."[39] In an echo of Jesus' statement in Matthew 19:24 on the rich man and the eye of the needle, Sobrino frames this point in typical dialectical fashion by arguing that there is no salvation outside the poor (*Extra Pauperes Nulla Salus*).[40]

A fundamental conviction of the Christian tradition—shared by a variety of Christians from Popes John Paul II, Benedict XVI, and Francis to Latin American liberation theologians Gustavo Gutiérrez, Ignacio Ellacuría, and Jon Sobrino—is that the Christian option for the poor is at the center of the Christian life and entails the dual commitment to charity (Singer) and distributive justice (Pogge). Indeed, Gutiérrez contends that the "option for the poor" is not optional for Christians. It is the option God has taken, and is central to who

---

[36] Ibid., 1–2.

[37] Pogge, *World Poverty and Human Rights*, 31. See also idem, *Politics as Usual*, 2.

[38] Jon Sobrino, *The Principle of Mercy: Taking the Crucified People from the Cross* (Maryknoll, NY: Orbis Books, 1994), 50.

[39] Sobrino, *No Salvation Outside the Poor*, 19.

[40] Ibid., 35–76.

Christians are called to be.[41] In contemporary culture, however, there exist realities that obstruct Christians from seeing their concrete obligations to the world's poor and making this option central to their lives. The next two sections will examine how the logic of the market habituates individuals to a consumeristic vision of the world that marginalizes the needs of the poor. The next chapter will describe an alternative to this consumerist "globalization of indifference" (Pope Francis) by examining the "globalization of solidarity" (John Paul II) that is rooted in the Christian option for the poor.[42]

The Religion of the Market

In an article entitled "The Religion of the Market," David Loy argues that the market is "already the most successful religion of all time, winning more converts more quickly than any previous belief system or value-system in human history."[43] Loy contends that the market is the first truly global religion; the only reason we do not describe the market as a religion is that we mistakenly view it as a secular reality. However, when the distinction between the sacred and the secular collapses—as it should—it becomes evident that the market represents the dominant rival to monotheistic religion insofar as the market demands the type of total devotion previously reserved for God. Loy argues that the success of the market economy is rooted in the view that the market expresses the natural order of things, notwithstanding the fact that the current economic order is "leading to extreme social inequity and environmental catastrophe."[44] He contests the claim that the market represents the natural order of things and instead argues that it is "the false religion of our age." Accordingly, he claims that the task of traditional religions is to resist the religion of the market

---

[41] Gustavo Gutiérrez, "Remembering the Poor: An Interview with Gustavo Gutirrez [sic]," *America*, 3 February 2003, at http://americamagazine.org/issue/420/article/remembering-poor-interview-gustavo-gutirrez.

[42] Pope Francis, "Homily at Lampedusa," July 8, 2013, http://www.news.va/en/news/pope-on-lampedusa-the-globalization-of-indifference; Pope Francis, *Evangelii Gaudium* 54 at http://www.vatican.va/holy_father/francesco/apost_exhortations/documents/papa-francesco_esortazione-ap_20131124_evangelii-gaudium_en.html; John Paul II, *Ecclesia in America*, 22 January 1999, http://www.vatican.va/holy_father/john_paul_ii/apost_exhortations/documents/hf_jp-ii_exh_22011999_ecclesia-in-america_en.html.

[43] David Loy, "The Religion of the Market," *Journal of the American Academy of Religion* 65 (1997): 275–90, at 275. See also Dwight N. Hopkins, "The Religion of Globalization," 7–32 in *Religions/Globalizations: Theories and Cases* (Durham, NC: Duke University Press, 2001), at 14.

[44] Loy, "The Religion of the Market," 277.

by making it clear that the market "is the ascendancy of one particular way of understanding and valuing the world that need not be taken for granted. Far from being inevitable, this economic system is one historically-conditioned way of organizing/reorganizing the world. . . ."[45]

As noted previously, from a Christian perspective the market economy is not itself the problem. The issue is that the market has displaced all other value systems and submitted the entirety of life to its narrow logic. In "The Market as God," Harvey Cox has written:

> Since the earliest stages of human history, of course, there have been bazaars, rialtos and trading posts—all markets. But The Market was never God, because there were other centers of value and meaning, other "gods." The Market operated within a plethora of other institutions that restrained it. As Karl Polanyi has demonstrated in his classic work *The Great Transformation*, only in the past two centuries has The Market risen above these demigods and chthonic spirits to become today's First Cause.[46]

Thus Cox concludes that the religion of the market has become a formidable rival to traditional religions precisely because it is rarely viewed as a religion.[47] The reason for this rivalry is that both religion and the market "direct and distribute time, attention, and devotion." Philip Goodchild observes: "in a society organized primarily for the pursuit of wealth, nothing could seem more evident and unquestionable than that time, attention, and devotion should be allocated to the pursuit of wealth. It is the very obligation to do so that constitutes the spiritual power of money."[48] The goal of wealth accumulation supplants all other values and loyalties within market culture and reduces the human person to an entity driven by the market values of competition, exchange, symmetry, and cost-benefit analysis.[49] The problem with this is that realities surpassing the logic of self-interest and profit motives—e.g., solidarity, self-sacrifice, compassion, and justice—become marginal to what it means to be human.[50] This narrow focus on wealth as the *telos* of human existence legitimates a social order that

[45] Ibid., 277–78.

[46] Harvey Cox, "The Market as God: Living in the New Dispensation," *The Atlantic*, 1 March 1999, http://www.theatlantic.com/magazine/archive/1999/03/the-market-as-god/306397.

[47] Ibid.

[48] Philip Goodchild, *Theology of Money* (Durham, NC: Duke University Press, 2009), 6.

[49] See also Daniel M. Bell, *The Economy of Desire: Christianity and Capitalism in a Postmodern World* (Grand Rapids: Baker Academic, 2012), 94–96.

[50] See Metz, *Faith in History and Society*, 49; Joerg Rieger, *No Rising Tide: Theology, Economics, and the Future* (Minneapolis: Fortress Press, 2009), 89.

produces agonistic and unjust relations between individuals. For example, the exclusion of the poor from the benefits of the market is viewed as necessary for the system to function properly insofar as it provides incentive for competition and leads to "progress." Moreover, the search for the cheapest labor abroad is justified because it serves to secure the lowest prices and highest profits at home. This dynamic fuels the so-called race to the bottom, in which poorer countries lower their wages and create inhumane labor conditions in order to make their countries more attractive to the profit interests of global corporations.[51]

In addition to promulgating the view that wealth accumulation is the goal of life, the religion of the market offers a distinctive theory of secular salvation known as the invisible hand.[52] The invisible hand of the market is the theory that if people pursue their own self-interest—even toward manifestly selfish ends—the invisible force of the market will guide those actions toward an end that benefits all members of society. Those committed to the market are asked to invest absolute faith in its capacity to guide economic activity toward just ends that serve the common good. The invisible hand of the market, then, represents a rather straightforward secularization of the Christian doctrine of providence or, even more problematically, a destructive parody of this Christian doctrine. The market itself functions as God and possesses the attributes of omniscience, omnipotence, and omnibenevolence. These attributes supposedly enable the market to guide economic activity toward an end that serves the good of all. Thus any call to intervene in the market to attempt to steer it toward more humane ends is viewed as a blasphemous deviation from market orthodoxy.[53] Furthermore, the idea of the invisible hand of the market engenders the view that the most virtuous act an individual can pursue is to follow his or her own self-interest. The result is that self-interest (or greed) is transformed into the central virtue of the market— a transformation, it should be noted, that is all the more remarkable when it is viewed alongside the Christian interpretation of greed (*pleonexia*) as a sin.[54]

---

[51] See Jeffry Odell Korgen and Vincent A. Gallagher, *The True Cost of Low Prices: The Violence of Globalization* (Maryknoll, NY: Orbis Books, 2013), 10–34.

[52] Jung Mo Sung, *Desire, Market and Religion* (London: SCM Press, 2007), 56.

[53] Pope Francis has criticized faith in the invisible hand of the market by arguing that proponents of "trickle-down theories" of the free market possess a "naïve trust in the goodness of those wielding economic power." *Evangelii Gaudium* 55; available at http://www.vatican.va/holy_father/francesco/apost_exhortations/documents /papa-francesco_esortazione-ap_20131124_evangelii-gaudium_en.html.

[54] Daniel Bell Jr. "What is Wrong with Capitalism? The Problem with the Problem with Capitalism," *The Other Journal: An Intersection of Theology and Culture* 5 (4 April 2005), at http://theotherjournal.com/2005/04/04/what-is-wrong-with-capitalism-the-problem -with-the-problem-with-capitalism.

Furthermore, the market functions not only as a secularized version of providence but also as a theodicy that doles out rewards and punishments to those who either embody or fail to embody its vision of the good life. This strand of theodicy—the temporal theory of retribution—posits that if you suffer, you have sinned, and the suffering experienced is the punishment for that sin (or conversely, if you are rich and healthy, you are virtuous).[55] The theodicy of the market makes the judgment that the poor are guilty of some offense (e.g., the failure to practice the virtues of the religion of the market), and their suffering is viewed as just punishment for that failure.[56]

Similarly, because the worth of a human being is determined by an individual's capacity to accumulate wealth and to purchase commodities, the poor are judged to be deficient and less valuable by the standards of the market.[57] This view was made explicit by Larry Summers, the former chief economist and vice president of the World Bank and president of Harvard University, when he argued that "the economic logic" behind unloading toxic waste in the poorest and least-developed countries "is impeccable and we should face up to that."[58] This argument is rooted in the view that the poor are less productive by market standards. Thus if toxic waste results in disease or negatively affects the populations surrounding it, the waste should be placed in a country where the people are less valuable by the standards of the market. Summers's argument represents an example of the way faith in the market compels those committed to its logic to view human beings as mere commodities (or raw material) who are assigned a value exclusively on the basis of their capacity to produce and consume.

As discussed in the second chapter, the rites and rituals of consumer culture represent the most potent means for habituating individuals to the values of the market insofar as they train individuals to acquire their identity through the acquisition and display of commodities.[59] This process of identity formation is rooted in the attempt to imitate what advertisers promote as the vision of the good life. Consumer culture trains individuals to desire what others have purchased and attempt to imitate the lives most valued within the market

---

[55] Sung, *Desire, Market and Religion*, 69. For a deconstruction of the temporal theory of retribution see Gustavo Gutiérrez, *On Job: God-Talk and the Suffering of the Innocent* (Maryknoll, NY: Orbis Books, 1987).

[56] Rieger, *No Rising Tide*, 65–68.

[57] Zygmunt Bauman, *Work, Consumerism, and the New Poor* (Philadelphia: Open University Press, 1998).

[58] David Naguib Pellow, *Resisting Global Toxics* (Cambridge, MA: MIT Press, 2007), 9.

[59] See Peter N. Stearns, *Consumerism in World History: The Global Transformation of Desire* (London: Routledge, 2001), ix.

system: celebrities, athletes, and the wealthy.[60] This imitative form of desire is stoked by advertising and marketing strategies that attempt to convince individuals that what they possess is inadequate. Zygmunt Bauman contends that "consumer society thrives as long as it manages to render the non-satisfaction of its members (and so, in its own terms, their unhappiness) perpetual. The explicit method of achieving such an effect is to denigrate and devalue consumer products shortly after they have been hyped into the universe of consumers' desires."[61] The dialectical structure of consumerism is such that commodities are offered as an antidote to the human experience of restlessness, but once the commodity is acquired, advertisers trot out new commodities that make the purchase appear inadequate. This fuels a renewed experience of restlessness. The cycle of consumerism repeats itself endlessly with the result that the more individuals consume, the more they desire.[62]

While the invisible hand represents the communal vision of salvation within the religion of the market, the individual vision of salvation is attained through the pursuit of the consumer picture of the good life. David Loy writes:

> If we are not blinded by the distinction usually made between secular and sacred, we can see that advertising promises another kind of salvation, i.e., another way to solve our lack. Insofar as this strikes at the heart of the truly religious perspective   which offers an alternative explanation for our inability to be happy and a very different path to become happy—religions are not fulfilling their responsibility if they ignore this religious dimension of capitalism.[63]

In this sense consumerism represents a toxic rival to Christianity insofar as it captures desire and directs it toward ends that stand in fundamental tension with the Christian tradition. Consumerism provides a story about who we are (consumers) and the ends toward which we should devote our lives (making money).[64] The problem, of course, is that this story has become parasitic on

---

[60] Arthur Asa Berger, *Ads, Fads, and Consumer Culture: Advertising's Impact on American Character* (Lanham, MD: Rowman & Littlefield, 2004), 45.

[61] Zygmunt Bauman, *Consuming Life* (Malden, MA: Polity Press, 2007), 47. See also idem, *44 Letters from the Liquid Modern World* (Malden, MA: Polity Press, 2010), 67.

[62] Bauman, *Work, Consumerism, and the New Poor*, 26.

[63] David Loy, *A Buddhist History of the West: Studies in Lack* (Albany: SUNY Press, 2002), 200.

[64] Sallie McFague, *Life Abundant: Rethinking Theology and Economy for a Planet in Peril* (Minneapolis: Fortress Press, 2001), xi.

Christianity. Thus Christianity has been employed as a tool to spread the religion of the market (the prosperity gospel). Or, alternatively, it has purged the traditional religious elements from Christianity itself—for example, by transforming Christmas into a sustained ritual of consumption.[65]

This section has examined how the market has taken on a religious status in contemporary culture, articulating a secular view of providence and theodicy, a vision of the human person shaped by the values of self-interest, competition, and exchange principles, and an overarching system that disciplines desire and habituates individuals into forms of life focused on the acquisition of commodities. The next section will examine how Christianity, rightly understood and lived, stands in fundamental opposition to the religion of the market and the consumer spirituality it supports.

Consumerism and Christianity

In view of the foregoing analysis it is clear that the market represents a rival to God in the contemporary cultural imaginary.[66] John Paul II argued as much when he pointed to the fact that there exists "an idolatry of the market" in which the market takes on ultimacy in the lives of individuals in a way that rivals the devotion traditionally displayed toward God.[67] In a similar vein Pope Francis contends that "the worship of the golden calf of old (cf. Ex 32:15-34) has found a new and heartless image in the cult of money and the dictatorship of an economy which is faceless and lacking any truly human goal . . . in circumstances like these, solidarity, which is the treasure of the poor, is often considered

---

[65] Richard Horsley, "Christmas: The Religion of Consumer Capitalism," in Richard Horsley and James Tracy, *Christmas Unwrapped: Consumerism, Christ, and Culture* (Harrisburg, PA: Trinity Press International, 2001), 174. On the religious dimensions of consumer culture see Dell deChant, *The Sacred Santa: Religious Dimensions of Consumer Culture* (Cleveland: Pilgrim Press, 2002); Leigh Eric Schmidt, *Consumer Rites: The Buying & Selling of American Holidays* (Princeton, NJ: Princeton University Press, 1995); George Ritzer, *Enchanting a Disenchanted World: Revolutionizing the Means of Consumption* (Thousand Oaks, CA: Pine Forge, 2005). See also John Pahl, *Shopping Malls and Other Sacred Spaces: Putting God in Place* (Grand Rapids: Brazos Press, 2003); Bryan D. Spinks, *The Worship Mall: Contemporary Responses to Contemporary Culture* (London: SPCK, 2010).

[66] Gustavo Gutiérrez, "Liberation Theology and the Future of the Poor," 96–123 in *Liberating the Future: God, Mammon and Theology*, ed. Joerg Rieger (Minneapolis: Fortress Press, 1998), at 116.

[67] John Paul II, *Centesimus Annus*, § 40, available at http://www.vatican.va/holy_father /john_paul_ii/encyclicals/documents/hf_jp-ii_enc_01051991_centesimus-annus_en.html.

counter-productive, opposed to the logic of finance and the economy."[68] For Francis the fundamental problem with the current market system is that its logic and commitments are faceless and demand the sacrifice of victims in order to function properly. He argues that in contemporary culture "money is in charge, money rules" and the ultimate effect of this devotion to wealth is that "men and women are sacrificed to the idols of profit and consumption."[69]

Gustavo Gutiérrez echoes this view and invokes the biblical prophets to underscore the link between idolatry and murder. He observes that the reason for this is simple: "If . . . Jesus Christ ranks money as an antigod and sets before us the inescapable choice of following one or the other, it is, in the final analysis, because the worship of mammon entails shedding the blood of the poor."[70] For Gutiérrez the persons excluded from the current global economic order are the victims of the idol of money and wealth.[71] The loss of the lives of the poor is justified as the necessary price that must be paid for the market system to flourish and continue to deliver wealth to the chosen few in the developed world. According to Gutiérrez a system that needs victims in order to function should be denounced, and with it "the idolatrous nature of human profit as promoted by 'savage capitalism.'"[72] In this sense, he argues, the most widespread form of idolatry in contemporary culture is the market form of life to which people devote their own lives. Gutiérrez observes that people describe themselves as Christians "while in practice serving mammon by mistreating and murdering God's favorites, the poor."[73]

[68] "Address of Pope Francis to the New Non-Resident Ambassadors to the Holy See," 16 May 2013, at http://www.vatican.va/holy_father/francesco/speeches/2013/may/documents /papa-francesco_20130516_nuovi-ambasciatori_en.html. See also Pope Francis, *Evangelii Gaudium* 55, http://www.vatican.va/holy_father/francesco/apost_exhortations/documents /papa-francesco_esortazione-ap_20131124_evangelii-gaudium_en.html.

[69] Pope Francis, "World Environment Day," June 5, 2013, http://en.radiovaticana .va/news/2013/06/05/pope_at_audience: counter_a_culture_of_waste_with_solidarity /en1-698604. Elsewhere Francis says it is necessary to resist the "ephemeral idols" of money, power, success, and pleasure. See "Homily of Pope Francis on July 24, 2013," http://www.vatican.va/holy_father/francesco/homilies/2013/documents/papa-francesco _20130724_gmg-omelia-aparecida_en.html.

[70] Gustavo Gutiérrez, *The God of Life* (Maryknoll, NY: Orbis Books, 1991), 55–56.

[71] Gutiérrez, "Liberation Theology and the Future of the Poor," 117. See also Archbishop Oscar Romero, *Voice of the Voiceless: The Four Pastoral Letters and Other Statements* (Maryknoll, NY: Orbis Books, 1985), 133.

[72] Gustavo Gutiérrez, *The Density of the Present: Selected Writings* (Maryknoll, NY: Orbis Books, 1999), 132–33.

[73] Ibid., 48.

Thus while it is important to recognize that idolatry functions at a discursive level as a means of legitimating a social order, it is also necessary to recognize that idolatry manifests itself in more subtle ways in the forms of life produced by market culture. As noted in the second chapter, the market shapes individuals, through the discipline of consumerism, to desire certain things and devote themselves to particular ends. This discipline is inhospitable to the formation of Christian subjects because it employs sophisticated techniques to capture desire through the endless flow of advertising messages.[74] According to Michael Budde:

> Christians spend thousands of hours a year interacting with complex systems that, in ways not fully understood, impact our desires, temperament, predispositions, and sense of normality. Far from being distinctive in themselves, Christians see their once-distinctive stories and symbols deployed against them in efforts to make them buy, desire, and dream like everyone else.[75]

Budde sees Christianity and consumerism both seeking to form people in ways that stand in opposition to each other. In terms of the time given to these realities, consumerism has the upper hand. It has been estimated that the average American is exposed to nearly 16,000 marketing messages and advertisements every single day.[76] This presents a unique challenge to the formation of Christian subjects, since the time and attention devoted to consumer culture far outstrips the time devoted to prayer, liturgy, the works of mercy, or other activities related to Christian formation. This means that individuals in contemporary culture are habituated to a consumer ethos in a much more decisive way than they are trained in Christian forms of life. As Budde rightly remarks,

> one would be hard-pressed to learn any demanding set of skills or competencies with the amount of time most Catholics in advanced industrial countries devote to their faith tradition. On the other hand, there are few competencies that cannot be acquired with three to four hours per day of time invested—and people in the West use that much time to develop "competence" in television watching.[77]

Thus just as the market represents one of the most successful religions in the history of the world, consumerism also constitutes one of the most successful

---

[74] Michael Budde, *The (Magic) Kingdom of God: Christianity and Global Culture Industries* (Boulder, CO: Westview Press, 1997), 70.

[75] Ibid., 95.

[76] Michael Budde and Robert Brimlow, *Christianity Incorporated: How Big Business Is Buying the Church* (Grand Rapids: Brazos Press, 2002), 14.

[77] Budde, *The (Magic) Kingdom of God*, 82.

systems of desire formation in world history. This consumer system of desire formation is problematic in both the negative byproducts it produces—environmental degradation and poverty—and in its effect on the individuals who succeed by its standards. Jon Sobrino argues that consumer culture creates subjects who are trained to pursue unlimited luxuries without "considering that it may also be dehumanizing both for those who enjoy it and for those who pay the costs."[78] In this sense consumer culture is not only problematic for what it fails to do but also because of what it succeeds in doing: deforming human desire and reducing the human person to an entity driven by self-interest, competition, and excess consumption.[79]

At its most basic level consumerism constitutes a particular aesthetic or way of seeing the world.[80] Consumerism trains consumers to perceive reality through the prism of the manufactured desires of the market. This aesthetic collapses the distinction between genuine needs and manufactured desires. The result of this attempt by consumer culture to direct desire toward the end of conspicuous consumption is that, as Jung Mo Sung puts it, there is "no significant place for the suffering of the poor and the socially excluded."[81] By collapsing the distinction between need and desire, consumer desire diverts attention away from the suffering of the poor and directs it toward the consumption of commodities that make life more enjoyable.[82] As a result, according to Bauman, in a consumer society any sense of collective responsibility for the poor has been exchanged for the individual pursuit of pleasurable consumer experiences. He specifically argues that in contemporary culture an aesthetic of consumption has replaced an ethics of responsibility: "it is aesthetics, not ethics, that is deployed to integrate the society of consumers, to keep it on course and time. If ethics accord supreme value to duty well done, aesthetics put a premium on sublime experience."[83] Bauman contends that consumers are driven by their perceived right to enjoy

---

[78] Jon Sobrino, *No Salvation Outside the Poor*, 13.

[79] On this point see also the important criticism of Alasdair MacIntyre, *Marxism and Christianity* (London: Duckworth, 1995), xiv, and Bell, "What Is Wrong with Capitalism?" (n. 54 above).

[80] William T. Cavanaugh, *Being Consumed: Economics and Christian Desire* (Grand Rapids: Eerdmans, 2008), 47.

[81] Jung Mo Sung, *The Subject, Capitalism, and Religion* (New York: Palgrave Macmillan, 2011), 2. Cavanaugh observes: "desire in consumer society keeps us distracted from the desires of the truly hungry, those who experience hunger as life-threatening deprivation." Cavanaugh, *Being Consumed*, 91.

[82] Cavanaugh, *Being Consumed*, 91.

[83] Bauman, *Work, Consumerism and the New Poor*, 31. According to him this erosion is evident in the recent "approval given in the US and elsewhere to the reduction of social

whatever they desire without limits with the result that they "must be guided by aesthetic interests, not ethical norms."[84] Indeed, the consumer economy is based not on the satisfaction of basic needs, but on the satisfaction of consumer preferences and the attempt to sell the public enjoyable aesthetic experiences.[85] Bauman observes: "consumers are sensation-seekers and collectors of experiences; their relationship to the world is primarily *aesthetic*: they perceive the world as a food for sensibility—a matrix of possible experiences."[86]

The problem with this aesthetic sensibility is that it is antithetical to another form of sensibility that, following Emmanuel Lévinas, Bauman describes as the sensibility of the face of the other. According to Bauman the face of the other makes an ethical demand on the self that summons it into a relationship of responsibility. For him the omnipresence of images in consumer culture constitute an aesthetic that attracts, seduces, and diverts the attention of individuals away from the suffering faces of the poor. In *Postmodern Ethics*, Bauman describes this as the "aestheticization of social space" and suggests "moral proximity was the nearness of the Face. This one, the aesthetic proximity, is the nearness of the crowd; and the meaning of the crowd is facelessness."[87]

In response to the dominance of this consumer aesthetic in contemporary culture, the task of Christians is to make the faces of the poor visible, as Sung observes:

> a basic task for the Christian churches and for ecumenical organizations is to give visibility to the lives of those living on the periphery or outside the system, and then to make it possible for their voices to be heard by the privileged. Actually seeing the people who are suffering and hearing their cry (Ex. 3:7) can lead people to want to understand the connection between their desire to improve their standard of living, their pattern of consumption and the suffering of the poor. In that way, people will be better able to perceive that the spirituality of consumption is dehumanizing and to opt for a more humane way of life that holds together their human condition and their pursuit of "being" in relationships of solidarity.[88]

services—centrally administered and guaranteed provisions of necessities—providing the reduction goes hand in hand with the lowering of taxes." Ibid., 30.

[84] Ibid.

[85] Jung Mo Sung, *The Subject, Capitalism, and Religion*, 52.

[86] Zygmunt Bauman, *Globalization: The Human Consequences* (New York: Columbia University Press, 1998), 94. Emphasis in original.

[87] Bauman, *Postmodern Ethics* (Oxford and Cambridge, MA: Blackwell, 1993), 130.

[88] Jung Mo Sung, "Greed, Desire, and Theology," *Ecumenical Review* 63 (2011): 251–62, at 261–62.

The market legitimates a social order that perpetuates extreme poverty while simultaneously creating, stoking, and sustaining excessive forms of consumption. It has been argued in this chapter that these two realities—excessive consumption and extreme poverty—are connected, because the consumer aesthetic limits the capacity of individuals to perceive and be affected by the suffering of the poor.

Conclusion

This chapter has examined the relationship between the crisis of global poverty and consumer culture. It has argued that the religion of the market creates and sustains an ethos in which exchange principles, self-interest, and consumer pleasure dominate the lives of individuals in the developed world. In this regard the facelessness of the consumer aesthetic stands in fundamental opposition to the "face-seeking mysticism" (Benedict XVI) that is at the core of Christian spirituality.[89] The next chapter will analyze the significance of a mysticism of open eyes for the cultivation of a prophetic spirituality responsive to the suffering of the poor.

---

[89] Johann Baptist Metz, "Wer steht für die unschuldigen Opfer ein? Ein Gespräch mit Johann Baptist Metz," *Orientierung* 72 13/14 (Zürich, 15–31 July 2008), 148–50, at 150.

Chapter 6

Prophetic Vision

Introduction

The previous chapter described the way in which the religion of the market and the dominance of a consumer aesthetic foster a culture in which the suffering of the poor is marginalized by the demands of profit and the allure of commodities. In particular we examined Zygmunt Bauman's argument that the ethical call that emerges from the face of the other has been obstructed by the proliferation of images presented by consumer culture as the keys to participation in its vision of the good life. This chapter will analyze the prophetic mode of perception, as narrated in the parable of the Good Samaritan, as an alternative to the consumer aesthetic. This prophetic vision is rooted in what Johann Baptist Metz terms a "mysticism of open eyes" (or "face-seeking mysticism") that "sees more and not less. It is a mysticism that especially makes visible all invisible and inconvenient suffering, and—convenient or not—pays attention to it and takes responsibility for it."[1]

The first section of the chapter will examine the theologies of Johann Baptist Metz and Jon Sobrino as focused attempts to foreground the suffering of the innocent, which they insist is one of the most basic challenges to contemporary Christian spirituality. In particular, this section focuses on both Metz's and So-

---

[1] Johann Baptist Metz, *A Passion for God: The Mystical-Political Dimension of Christianity*, trans. J. Matthew (New York: Paulist Press, 1998), 163. In terms that are consistent with the emphases placed on vision in Metz's work, Jon Sobrino contends that the failure to encounter the suffering of others with open eyes constitutes an evasion of reality because "'not seeing' is sin." Jon Sobrino, *Where Is God? Earthquake, Terrorism, Barbarity, and Hope* (Maryknoll, NY: Orbis Books, 2004), 38.

brino's interpretation of the parable of the Good Samaritan as the paradigmatic example of a mysticism of open eyes in the Christian tradition. Next, I will turn to the spiritual exercises that can form persons in this mysticism of open eyes: liturgy and the Eucharist, *memoria passionis,* the encounter with the face of the other, and contemplative prayer. Finally, the chapter examines the lives of Dorothy Day and Martin Luther King Jr. as icons of a prophetic spirituality rooted in the commitment to justice for the poor.

The Eyes of the Samaritan

Chapter 4 examined the significance of theological aesthetics for the cultivation of a form of perception that sees the sacramentality of creation. That chapter focused on the cultivation of this sacramental vision of reality as a means of responding to the crisis of environmental degradation. In parallel fashion, this section examines the significance of a prophetic vision of reality as a means of responding to the crisis of global poverty.[2] In particular, it examines the theologies of Metz and Sobrino and their contention that the fundamental sign of the times is the experience of widespread suffering in history, from the Gulag and the Shoah to the Killing Fields of Cambodia, El Mozote, and Rwanda. The problem of innocent suffering has emerged as a theological concern for them as a result of their concrete encounter with victims of oppression and persecution in history—specifically in relation to the victims of the Shoah (Metz) and the dehumanizing poverty experienced in Latin America (Sobrino). In response to these experiences of suffering, Metz and Sobrino argue that there is no more important problem than that of innocent suffering. This emphasis on the problem of suffering manifests itself as a methodological priority in their theologies in a number of ways, from their sustained attention to the irreconcilable problem of theodicy to their recognition that the absolute authority in history is that of those who suffer. Metz and Sobrino maintain that the primary task of Christian spirituality is to facilitate an awakening in which Christians open their eyes to the reality of a suffering world.[3]

---

[2] A version of this section appeared in Matthew T. Eggemeier, "A Mysticism of Open Eyes: Compassion for a Suffering World and the *Askesis* of Contemplative Prayer," *Spiritus: A Journal of Christian Spirituality* 12 (2012): 43–62.

[3] Johann Baptist Metz, *Memoria Passionis: ein provozierendes Gedächtnis in pluralistischer Gesellschaft* (Freiburg: Herder, 2006), 166. See also idem, *The Emergent Church: The Future of Christianity in a Postbourgeois World* (New York: Crossroad, 1981), 61. On adopting the view of the other see Jon Sobrino, *Christ the Liberator: A View from the Victims* (Maryknoll, NY: Orbis Books, 2001), 8, and idem, *The Principle of Mercy: Taking the Crucified People from the Cross* (Maryknoll, NY: Orbis Books, 1994), 4, 11.

The central event that animates Metz's mature theology is the Shoah and his decision—which came "slowly, much too slowly"—to face this catastrophe as a fundamental challenge to Christian theology.[4] Metz confesses that by confronting it he realized that it was no longer possible to practice theology "with my back turned to the invisible, or forcefully made-invisible, sufferings in the world; with my back toward the Holocaust; with my back turned to the speechless sufferings of the poor and oppressed in the world."[5] His confrontation with this event led him to recognize the reality of suffering as the privileged lens through which to view history, and to define it as a history of suffering.[6] The interpretation of history as one of suffering contrasts with discourses that name reality in ways that cover over and marginalize the suffering of the oppressed.

Metz sees a variety of Western interpretations of history as having defined reality without recognizing the suffering of the innocent as *the* reality that demands the most fundamental attention. In particular, he points to the triumphalism of those Christian theologies of redemption that ahistorically discuss reconciliation without reference to the cries of the victims,[7] the theories of progress in modernity that justify suffering by interpreting it as a byproduct of technological and economic development,[8] and finally, those postmodern discourses that subsume humanity within the anonymous forces of the cosmos (Nietzsche) or Being (Heidegger).[9] These interpretations of history share the common tendency to interpret the significance of history in a way that fails to acknowledge the absolute authority of the victims. Therefore these histories function as ideologies for the victors.

In contrast to what he characterizes as the "faceless metaphysics" of these ideologies, Metz maintains that a post-Shoah theology recognizes the faces of

---

[4] See Metz, *A Passion for God*, 54.

[5] Johann Baptist Metz, *Faith and the Future: Essays on Theology, Solidarity, and Modernity* (Maryknoll, NY: Orbis Books, 1995), 41.

[6] Johann Baptist Metz, *Love's Strategy: The Political Theology of Johann Baptist Metz,* ed. John K. Downey (Harrisburg, PA: Trinity Press International, 1999), 128, 139, and Metz, *A Passion for God*, 54, 56–60, 186.

[7] See, e.g., Johann Baptist Metz, "On the Way to a Christology after Auschwitz," 147–55, in *Who Do You Say That I Am? Confessing the Mystery of Christ*, ed. John C. Cavadini and Laura Holt, trans. J. Matthew Ashley (Notre Dame, IN: University of Notre Dame Press, 2004), at 148–49. See also, Metz, *A Passion for God*, 69, 86.

[8] See Metz's critique of the interpretation of history as progress in *Faith in History and Society: Toward a Practical Fundamental Theology*, trans. J. Matthew Ashley (New York: Crossroad, 2007), 97–98, 118–27.

[9] Metz, *A Passion for God*, 55, 78; idem, Elie Wiesel, Ekkehard Schuster, and Reinhold Boschert-Kimmig, *Hope Against Hope: Johann Baptist Metz and Elie Wiesel Speak Out on the Holocaust* (New York: Paulist Press, 1999), 28.

the victims as absolute and practices theology facing these victims.[10] According to Metz, "Christian theology after Auschwitz must—at long last—be guided by the insight that Christians can form and sufficiently understand their identity only in the face of the Jews. . . . For the sake of Auschwitz, they must be seen—the destroyed faces, the burned eyes."[11] After the Shoah it is necessary to look at the mutilated and burned bodies of the Jewish victims and permit the horror of these bodies to interrupt the strategies of evasion that explain away the suffering of the victims or dismiss the significance for the present of what has happened in the past. In contrast to ideologies that cultivate amnesia about past suffering and encourage apathy in the face of suffering in the present, Metz argues, the "categorical imperative" of this spirituality reads "awaken, open your eyes!"[12] Keeping one's eyes open allows one to see and be affected by past suffering, so that one might recognize the authority of those who suffer now.[13] It is this authority, after all, to which Jesus subjected all of humanity in the parable of the last judgment (Matt 25:31-46).[14] Furthermore, it is on the basis of this authority that individuals make their fundamental decision about God because, for Metz, "the only image of God is the face of our neighbor," which is a "sacrament of God's hidden presence."[15]

While Sobrino shares Metz's concern to give priority to the problem of suffering, his theological context differs from that of Metz's post-Shoah theology. Sobrino describes the difference:

> for years people have been asking "whether and how it is possible to do theology after Auschwitz," a challenge raised by visionary pioneers like Metz and Moltmann. But in reality, even Auschwitz seems not to be very present

---

[10] Metz, *Love's Strategy*, 138.

[11] Metz, *Faith and the Future*, 38–39.

[12] Metz, *Memoria Passionis*, 177. See also idem, *Armut im Geiste/Passion und Passionen* (Münster: Aschendorff, 2007), 72.

[13] Metz, *Hope against Hope*, 35. On the authority of suffering see idem, *Memoria Passionis*, 173; *A Passion for God*, 4; *Love's Strategy*, 170; *Hope against Hope*, 24; "The Provocation of Talking About God: A Discussion," 78–99 in J. Matthew Ashley, et al., eds., *The End of Time? The Provocation of Talking About God, Proceedings of a Meeting of Joseph Cardinal Ratzinger, Johann Baptist Metz, Jürgen Moltmann, and Eveline Goodman-Thau in Ahaus* (Mahwah, NJ: Paulist Press, 2004), at 89–90.

[14] Metz, *Love's Strategy*, 172; Metz, *Memoria Passionis*, 106. On Matthew 25 see Metz, *A Passion for God*, 163; Metz, "God: Against the Myth of the Eternity of Time," 26–46 in *The End of Time?* at 46; *Armut im Geiste/Passion und Passionen*, 72.

[15] Johann Baptist Metz, *Poverty of Spirit*, trans. John Drury (New York: Paulist Press, 1968), 32.

in today's theology, and when it is mentioned, the accent tends to fall on the word "after." Moreover, to focus on Auschwitz—a barbarity that occurred a half a century ago—may lead us to overlook contemporary Auschwitzes.[16]

Thus for Sobrino the critical question for theologians in Latin America is not "how to do theology after Auschwitz, but doing it in Auschwitz."[17] Although the task of doing theology in response to the experience of extreme poverty in Latin America expresses Sobrino's mature theological commitment, it took him years to awaken to this reality and to recognize as fundamental the authority of those who continue to suffer "in Auschwitz."

In an autobiographical text entitled "Awakening from the Sleep of Inhumanity," Sobrino describes an experience similar to Metz's, during which he gradually moved beyond his training in European theology and came to view his Christian faith from the perspective of the suffering poor in Latin America. According to Sobrino his studies in Europe had awakened him from his "dogmatic slumber," but he had yet to traverse the "sleep of inhumanity—the sleep of egocentrism and selfishness."[18] It was not until 1974, when he returned to El Salvador from Europe, that Sobrino encountered "the world of the poor—the real world."[19] In view of this encounter, Sobrino observes: "I saw that my life and studies had not given me new eyes to see this world as it really is, and they hadn't taken from me the heart of stone I had for the suffering of this world."[20] This awakening gave him the eyes to see the reality of the world from the perspective of the dehumanizing poverty that condemns millions to unjust death each year.[21]

Sobrino names this reality a crucified people. He argues, "the sign of the times *per antonomasiam,* par excellence, is 'the existence of a crucified people.'"[22] Because Sobrino describes reality as a crucified people, the authority of those who suffer becomes absolute. Sobrino invokes Metz on this point, arguing that "the highest authority on the planet is the authority of those who suffer, from

---

[16] Jon Sobrino, *Witnesses to the Kingdom: The Martyrs of El Salvador and the Crucified Peoples* (Maryknoll, NY: Orbis Books, 2003), 126.

[17] Jon Sobrino, *Jesus the Liberator: A Historical-Theological Reading of Jesus of Nazareth* (New York: Burns & Oates, 1994), 195.

[18] Sobrino, *Principle of Mercy*, 3.

[19] Ibid., 2.

[20] Ibid., 3.

[21] Jon Sobrino, "The Kingdom of God and the Theologal Dimension of the Poor: the Jesuanic Principle," 109–45 in *Who Do You Say That I Am? Confessing the Mystery of Christ,* ed. John C. Cavadini and Laura Holt, trans. J. Matthew Ashley (Notre Dame, IN: University of Notre Dame Press, 2004), at 136.

[22] Sobrino, *Principle of Mercy*, vii.

which there is no appeal" and that "suffering and compassion relativize—put in its place—anything else that tries to claim ultimacy: churches and religions, and also—lest we forget—the socialisms of the past, the Western democracies of the present."[23] For Sobrino the authorities to which people devote themselves—religious, political, and economic—should be displaced by the authority of the suffering of a crucified people. Accordingly, Christianity is given the task of forming Christians capable of being honest with this reality of a crucified people. For Sobrino, being honest with reality "is an option of whether to look at the truth of things or not," and this honesty is practiced concretely when one's life is "shaped by the fifty million people who die of hunger every year, or by El Mozote or Rwanda, or by the economic embargo against women, children, and the elderly in Iraq, or by the horrors that Congolese women suffer."[24] The normal response to unjust experiences of suffering is not honesty with reality, but rather a slumber of unreality in which people close their eyes to a suffering world in order to keep the painful questions about their complicity in these injustices at a safe distance.[25] But Sobrino, like Metz, contends that our relationship to God is decided by our response to a crucified people. Jesus proclaimed that it is through "showing love to the suffering 'people' that human life (Luke 10:29-37) and the life of salvation (Matt 25:34-40) are judged."[26] Indeed, for Sobrino the primary location of God's presence in a suffering world is in the primordial "sacrament" of the faces of the poor.[27]

Metz and Sobrino maintain that the fundamental task of Christian spirituality is to wake up, open one's eyes, and be honest with the real by acknowledging the absolute authority of those who suffer. However, the discipline of opening one's eyes to the suffering of others is only the first step in a form of spirituality that culminates in a liberating praxis of compassion (Metz) or mercy (Sobrino) for the victims. Both Metz and Sobrino understand the parable of the Good Samaritan as the foundational biblical narrative of a spirituality that sees a

---

[23] Sobrino, *Where Is God?*, 111. See also idem, *No Salvation Outside the Poor: Prophetic-Utopian Essays* (Maryknoll, NY: Orbis Books, 2008), 34, 50; idem, *Christ the Liberator*, 270, and idem, "Karl Rahner and Liberation Theology," *The Way* 43 (2004): 53–66, at 63.

[24] Sobrino, *Principle of Mercy*, 18; idem, "Kingdom of God and the Theologal Dimension of the Poor," 136.

[25] Sobrino, *Principle of Mercy*, 77. See also Sobrino, *Christ the Liberator*, 5, where he invokes Metz in relation to this "faceless distance."

[26] Sobrino, *No Salvation Outside the Poor*, 116. See also Sobrino, *The Principle of Mercy*, 5.

[27] Sobrino, *Where is God?*, 23, 74. Elsewhere (*Witnesses to the Kingdom*, 67) Sobrino maintains that God is "hidden in the suffering face of the poor" and in "God crucified in the crucified people."

suffering world and responds to it with compassion or mercy. These two theologians describe a threefold logic in the spirituality disclosed in the parable: (1) the encounter with the embodied suffering of the other makes an unconditional ethical demand on the subject; (2) in response to the encounter with the suffering of the other, the subject is called to a movement of self-abandonment or *kenosis* in which one relinquishes self-interest before the authority of the sufferer; (3) the subject is called to respond with political compassion (Metz) or structural mercy (Sobrino) to those who suffer unjustly by taking the crucified down from their cross and by contesting the structures that cause the suffering of the innocent.

Metz observes that there are parables with which Jesus has found a narrative place in the memory of humanity, and that the "'Good Samaritan' belongs first and foremost among these."[28] The significance of this parable lies in narration of the central concern of Jesus' life and ministry: his primordial sensitivity to the suffering of others.[29] As the parable is narrated, the priest and Levite simply pass by the victim on the side of the road "'for the sake of a higher concern'" and fail to see the victim's suffering as of ultimate significance.[30] In contrast to the moral blindness of the priest and Levite, Jesus points to the Samaritan as the one who embodied primordial sensitivity to the suffering of others by seeing and responding to the wounded victim. In the parable the ethical event takes place at the level of the body, in a visceral encounter with the suffering victim. Following the analysis of Hans Jonas, who claims that the very fact that a human being is breathing lays an obligation on the self, Metz contends that the "categorical imperative" of the mysticism of open eyes is "'just look and you know!' (H. Jonas)."[31] It is a question not of applying abstract rules of justice or theories of morality to a concrete situation, but of opening one's eyes to the face of the other and the ethical call that arises from an encounter with the suffering of the poor and the oppressed. In the parable of the Good Samarian, Metz maintains, Jesus "depicted a situation in which it is not possible for one to think through—Do I have to do this or that? Can I ascertain where the meaningful action lies? Rather, it is a situation in which one has to obey. Here I can only stand by the one who is lying on the side of the road, fallen into the hands of

---

[28] Metz, "Toward a Christianity of Political Compassion," 250–53, in *Love That Produces Hope*, ed. Kevin F. Burke and Robert Lassalle-Klein, trans. J. Matthew Ashley (Collegeville, MN: Liturgical Press, 2006), at 250.

[29] Metz, *Memoria Passionis*, 163–64.

[30] Metz, "Toward a Christianity of Political Compassion," 250.

[31] Metz, *Memoria Passionis*, 166. For Jonas's analysis see Hans Jonas, *The Imperative of Responsibility: In Search of an Ethics for the Technological Age*, trans. Hans Jonas in collaboration with David Herr (Chicago: University of Chicago Press, 1984), 131.

robbers."[32] In addition to describing this ethics as a form of responsibility that takes place at the level of embodiment and demands immediate recognition, Metz claims that the parable also narrates a form of ethics in which it is not possible to delimit or circumscribe the range of one's responsibility.[33] Instead, the sole criterion for action is the authority of the suffering of the other.[34]

For Metz an open-eyed spirituality is structured around a "death of the self" or a "relativization of the self" in which the human person is called to surrender his or her self-interest before the authority of the sufferer.[35] He observes: "Christian mysticism of suffering is not egocentric, because it knows something like a mystical 'abandonment of the self.'" It is characterized by "a deeper and deeper growth into a covenant, in the mystical covenant between God and the human person, in which the subject's responsibility for the other is not disintegrated, but summoned."[36] Against the various proclamations of the death of the subject in postmodern thought, Metz defends the subject as intersubjective.[37] For Metz, the subject receives its identity through its relationship with the suffering and threatened other in whom the authority of the God of biblical monotheism manifests itself.[38]

The term Metz has employed recently to characterize this spirituality is compassion. Compassion denotes both primordial sensitivity to the suffering of others and the task of assuming some form of political responsibility for that suffering. Metz describes this compassion as asymmetrical insofar as it involves "the strange notion of caring for others without getting something in return," and as a form of unlimited responsibility that exists "prior to any contractual exchange relationship."[39] In this sense compassion ruptures the dominant ways of relating to others in a market-driven society, because those relationships are based on principles of symmetry, exchange, and self-interest.[40] Furthermore, Metz argues that, in an era of globalization, compassion cannot be limited merely to aiding the wounded victim on the side of the road. It must also involve a comprehensive justice for the global poor that takes the form of what

---

[32] Metz, *The End of Time?*, 89. See also Metz, *Love's Strategy*, 170; Metz, *A Passion for God*, 163.

[33] Metz, *Love's Strategy*, 170.

[34] Metz, *A Passion for God*, 3, 134, 144; Metz, *Love's Strategy*, 170.

[35] Metz, *Memoria Passionis*, 166.

[36] Ibid., 106, 167, and idem, "God: Against the Myth of the Eternity of Time," 43.

[37] Metz, *A Passion for God*, 180n7.

[38] Metz, "God: Against the Myth of the Eternity of Time," 43.

[39] Metz, *Love's Strategy*, 175; "God: Against the Myth of the Eternity of Time," 43.

[40] Metz, "Toward a Christianity of Political Compassion," 252.

he describes as a "uniquely biblical" politics of compassion.[41] Concretely, this entails a critical confrontation with the logic of the market insofar as it only acknowledges the authority of profit, power, and technical efficiency and fails to recognize the more fundamental authority of the suffering poor.[42]

Like Metz, Jon Sobrino seizes upon the parable of the Good Samaritan as the paradigmatic example of being honest with reality: "When Jesus wishes to show what it is to be an ideal, total human being, he narrates the parable of the Good Samaritan."[43] According to Sobrino the parable demonstrates that

> the ideal human being, the complete human being, is the one who interiorizes, absorbs in her innards, the suffering of another—in the case of the parable, unjustly afflicted suffering—in such a way that this interiorized suffering becomes a part of her, is transformed into an internal principle, the first and the last, of her activity.[44]

In his description of mercy as a form of responsibility Sobrino uses extreme, visceral imagery of innards absorbing the pain of the other and entrails wrenching in the presence of the suffering flesh of the other to describe how "the victim lying in the road touches the deepest fiber of the human: *splachnon*, entrails, heart."[45]

Sobrino's interpretation of the parable of the Good Samaritan is consistent with Metz's reflections: the embodied encounter with the other makes an immediate ethical demand. For Sobrino the basis for this responsibility is neither "a disembodied categorical imperative" nor "an aesthetic attraction to putting some theory of justice into practice," but rather results from opening one's eyes to the reality of a crucified people.[46] He invokes Ignacio Ellacuría's challenge to "look with your eyes and heart at these peoples who are suffering so much" and ask yourself "What have I done to crucify them? What am I doing to end their crucifixion? What should I do so that this people might rise from the dead?"[47] The response to this challenge hinges on the capacity to use one's eyes to look at the crucified bodies of the victims and to respond to their suffering by taking

[41] Metz, *Memoria Passionis*, 171, 177; Metz, "Toward a Christianity of Political Compassion," 251; Metz, *Love's Strategy*, 168.

[42] Metz, *A Passion for God*, 3; Metz, *Memoria Passionis*, 170.

[43] Sobrino, *Principle of Mercy*, 17.

[44] Ibid.

[45] Jon Sobrino, "Jesus of Galilee from the Salvadoran Context: Compassion, Hope, and Following the Light of the Cross," *Theological Studies* 70 (2009): 436–60, at 454.

[46] Jon Sobrino, "Ignacio Ellacuría, the Human Being and the Christian: 'Taking the Crucified People Down from the Cross,'" 1–67, in *Love That Produces Hope*, at 5.

[47] Ibid., 17–18.

their bodies down from the crosses. Responding with mercy to a crucified people entails "fundamental Christian ascesis: *kenosis*," a "stripping of self" before the authority of the sufferer.[48] This *kenosis* involves displacement of self-interest and acceptance of a radical responsibility for the suffering of another human being "without ulterior motives, without any more motive than the enormous suffering of the crucified people."[49]

The praxis of mercy has a very specific content in relation to those who suffer innocently. This is the place for taking the crucified down from their crosses.[50] Sobrino argues that the task for the Christian who practices structural mercy is to respond to individual, concrete experiences of suffering with mercy but also to connect this practice of mercy to a critical confrontation with structural injustice. Because the suffering of the global poor is caused by structural injustices it is necessary for the mercy of the Samaritan to take form as structural mercy. Sobrino dissects this structural dimension of mercy by returning to the parable of the Good Samaritan and pointing to the often-overlooked role played by the robbers in the parable. According to Sobrino the robbers who inflicted the wounds on the victim lying on the side of the road represent those contemporary social structures that perpetuate the status quo by supporting unjust economic arrangements.[51] While the presence of apathy and blindness (the priest and Levite) is a pervasive reality and demands a response, Sobrino claims that what is more problematic and warrants prophetic condemnation is the set of structures (highway robbers) that causes the crucifixion of entire peoples.[52] Thus, as with Metz's description of the political compassion that emerges from the parable of the Good Samaritan, Sobrino insists that the mercy of the Samaritan must have a structural dimension in which responding to a crucified people involves both aiding the victims and a critical confrontation with structures of anti-mercy.

The scandal of innocent suffering demands that Christians look at that suffering, view the encounter with it as a call to conversion, and practice a form of political compassion (Metz) or structural mercy (Sobrino) to alleviate the suffering caused by the injustice of extreme poverty.[53] The next section of

---

[48] Jon Sobrino, *Spirituality of Liberation: Toward Political Holiness*, trans. Robert Barr (Maryknoll, NY: Orbis Books, 1988), 82. See also idem, *Jesus the Liberator*, 128.

[49] Sobrino, *Witnesses to the Kingdom*, 198; Sobrino, "Ignacio Ellacuría," 5; Sobrino, *Principle of Mercy*, 16, 18.

[50] Ibid., 10.

[51] Ibid., 200–201.

[52] Sobrino, *Witnesses to the Kingdom*, 200.

[53] Johann Baptist Metz, "Wer steht für die unschuldigen Opfer ein? Ein Gespräch mit Johann Baptist Metz," *Orientierung* 72 13/14 (Zürich, 15–31 July 2008), 148–50, at 150.

this chapter will examine the types of spiritual exercises that can facilitate the capacity to see the world from the perspective of the faces of a crucified people.

A Mysticism of Open Eyes

The previous section described the scandal of innocent suffering as the reality that animates the theologies of Johann Baptist Metz and Jon Sobrino and leads them to develop what, following Metz, we have characterized as a mysticism of open eyes. This section will deliberate on the question: which spiritual exercises are capable of forming individuals in this prophetic mysticism of open eyes in a cultural context shaped by the valorization of self-interest in the public realm and the proliferation of exculpatory strategies in the private lives of individuals? As with the discussion of contemplative-sacramental mysticism in the fourth chapter, this section will focus on four spiritual exercises that possess the capacity to cultivate this prophetic form of mysticism: liturgy and the Eucharist, *memoria passionis*, the encounter with the face of the other, and contemplative prayer. In this section particular emphasis will be placed on how these spiritual exercises constitute practices of resistance to the apathy of the consumer aesthetic and the dominance of relationships of symmetry and principles of exchange in market culture.

(1) As noted in the second chapter, in contemporary liturgical theology a great deal of attention has been paid to the significance of worship as a form of asceticism that trains individuals in a Christian vision of reality. In particular, Louis-Marie Chauvet has examined the capacity of liturgy to transform Christians' perceptions. Chauvet claims that "reality is never present to us except in a mediated way, which is to say, constructed out of the symbolic network of culture which fashions us."[54] For Chauvet, the manner in which culture influences us is analogous to the way in which a contact lens imperceptibly affects our vision. Indeed, for him, it is undeniable that our "vision of the real is filtered."[55] Chauvet observes that the problem with this situation is that "our perception has become so accustomed to this lens and this lens adheres so tightly to our perception that, almost as a reflex, we take the cultural for the natural and our desires for the real."[56]

For Chauvet, liturgy represents the crucible through which the cultural lens is replaced with a distinctively Christian vision. A central component is the work that liturgy performs on an individual at the level of embodiment, desire, and

---

[54] Louis-Marie Chauvet, *Symbol and Sacrament*, trans. Patrick Madigan and Madeleine Beaumont (Collegeville, MN: Liturgical Press, 1995), 84.

[55] Ibid., 86.

[56] Ibid.

perception. Indeed, liturgical worship is focused on the task of presenting the Gospel at the level of the senses: "to be initiated is not to have learned 'truths to believe' but to have received a tradition, in a way through all the pores of one's skin. Initiation comes about through a process of education which is like life: it is not the end of a simple intellectual course (indispensable though such courses may be today), but originally an identity."[57] Chauvet invokes psychoanalytic theory to argue that ritual and sacraments represent more effective mechanisms of conversion than intellectual debate or theological analysis. Worship and the reception of the sacraments are rituals that transform unconscious desire and embodied dispositions. As Chauvet describes it, "faith cannot be lived in any other way, including what is most spiritual in it, than in the mediation of the body, the body of a society, of a desire, of a tradition, of a history, of an institution, and so on. What is most spiritual always takes place in the most corporeal."[58]

This analysis is relevant to the cultivation of a prophetic spirituality committed to justice for the poor because Chauvet recounts the way in which liturgy serves to contest the dominance of the principles of exchange and symmetry in market culture and open the space for the practice of solidarity without expecting anything in return. According to Chauvet "the logic of the marketplace (under the form of barter or money) is that of value; it belongs to the regime of need which seeks to satisfy itself immediately through the possession of objects. The logic of symbolic exchange is of another order."[59] The logic of the marketplace is that of exchange and utility in which everything is turned into a commodity. Chauvet argues that the order of symbolic exchange supersedes the market's exchange of commodities. It enters the order of the gift.

Chauvet observes of symbolic exchange: "one is here outside or beyond the regime of usefulness and immediacy. Rather, the principle which rules here is one of super-abundance. The true objects being exchanged are the subjects themselves."[60] Chauvet contends that in symbolic exchange what is given is received as a gift. The reception of the gift represents a rupture with the dominant order of things in which everything is reduced to a symmetrical exchange of commodities.

The sacraments are the primary means for initiating Christians into this symbolic realm, through which the cultural logic of exchange is replaced by

---

[57] Louis-Marie Chauvet, "The Liturgy in its Symbolic Space," 29–40, in *Liturgy and the Body*, ed. idem and François Kabasele Lumbaba, *Concilium* 1995/3 (London: SCM; Maryknoll, NY: Orbis Books, 1995), 31.

[58] Louis-Marie Chauvet, *The Sacraments: The Word of God at the Mercy of the Body*, trans. Madeleine Beaumont (Collegeville, MN: Liturgical Press, 2001), xii.

[59] Chauvet, *Symbol and Sacrament*, 106.

[60] Ibid.

the Christian logic of the gift. Chauvet maintains that the response to this gift, or the "return-gift," is not rendered to the original giver. Instead, the gift is "returned" by giving a gift to another. This means that when God offers the Eucharist as a gift to Christians, the recipient is called to offer a "return-gift" to others in the world and not to God. Chauvet calls this the work of giving Christ a body in the world by making God's mercy present among the poor and oppressed.[61] The eucharistic sacrifice "seeks to be enfleshed in the *living-in-grace* between brothers and sisters. This ethical dimension is not simply an extrinsic consequence of the Eucharistic process; it belongs to it as an *intrinsic element*."[62] Indeed, following the Jewish philosopher Emmanuel Lévinas, Chauvet returns liturgy to its primordial meaning as a service (*leitourgia*) of hospitality to the other, or, quite simply, a "liturgy of the neighbor."[63]

Chauvet's analysis of the relationship between the liturgical imagination and the cultural imagination finds an interesting analogue in William Cavanaugh's reflections on the role of the Eucharist in the cultivation of what he describes as the "theopolitical imagination."[64] Cavanaugh's theological work is focused on the way in which the nation-state and the market represent realities that obstruct the cultivation of distinctive Christian lives in contemporary culture. In his reflections on these issues Cavanaugh focuses on the significance of the Eucharist as a reality that not only tells a story about the nature of reality that differs from those told by the nation-state or the market but also embodies a communal celebration that creates spaces of peace and justice in a world dominated by the violence of the nation-state and the injustice of the market.[65]

In relation to the nation-state, Cavanaugh argues that "the imagination of the state has a tremendous power to discipline bodies" and to divide human beings against one another in order to perpetuate its own existence and legitimate its use of force, violence, and even torture.[66] Cavanaugh maintains that the celebration of the Eucharist in the church is the site at which Christians

---

[61] Ibid., 265.

[62] Ibid., 277. Emphasis in original.

[63] Chauvet, *The Sacraments*, 58. For Lévinas's reflections on this point see Emmanuel Lévinas, *Of God Who Comes to Mind*, trans. Bettina Bergo (Palo Alto: Stanford University Press, 1998), 150–51. See also Jeffrey Bloechl, *Liturgy of the Neighbor: Emmanuel Lévinas and the Religion of Responsibility* (Pittsburgh: Duquesne University Press, 2000).

[64] William Cavanaugh, *Theopolitical Imagination: Christian Practices of Space and Time* (New York: T & T Clark, 2002).

[65] William Cavanaugh, "Liturgy and Politics: An Interview with William Cavanaugh," http://www.religion-online.org/showarticle.asp?title=3308.

[66] William Cavanaugh, *Torture and the Eucharist: Theology, Politics, and the Body of Christ* (Oxford, UK, and Malden, MA: Blackwell, 1998), 31.

are trained both to see the world differently and to act in the world differently. He stresses the ineluctability of seeing and action: "the Eucharist is not just about seeing the world in a certain way, but about acting. Social imagination is not merely a mental act. The Eucharist is about the construction of a social body—the Body of Christ—that is capable of resisting the imagination of the state when resistance is called for."[67] The borders the nation-state so tightly patrols and the divisions it creates are called into question in the church when Christians are invited into God's imagination where the divisions of class, creed, and nationality are dissolved.

Cavanaugh maintains that the Eucharist also serves as the discipline that permits Christians to confront the perverted liturgies of the market. Like the advocates of the nation-state, the advocates of the free market tell a particular story about the world that is rooted in a view of competition between individuals over scarce resources. The story of the market is a story of endless desire in which the desire for goods can never be fulfilled. It is grounded in the view that scarcity is the fundamental law of reality, so that "hunger is written into the conditions under which economics operates. There is never enough to go around."[68] The economic law of scarcity describes both those who experience physical hunger and the affluent who have been trained to be dissatisfied with what they possess. The result is that "my desires to feed the hungry are always being distracted by the competition between their desires and my own."[69]

The story of the market is therefore one of hunger and consumption.[70] But it differs from the Christian story about hunger and consumption as that story is disclosed in the Eucharist. The Eucharist is grounded in a view of the world that is based not on scarcity but on "life in abundance" (John 10:10). It is a story not about the endless desire for new things but about a desire formed and shaped by God's desire as revealed in the gift of the Eucharist.[71] Cavanaugh argues that participation in the Eucharist initiates individuals into a form of consumption that represents an alternative to the consumer model: "the Eucharist effects a radical decentering of the individual by incorporating the person into a larger body. In the process, the act of consumption is turned inside-out,

---

[67] William Cavanaugh, "Telling the Truth About Ourselves: Torture and Eucharist in the U.S. Popular Imagination," http://theotherjournal.com/2009/05/08/telling-the-truth-about-ourselves-torture-and-eucharist-in-the-u-s-popular-imaginat/.

[68] William Cavanaugh, *Being Consumed: Economics and Christian Desire* (Grand Rapids: Eerdmans, 2008), 90.

[69] Ibid., 91–92.

[70] Ibid., 89.

[71] Ibid., 98.

such that the consumer is consumed."[72] Cavanaugh maintains that, in contrast
to the model of consumption in which the individual searches for new commodities as a means of participating in the consumer vision of salvation, the
Eucharist is a *kenotic* reality that calls those who receive it to offer themselves
"to be consumed by the world."[73]

To be consumed in the Eucharist is to be placed within the larger story of
the mystical Body of Christ and to enter into relationships of solidarity with
those members of the body who live under brutal conditions of deprivation.
Furthermore, this mystical body is held together by physical ties:

> the enacting of the Body of Christ in the Eucharist has a dramatic effect on
> the communicability of pain from one person to another, for individuals
> are now united in one body, connected by one nervous system. Not only
> can the eye not say to the hand "I have no need of you" (I Cor. 12:21), but
> the eye and the hand suffer or rejoice in the same fate.[74]

The Eucharist serves as a spiritual practice that trains those who receive it to
be affected by the pain of others in a manner reminiscent of the last judgment
scene (Matthew 25) in which Christ himself is encountered in the hungry and
thirsty. It follows, therefore, that refusal to respond to the suffering of the poor
and the hungry is a refusal to receive Christ in the world.[75] Cavanaugh concludes:
"those of us who partake in the Eucharist while ignoring the hungry may be
eating and drinking our own damnation" (cf. 1 Cor. 11:29).[76]

(2) As described in the second chapter, the Eucharist is a central practice of
remembrance in the Christian tradition. As the ritualized remembrance (*memoria passionis*) of the suffering of Jesus Christ, the Eucharist makes those who receive it aware of the ongoing crucifixion of the poor in the contemporary world.
Cavanaugh emphasizes the significance of the Eucharist as *memoria passionis*:

> In the Eucharistic rite, the commemoration of the passion, death, resur-
> rection, and ascension of Christ spoken after the words of institution is
> called the *anamnesis*. This is the Greek word used by the New Testament
> in rendering Jesus's command "Do this in remembrance of me" (e.g., Luke
> 22:19). The Greek word an-amnesis is the opposite of amnesia; it is literally
> an "unforgetting." It is an odd term, for how could we forget about God?

---

[72] Ibid., 95.
[73] Ibid., 84, 95.
[74] Ibid., 96.
[75] Ibid.
[76] Ibid., 98.

Perhaps it is because we are constantly tempted to forget the victims of this world. We contrive to blame the poor for their poverty, or claim that their poverty is necessary for the smooth functioning of the free market.[77]

This specific *anamnesis* of the passion of Jesus Christ serves to sensitize Christians to the plural histories of suffering in the world and encourages them to cultivate a way of being in the world that is rooted in an option for the poor and the oppressed. As Metz suggests in *Love's Strategy*, a Christian spirituality rooted in *memoria passionis* serves to liberate individuals not from their poverty but from their wealth and "excessive prosperity," not from their lack but from their consumerism, not from their suffering but from their apathy before the suffering of others, not from their guilt but from their innocence.[78]

While Metz contends that *memoria passionis* is a central dimension of Christian spirituality, he argues that we live in the midst of a "culture of amnesia" that purges from public awareness any unreconciled memories that disturb the pursuit of guilt-free experiences of consumption.[79] For him a culture of amnesia is a culture of apathy that supports the view that the suffering of others is "insignificant, ugly and better kept out of sight."[80] Because consumer culture habituates individuals to forms of life that are numb to the deprivation of others, the human experience of restlessness or dissatisfaction is interpreted through the lens of consumer desire and remedied through the acquisition of new commodities. This stands in marked contrast to the interpretation of restlessness within the traditions of prophetic Christianity. In particular, a spirituality rooted in *memoria passionis* places this experience of restlessness within the broader horizon of unreconciled suffering from the past and therefore interprets it not in terms of some private sense of lack or the experience of spiritual *Angst*, but rather as sociopolitical "awareness of what is missing" and as a particular sensitivity to the absence of justice in the world.[81]

Furthermore, as argued in chapter 5, the apathy of consumer culture is supported by the market system that trains individuals to pursue only those activities that possess exchange value and bear the promise of profit.[82] Whereas

[77] Cavanaugh, "Telling the Truth About Ourselves."

[78] Metz, *Love's Strategy*, 60, in the section "The Future Church."

[79] Metz, *Memoria Passionis*, 74.

[80] Metz, *Faith and the Future*, 6. See also, idem, *Faith in History and Society*, 101.

[81] Metz, *A Passion for God*, 25, 28. According to Metz, from the perspective of prophetic Christianity, "being attentive to God means hearing the silence of those who have disappeared." Johann Baptist Metz, "Suffering unto God," trans. J. Matthew Ashley, *Critical Inquiry* 20 (1994): 611–22, at 615.

[82] Metz, *Love's Strategy*, 173.

the market reduces all human relationships to exchange principles, Metz maintains that *memoria passionis* resists this formation by cultivating a relationship of solidarity with the dead and vanquished. Relating to such "disappeared" persons breaks the market standard for relationships: "when it comes to the dead there is no exchange relationship, no *do ut des* [principle of reciprocity]. The love that mourns for the dead is that form of love (the only form according to Kierkegaard) that cannot be taken up into a consumer society's exploitation structures."[83]

Remembering the suffering and death of the victims of history is a practice from which a person receives no benefit, no exchange value, and no profit. As a consequence, this form of remembrance resists the logic of the market by training individuals to be attentive to those relationships that are deemed irrelevant and insignificant by cultural standards. The act of remembering past suffering sensitizes individuals to the cries of the poor and brings about "a new moral imagination with regard to others' suffering which should bear fruit in an excessive, uncalculated partiality for the weak and the voiceless."[84] Indeed, Metz argues that entering into asymmetrical relationships of solidarity and responsibility for the "threatened and destroyed other" is the only way to break "the violence of the logic of the marketplace in politics."[85] *Memoria passionis* is, therefore, not only a central discipline of Christian spirituality but also serves to cultivate resistance to the market reduction of all relationships to the Darwinian logic of the survival of the fittest.[86]

(3) As with Metz, the memory of the victims of the Shoah haunts Emmanuel Lévinas's entire philosophy and is at the root of his attempt to foreground ethics as first philosophy. This memory—particularly the specific memory of Lévinas's family members murdered at the death camp in Dachau—is invoked explicitly in his most significant philosophical work, *Otherwise than Being*. He dedicates the book "to the memory of those who were closest among the six million assassinated by the National Socialists, and of the millions on millions of all confessions and all nations, victims of the same hatred of the other man, the same anti-semitism."[87] While Metz and Lévinas share this common horizon, where Metz emphasizes the significance of *memoria passionis* as a response to

---

[83] Metz, *Faith in History and Society*, 51.

[84] Metz, Ibid., 113.

[85] Metz, "Toward a Christianity of Political Compassion," 252. See also idem, "God: The Myth of the Eternity of Time," 39, and *Memoria Passionis*, 170.

[86] On Metz's resistance to this Darwinian (and Nietzschean) logic see Matthew T. Eggemeier, "Christianity or Nihilism? The Apocalyptic Discourses of Johann Baptist Metz and Friedrich Nietzsche," *Horizons* 39:1 (2012), 7–26.

[87] Emmanuel Lévinas, *Otherwise than Being*, trans. Alphonso Lingis (The Hague: Martinus Nijhoff, 1981), dedication.

the Shoah, Lévinas responds by analyzing the ethical and spiritual significance of the embodied encounter with the suffering flesh of another human being.[88]

Lévinas employs a complex phenomenological description of embodied experience in the world to describe ethics as an event that takes place in the encounter with the suffering flesh of the other. He first describes the primordial experience of human embodiment in terms of the pleasure we take in the things of the world. According to Lévinas, to be human is to receive enjoyment from the basic elements of existence: "life is *love of life*, a relation with contents that are not my being but more dear than my being: thinking, eating, sleeping, reading, working, warming oneself in the sun."[89] For Lévinas, life at its most basic level is the enjoyment of the things of the world like good soup and fresh air. He contends, however, that this primordial experience of enjoyment is interrupted by the suffering flesh of another human being that affects the subject "on the surface of the skin" and "at the edge of the nerves."[90] Concretely, the encounter with the emaciated body of another human being suffering from hunger is an event that interrupts the simple pleasure of a full stomach. Thus the exclusive pursuit of the enjoyment of food or pleasurable aesthetic experiences is called into question by the embodied encounter with those who are denied access to the most basic necessities of life.

In this sense ethics is a flesh-and-blood affair that is grounded in human embodiment. Lévinas straightforwardly asserts that "only a subject that eats can be for-the-other."[91] The encounter with the suffering body of another human being makes a demand on the self and calls it beyond the exclusive pursuit of egoistic pleasure and into a relationship of responsibility. This form of responsibility manifests itself concretely in terms of "taking care of the other's need" and "snatching the bread from one's mouth" to give it to the other. Furthermore, it involves sacrifice and self-denial insofar as it entails this taking of bread from oneself and giving it to another. Or, even more dramatically, it might mean placing oneself in a situation in which taking responsibility for the other could imply suffering, to the point of dying for the other. Lévinas explicitly invokes the "suffering servant" of Isaiah 58 and the Christian concept of *kenosis* to describe the self-emptying character of ethical subjectivity, as individuals are called

---

[88] For Lévinas the type of holiness described in Matthew 25 is "the holiness of a social problem. All the problems of eating and drinking, insofar as they concern the other, become sacred." Emmanuel Lévinas, *Is It Righteous to Be?* trans. Jill Robbins (Stanford, CA: Stanford University Press, 2001), 52.

[89] Emmanuel Lévinas, *Totality and Infinity*, trans. Alphonso Lingis (Pittsburgh: Duquesne University Press, 1969), 112. Emphasis in original.

[90] Lévinas, *Otherwise than Being*, 64.

[91] Ibid., 74.

to pour out their own lives to alleviate the suffering of another.[92] It is through this movement toward the other that the self encounters God, because God is available as a trace inscribed in the other person: "the relation to God is already ethics, or, as Isaiah 58 would have it, the proximity to God, devotion itself, is devotion to the other man."[93]

Lévinas uses the visual metaphor of "the face of the other" to signify the ethical call that emerges from the suffering body of the other. The authority of the face of the other is an ethical revelation that exists prior to any rational deliberation and consensus about moral norms. Lévinas specifies this ethical revelation: "there is a commandment in the appearance of the face, as if a master spoke to me. However, at the same time, the face of the Other is destitute; it is the poor for whom I can do all and to whom I owe all."[94] Ethics does not depend on any prior agreement, contract, or relationship of reciprocity. The structure of responsibility is asymmetrical and involves a movement toward the other without expecting anything in return. This asymmetrical responsibility is, furthermore, infinite and without limit, so it is impossible ever to fulfill the obligation to alleviate the suffering of others.

In terms that are remarkably similar to those employed by Lévinas, Benedict XVI has argued that the enfleshed encounter with the other is an experience of moral and spiritual significance. In an essay entitled "We Must Use Our Eyes!" Benedict XVI analyzes the meaning of face-to-face encounter by arguing that the face of the other summons an individual to relinquish his or her self-interest and to make room for the other. He writes:

> The face of the other addresses an appeal to my liberty, asking me to welcome him and take care of him, asking me to affirm his value per se, not

[92] For further reflections on the *kenosis* of God, see "Judaism and Kenosis," 114–32, in Emmanuel Lévinas, *In the Time of the Nations*, trans. Michael B. Smith (Bloomington: Indiana University Press, 1994), and "A Man-God?" 46–52 in idem, *Entre Nous: Thinking of the Other,* trans. Michael B. Smith and Barbara Harshav (New York: Columbia University Press, 1998).

[93] Lévinas, *Is It Righteous to Be?* 243. Lévinas invokes Matthew 25 in much the same way as do both Metz and Benedict XVI: "I cannot describe the relation to God without speaking of my concern for the other. When I speak to a Christian, I always quote Matthew 25: the relation to God is presented there as a relation to another person. It is not a metaphor; in the other, there is a real presence of God. In my relation to the other, I hear the word of God. It is not a metaphor. It is not only extremely important; it is literally true. I'm not saying that the other is God, but that in his or her face I hear the word of God." Ibid., 171.

[94] Emmanuel Lévinas, *Ethics and Infinity: Conversations with Philippe Nemo*, trans. Richard Cohen (Pittsburgh: Duquesne University Press, 1985), 89.

merely to the extent to which he may happen to coincide with my own interests. . . . When I decide to look him in the face, I am deciding on conversion, I am resolving to let the other address his appeal to me, to go beyond the confines of my own self and to make space for him. This is why even the evidential character of this moral value depends to a large extent on a secret decision by my liberty to agree to look at the other and thus be provoked to change my life.[95]

This encounter is a conversion experience in which the face issues a call to recognize responsibility for the other in whom God is revealed. Indeed, for Benedict XVI one of the basic tasks of Christian spirituality is to "learn to recognize the image of God in the face of every man, however disagreeable or strange he may seem to us."[96]

The Jewish Lévinas and the Roman Catholic Benedict XVI converge in their conviction that the enfleshed encounter with the other is not only a decisive event in the moral life but also one of the fundamental ways in which the human person encounters God in the world. This type of embodied encounter is a spiritual exercise, one that may take different forms, from Peter Hans Kolvenbach's and Jon Sobrino's emphasis on immersion in the world of the poor as a practice of moral and spiritual formation to Dorothy Day's commitment to the corporal works of mercy in the Catholic Worker houses of hospitality.[97] The fundamental point is that the call of Christ is not abstract. It is a call to express the Christian faith concretely by entering into relationships of solidarity with the poor. This means that solidarity involves coming to know the poor as human beings and not as mere statistics.[98] As Gustavo Gutiérrez often emphasizes, it is important to know the names of the poor because "the preferential option for the poor is ultimately a question of friendship. Without friendship, an option for the poor can easily become commitment to an abstraction . . . when we become friends with the poor, their presence leaves an indelible imprint on our lives."[99]

[95] Benedict XVI, *Christianity and the Crisis of Cultures*, trans. Brian McNeil (San Francisco: Ignatius Press, 2006), 66.

[96] Benedict XVI, *Europe Today and Tomorrow* (San Francisco: Ignatius Press, 2007), 109. See also idem, *Values in a Time of Upheaval* (San Francisco: Ignatius Press, 2006), 158.

[97] See Sobrino, *Principle of Mercy*, 2, 4–5, 79, and idem, *No Salvation Outside the Poor*, 51–52.

[98] Gustavo Gutiérrez, "Renewing the Option for the Poor," 69–82 in *Liberation Theologies, Postmodernity, and the Americas* (New York: Routledge, 1997), at 72.

[99] Gustavo Gutiérrez, "Remembering the Poor: An Interview with Gustavo Gutiérrez," *America*, 3 February 2003. See also idem, "Renewing the Option for the Poor," 73.

(4) Finally, we turn to the importance of contemplative prayer as a practice capable of supporting a mysticism of open eyes. From the perspective of prophetic spirituality, contemplative prayer constitutes a significant, although often marginalized, spiritual exercise. The criticisms of contemplation are well known and often are rooted in the view that with such urgent social crises consuming the world it is unjustifiable to devote time to the silent, passive work of waiting for God in prayer.

Sarah Coakley and Simone Weil resist this interpretation and argue instead that contemplative prayer is a critical practice that prepares the self to attend to the suffering of the other. In particular, in a recent article Coakley articulates a forceful criticism of the tendency in much continental and post-colonial thought to focus on responsibility for the oppressed and marginalized without an adequate description of the types of embodied practices that might engender this activity. She proposes that contemplation offers an important corrective to this tendency: it is a means for developing the discipline necessary to attend to the sufferer.[100] She elaborates on this insight:

> . . . the ascetic practices of contemplation are themselves indispensable
> means of a *true* attentiveness to the despised or marginalized "other." . . .
> there is much talk of the problem of attending to the otherness of the
> "other" in contemporary post-Kantian ethics and post-colonial theory; but
> there is very little about the intentional and embodied practices that might
> enable such attention. The moral and epistemic stripping that is endemic
> to the act of contemplation is a vital key here: its practised self-emptying
> inculcates an attentiveness that is beyond merely good political intentions.
> Its practice is more discomforting, more destabilizing to settled presump-
> tions, than a simple intentional *design* on empathy.[101]

Following Talal Asad's assertion that disbelief is a consequence of untaught bodies, Coakley writes that inattention to the suffering of others is likewise a function of untaught bodies.[102] Coakley contends that contemplative prayer

---

[100] For a brief reflection on the sociopolitical implications of meditation in the context of a prison see Sarah Coakley, "Jail Break: Meditation as Subversive Activity," *Christian Century* 121/13 (29 June 2004): 18–21.

[101] Sarah Coakley, "Is There a Future for Gender and Theology? On Gender, Contemplation, and the Systematic Task," *Criterion* 47/1 (Spring/Summer 2002): 2–11, at 6–7. Emphasis in original.

[102] Talal Asad, "Remarks on the Anthropology of the Body," 42–52 in *Religion and the Body*, ed. Sarah Coakley (Cambridge and New York: Cambridge University Press, 1997). See also Sarah Coakley, "Deepening Practices: Perspectives from Ascetical and Mystical The-

cultivates the bodily and spiritual dispositions necessary to give one's attention to the oppressed and marginalized other.[103] It is the repeated, embodied practice of waiting for God in contemplative prayer that creates a space for God to transform the self. This self-emptying process in turn gives rise to "personal empowerment, prophetic resistance, courage in the face of oppression, and the destruction of false idolatry."[104]

Like Coakley, Simone Weil maintains that being truly attentive to those who experience suffering and oppression is a discipline that requires training. According to Weil the dominant mode of perceiving the world is one in which the self is largely inattentive to the suffering of the other because it remains absorbed in its own egocentric concerns. It is possible, however, to overcome this inattention: to see reality as it is and not merely view it from a self-absorbed perspective. Being genuinely attentive to what lies outside the self involves the long and painful process of eradicating idolatrous modes of perception. Because of the difficulty of this process, few develop the capacity to attend to what lies outside the self—a fact Weil deems particularly evident in relation to the pervasive inability to give attention to those who suffer: "The capacity to give one's attention to the sufferer is a very rare and difficult thing; it is almost a miracle; it *is* a miracle. Nearly all those who think they have this capacity do not possess it."[105] In order to develop this capacity, Weil maintains, it is necessary to undergo an "apprenticeship" in embodied practices.[106] In Weil's thought, attention is cultivated in a number of different activities from manual labor to study, but of particular importance is prayer.

Weil holds that attention is always oriented toward the other and never toward the self. The act of attention therefore involves a "stripping of the self" before the reality upon which it is focused.[107] Attention—and this is particularly true of prayer as "attention taken to the highest degree"[108]—is a passive

---

ology," 78–93, in *Practicing Theology: Beliefs and Practices in the Christian Life*, ed. Miroslav Volf and Dorothy Bass (Grand Rapids: Eerdmans, 2002), at 87.

[103] Coakley, "Deepening Practices," 80.

[104] Sarah Coakley, *Powers and Submissions: Spirituality, Philosophy, and Gender* (Oxford: Blackwell, 2002), 38. See also Constance Fitzgerald, "From Impasse to Prophetic Hope: Crisis of Memory" *CTSA Proceedings* 64 (2009): 21–42, at 37–40.

[105] Simone Weil, *Waiting for God* (New York: Putnam, 1951; repr. New York: HarperCollins, 1973, 2009), 64. Emphasis in original.

[106] On "apprenticeship," see ibid., 78–79, and Mario von der Ruhr, *Simone Weil: An Apprenticeship in Attention* (New York: Continuum, 2007).

[107] Simone Weil, *Notebooks: I*, trans. Arthur Wills (London: Routledge and Kegan Paul, 1956), 292.

[108] Simone Weil, *Gravity and Grace*, trans. Emma Crawford and Mario von der Ruhr (New York: Routledge, 2002), 117.

openness to what lies outside the self and involves the suspension of "thought, leaving it detached, empty, and ready to be penetrated by the object. . . . Our thought should be empty, waiting, not seeking anything, but ready to receive in its naked truth the object that is to penetrate it."[109]

Prayer involves a disciplined waiting for God in silence.[110] This silent passivity before God constitutes a practice of self-diminishment in which the ego is progressively stripped as a result of the bewildering experience of the darkness of "the void." Weil's description of the purgative transformation experienced in contemplative prayer is consistent with the reflections of John of the Cross on the dark night of the soul.[111] The spiritual discipline of waiting for God without the experience of consolation or spiritual gratification is a process by which the ego is stripped of its false idols and opened to the grace of God.[112] Weil will even go so far as to say that the "I" itself dissipates: "through grace, the individual 'I' can decreate itself, the 'I' little by little disappears, and God loves himself by way of the creature."[113] For Weil, the emptying of the self cultivated through the discipline of attentively waiting for God results in the transformation that is consonant with St. Paul's proclamation: "it is no longer I who live, but it is Christ who lives in me" (Gal 2:20). In Weil's thought this *kenotic* transformation experienced in contemplative prayer is intimately connected to the selfless act of attending to the sufferer.[114] Although attentiveness to the sufferer is possible without this practice of *kenosis*, Weil maintains that the person who has passed through the trial of waiting for God in prayer "has a deeper love than ever for those who suffer affliction."[115] This love takes form as an ethics of attention rooted in the concrete encounter with another human being. According to Weil, it is indispensable "to know how to look at him in a certain way. This way of looking is first of all attentive. The soul empties itself of all its own content in order to receive into itself the being it is looking at, just as he is, in all his truth. Only he who is capable of attention can do this."[116]

---

[109] Weil, *Waiting for God*, 62.

[110] Ibid., 126.

[111] See Weil, *Notebooks: I*, 215, 238, 545, and eadem, *Waiting for God*, 126.

[112] Weil, *Gravity and Grace*, 11.

[113] Weil, *Notebooks: I*, 145.

[114] Weil, *Waiting for God*, 64.

[115] Ibid., 138. See also *Simone Weil: An Anthology*, ed. Sian Miles (New York: Grove Press, 1986), 71.

[116] Weil, *Waiting for God*, 65.

Weil, like the other authors considered above, looks to the parable of the Good Samaritan as an exemplary description of this ethics of attentively seeing the other. In that parable the sufferer on the side of the road is

> only a little piece of flesh, naked, inert, and bleeding beside a ditch; he is nameless, no one knows anything about him. Those who pass by this thing scarcely notice it, and a few minutes afterward do not even know that they saw it. Only one stops and turns attention toward it. The actions that follow are just the automatic effect of this moment of attention. The attention is creative. But at the moment when it is engaged it is a renunciation.[117]

The priest and the Levite who pass by the wounded victim regard "it" as a mere "thing" and soon forget that they ever saw "it." By contrast, it is the Samaritan who possesses the eyes to see the wounded victim as a person because the Samaritan looked at the sufferer with attention. Weil comments: "the Samaritan who stops and looks gives his attention all the same to this absent humanity, and the actions which follow prove that it is a question of real attention."[118]

Weil regards responsibility as ultimately a question of attention because it involves the capacity both to see reality as it is and to respond selflessly to that reality. As noted above, according to Weil these are precisely the dispositions that are cultivated through the practice of waiting for God. In this sense Weil's reflections are an important account of the connection between the time spent before God in silent, passive prayer and the capacity to see with the eyes of the Samaritan.

Prophetic Witness

This section examines the lives and writings of Dorothy Day and Martin Luther King Jr. as Christians who witnessed to a form of prophetic spirituality responsive to the suffering of the poor. Although both Day and King were concerned with a variety of issues, from racism (King) to war and pacifism (Day and King), this section will focus on their approach to the problem of poverty.

Day responded to the obligation to the suffering poor through concrete works of mercy in Catholic Worker houses of hospitality. By contrast, King used local organization and nonviolent forms of resistance as a means of transforming the social order through the state. Thus while Day and King shared a commitment to retrieving the radicalism of Jesus' teaching in relation to the poor, they adopted different political and economic strategies for transforming

---

[117] Ibid., 90.
[118] Ibid., 92.

the social order. As will be evident in the conclusion, these tactics need not be in competition with one another and should be viewed as complementary Christian responses to poverty.

Dorothy Day was born in Brooklyn, New York, in November of 1897 and died in 1980 at the age of eighty-three. Baptized an Episcopalian and raised by nonreligious parents, Day became an atheist in her early twenties and joined the Socialist movement after dropping out of college. She converted to Catholicism in 1927, and with Peter Maurin (1877–1949) founded the Catholic Worker in 1933. To this day the Catholic Worker publishes a newspaper, runs houses of hospitality that serve the poor and homeless, and owns and operates agrarian farms. There are currently houses of hospitality in over 150 cities and farms in more than a dozen locations in the United States.[119]

Day's legacy in American Catholicism is immense, both in terms of the continued work of Catholic Worker houses of hospitality and of her provocative retrieval of a radical spirituality rooted in a literal adherence to the Sermon on the Mount and the parable of last judgment in Matthew 25. This commitment to the radicalism of the Gospel in the Catholic Worker movement was described by Maurin in potent terms:

> if the Catholic Church is not today the dominant social dynamic force, it is because Catholic scholars have taken the dynamite of the church, have wrapped it up in nice phraseology, placed it in a hermetic container and sat on the lid. It is about time to blow the lid off so the Catholic Church may again become the dominant social dynamic force.[120]

Because modern culture has devoted itself to the bank account rather than the Sermon on the Mount, Maurin argued, individuals have become incapable of recognizing Christ in the face of the poor. He proposed the practice of concrete works of mercy in houses of hospitality as the most effective antidote to the banality of modern Christianity: "we need Houses of Hospitality to give the rich the opportunity to serve the poor. . . . We need Houses of Hospitality to show what idealism looks like when it is practiced."[121]

While Day is often recognized for the radicalism of her prophetic spirituality, that radicalism was cultivated and nurtured by the contemplative and liturgical practices of the Christian tradition. Indeed, in this regard Day represents an

---

[119] Dan McKanan, *The Catholic Worker after Dorothy: Practicing the Works of Mercy in a New Generation* (Collegeville, MN: Liturgical Press, 2008), 2.

[120] Peter Maurin, *Easy Essays* (Chicago: Franciscan Herald Press, 1977), 3.

[121] Ibid.

important witness to the unity of contemplation and action or, as she put it, to the "retreat apostolate" and the "street apostolate."[122] Emphasis on the former is particularly evident in Day's focus on the significance of liturgical worship and the Mass.[123] She was convinced that all of life flowed from worship, so that the concrete works of mercy practiced in houses of hospitality were both the fruit of and the preparation for participation in the prayer life of the Catholic Church. She instructed those who worked at houses of hospitality to pray the Liturgy of the Hours and to go to daily Mass as a means of training their perception to "see Christ in each other."[124] As one former Catholic Worker recalled, Day once rebuked him for missing Mass and suggested that he was hurting the work of the Catholic Worker by failing to attend daily Mass.[125]

In her focus on the moral and religious significance of liturgy Day was particularly indebted to the work of Virgil Michel, OSB, and the attempt of the liturgical movement to retrieve the radicalism of liturgy as a means of transforming the social order.[126] Along with Michel, Day was committed to the view that the regular practice of corporate worship was the most effective means of resisting the pernicious character of American individualism by instilling in participants the sense that all are members of the mystical Body of Christ. The concrete implication of this view is that "we can never be indifferent to the social miseries and evils of the day. The dogma of the Mystical Body has tremendous

---

[122] *Dorothy Day: Writings from Commonweal*, ed. Patrick Jordan (Collegeville, MN: Liturgical Press, 2002), 106.

[123] See Margaret Pfiel, "Love and Poverty: Dorothy Day's Twofold *Diakonia*," *Journal of Moral Theology* 1 (2012): 61–71.

[124] Dorothy Day, *Selected Writings: By Little and By Little*, ed. Robert Ellsberg (Maryknoll, NY: Orbis Books, 1992), 91.

[125] Mark Zwick and Louise Zwick, *The Catholic Worker Movement: Intellectual and Spiritual Origins* (New York and Mahwah, NJ: Paulist Press, 2005), 67. It should be noted that while Day viewed the Mass as an important spiritual exercise that formed Catholic Workers to see Christ in the poor, the reverse was true as well. That is, Day viewed the works of mercy and the radical hospitality offered to the poor and dispossessed as preparation for individuals to experience the Mass as the culminating point of the day. Day argued that all activities in Catholic Worker houses were a preparation for "the climax of the Mass." Dorothy Day, "Creation," *The Catholic Worker* (June 1956), 2.

[126] Day recounts this movement's influence: "The Liturgical movement has meant everything to the Catholic Worker from its beginning. The Mass was the center of our lives and indeed I was convinced that the Catholic Worker had come about because I was going to daily Mass, daily receiving Holy Communion." See Michael Baxter, "Reintroducing Virgil Michel: Towards a Counter-Tradition of Catholic Social Ethics in the United States," *Communio* 24 (1997): 499–528, at 523.

social implications."[127] In particular, Day wrote that by participating in the liturgical worship of the church we begin to find that it is no longer we ourselves "but Christ in us, who is working to combat injustice and oppression. We are on our way to becoming 'other Christs.'"[128]

Day held that service to the poor has a similar effect on individuals because it brings Christ into their lives in a way that is otherwise unavailable to them. She framed this point in terms of the radicalism of Jesus' parable of the last judgment in Matthew 25:

> the mystery of the poor is this: That they are Jesus, and what you do for them you do for Him. It is the only way we have of knowing and believing in our love. The mystery of poverty is that by sharing in it, making ourselves poor in giving to others, we increase our knowledge of and belief in love.[129]

Accordingly, the spirituality of the Catholic Worker movement is rooted in the view that voluntary poverty, radical hospitality, and the encounter with Christ in the world are intrinsically connected. Specifically, Day argued that voluntary poverty strips the self of its egoism and liberates individuals from lifestyles that prevent them from practicing the option for the poor and seeing Christ in others.[130] She wrote:

> Poverty is good, because we share the poverty of others, we know them and so love them more. Also, by embracing poverty we can give away to others. If we eat less, others can have more. If we pay less rent, we can pay the rent of a dispossessed family. If we go with old clothes, we can clothe others. We can perform the corporal works of mercy by embracing poverty. If we embrace poverty we put on Christ. If we put off the world, if we put the world out of our hearts, there is room for Christ within.[131]

---

[127] Dorothy Day, "Liturgy and Sociology," *The Catholic Worker* (January 1936), 5.

[128] Ibid.

[129] Day, *Selected Writings*, 330. Day observes of Matthew 25 that Christ himself said: "a glass of water given to a beggar was given to Him. He made heaven hinge on the way we act toward Him in His disguise of commonplace, frail, ordinary humanity. Did you give Me [food] when I was hungry? Did you give Me to drink when I was thirsty? Did you give Me clothes when My own were all rags? Did you come to see Me when I was sick, or in prison or in trouble?" Ibid., 96–97.

[130] Dorothy Day, *Loaves and Fishes* (New York: Harper & Row, 1963), 86.

[131] Dorothy Day, "Notes by the Way—January 1944," *The Catholic Worker* (January 1944), 2.

The commitment to voluntary poverty that Day advocates entails the rejection of the nonessentials that inhibit persons from embodying the values of the Gospel in their lives: "Love of brother means voluntary poverty, stripping one's self, putting off the old man, denying one's self. . . . It also means nonparticipation in those comforts and luxuries which have been manufactured by the exploitation of others."[132]

Thus, for Day, voluntary poverty involved a form of practical resistance to the consumer ethos that elicits desires for inessential wants when countless people live daily without meeting their basic needs. She was uncompromising on this point and insisted that if a person's work does not contribute to the common good, that person is obliged to look for other work that does. Day trenchantly criticized consumer culture and the type of work that stokes desire for unnecessary commodities. For example, she enumerated the following charges:

> There have been many sins against the poor which cry out to high heaven for vengeance. The one listed as one of the seven deadly sins, is depriving the laborer of his share. There is another one, that is, instilling in him the paltry desires to satisfy that for which he must sell his liberty and his honor. . . . Newspapers, radio, TV and battalions of advertising people (woe to that generation!) deliberately stimulate his desires, the satisfaction of which mean the degradation of the family.[133]

Consequently, Day suggested that the proper exercise of Christian discernment

> would exclude jobs in advertising, which only increases people's useless desires. In insurance companies and banks, which are known to exploit the poor of the country and of others. Banks and insurance companies have taken over land, built up farms, ranches, plantations of 30,000, 100,000 acres, and have dispossessed the poor. Loan and finance companies have further defrauded him. . . . Whatever has contributed to his misery and degradation may be considered a bad job.[134]

The Catholic Worker movement offers an alternative to the commitments of consumer culture and the type of work that fuels that culture. Day thought the witness of those who commit themselves to the work of the Catholic Worker could particularly benefit others in terms of their discernment of proper Christian vocations: "We hope that those who come to us, as well as those who read

---

[132] Day, *Selected Writings*, 229.

[133] Zwick and Zwick, *The Catholic Worker Movement*, 149, quoting Day's essay in the April 1953 issue of *The Catholic Worker*.

[134] Dorothy Day, "Poverty and Pacifism," *The Catholic Worker* (December 1944), 1.

the paper, will be led to examine their consciences on their work—whether or not it contributes to the evil of the world, to wars—and then to have the courage and resolution to embrace voluntary poverty and give up their jobs, lower their standard of living, and raise their standard of thinking and loving."[135]

Voluntary poverty and the commitment to concrete acts of mercy as a response to the suffering of the poor were critical elements of Day's attempt to configure an approach to politics as personal and local responsibility. This move toward the personal and the local in relationship to the problem of poverty is analogous to Wendell Berry's localist approach to the environmental crisis. Berry appears to have recognized this link:

> a lot of our smartest, most concerned people want to come up with a big solution to a big problem. I don't think that planet-saving, if we take it seriously, can furnish employment to many such people. . . . When I think of the kind of worker the job requires, I think of Dorothy Day (if one can think of Dorothy Day herself, separate from the publicity that came as a result of her rarity), a person willing to go down and down into the daunting, humbling, almost hopeless local presence of the problem—to face the great problem one small life at a time.[136]

Berry and Day focused on the political as local as a means of resisting the profit-maximalizing commitments of global corporations and the anonymity of the bureaucratic state. Furthermore, this emphasis on the local underscores the fact that each individual has a personal responsibility to effect social change, one small act at a time.

Day found inspiration for her localism in Jesus Christ's method for effecting social transformation. Robert Coles notes that Day was committed to the use of "Christ's technique" as a response to social problems: "she was always trying to remember that He was an obscure carpenter who, in His early thirties, did not go talk with emperors and kings and important officials, but with equally obscure people."[137] Because Day was committed to the view that the proper approach to social change should be modeled on the life of Jesus Christ, she thought the standard approach to politics needed to be reconceived. In par-

---

[135] Quoted in Dorothy Day, *On Pilgrimage* (Grand Rapids: Eerdmans 1999), 24.

[136] Wendell Berry, *Sex, Economy, Freedom & Community: Eight Essays* (New York: Pantheon, 1993), 25.

[137] Robert Coles, *Dorothy Day: A Radical Devotion* (Reading, MA: Perseus, 1987), 90. For Day's reflections on this point, see Dorothy Day, *The Long Loneliness* (New York: Harper & Row, 1952; repr. 1997), 204–5.

ticular she was concerned to articulate a form of politics that could represent an alternative to large-scale political operations that attempt to transform the world from centers of economic and military power. Day was well aware that this alternative approach to politics would be viewed as a failure by the standards of the world because the world interprets small, discrete acts of mercy as ineffective and irrelevant. But, in response to the question of what good the discrete works of mercy could achieve in the world, Day drew an analogy between the work of the Catholic Worker and that of Jesus Christ: "what we do is very little but it is like the little boy with a few loaves and fishes. Christ took that little and increased it. He will do the rest. What we do is so little we may seem to be constantly failing. But so did he fail. He met with apparent failure on the Cross. But unless the seed fall into the earth and die, there is no harvest. And why must we see results? Our work is to sow."[138] Thus, rather than conceiving of politics as the attempt to control outcomes through the use of coercive state violence, Day proposes the alternative of a local politics that achieves its humble effects in history through the nonviolent practice of the works of mercy.[139]

Moreover, Day developed this account of politics through her engagement with the "little way" of Thérèse of Lisieux. Day regarded Thérèse as the saint every person should dread because she demonstrates the folly of refusing to act whenever we somehow think that our efforts will not succeed or things will never change. In this sense Thérèse is the "saint of the responsible" who demands small, everyday practices of holiness as a means of responding to the call of Christ. Day acknowledges the tepidity with which she initially encountered Thérèse: "I much preferred then to read about spectacular saints who were impossible to imitate. The message of Thérèse was too obviously meant for each one of us, confronting us with daily duties, simple and small, but constant."[140] Eventually, however, her experience in the Catholic Worker movement led her to see the little way of Thérèse as a template for the capacity of small, discrete acts of mercy to transform the broader social order. In particular, Day viewed Thérèse's spirituality as a challenge to the assumptions of American culture:

> The Little Flower has shown us her tremendous lesson of "the little way." We need that lesson especially in America where we want to do things in a big way or not at all.

---

[138] Day, *Selected Writings*, 92.

[139] See Frederick Bauerschmidt, "The Politics of the Little Way: Dorothy Day Reads Thérèse of Lisieux," 77–95, in *American Catholic Traditions: Resources for Renewal*, ed. Sandra Yocum Mize and William L. Portier (Maryknoll, NY: Orbis Books, 1997).

[140] Day, *Loaves and Fishes*, 127.

> A small store is sufficient to start the work. One pot of soup or a pot of coffee and some bread is sufficient to make a beginning. You can feed the immediate ones who come and God will send what is needed to continue the work.[141]

Day's approach to the economy was likewise rooted in this commitment to the radical personalism of the "little way." She was resolute in her criticisms of industrial capitalism and its tendency to create a divisive world in which extreme social misery stands alongside indecent wealth. She illustrates this contrast: "on the one hand, the capitalist-industrialist robber baron weeps that if he paid a living wage industry would go broke and the workers would be out of jobs. On the other hand, they have such huge surpluses of property and money and goods, and the worker remains in his pauper, proletariat, destitute state."[142] Despite her opposition to industrial and corporate capitalism, Day nevertheless defended the right to private property. This defense of private property is framed by her view that private property should be widely distributed and owned by as many persons as possible. In this sense Day advocated for Catholic distributism as a third way beyond capitalism and communism:

> we are working for the Communitarian revolution to oppose both the rugged individualism of the capitalist era and the collectivism of the Communist revolution. We are working for the Personalist revolution because we believe in the dignity of man, the temple of the Holy Ghost, so beloved by God that He sent His son to take upon Himself our sins and die an ignominious and disgraceful death for us. We are Personalists because we believe that man, a person, a creature of body and soul, is greater than the State, of which as an individual he is a part. We are Personalists because we oppose the vesting of all authority in the hands of the state instead of in the hands of Christ the King. We are Personalists because we believe in free will, and not in the economic determinism of the Communist philosophy.[143]

In the place of the economic ideologies of capitalism and communism, the Catholic Worker movement advocates a communitarian personalism that works toward a decentralized economy in which individuals own the means of production and cultivate the land on their own small farms and produce goods through local cottage industries.[144]

---

[141] Day, *Writings from Commonweal*, 63.

[142] Quoted in Zwick and Zwick, *The Catholic Worker Movement*, 148.

[143] From *The Catholic Worker* (September 1936), quoted in *On Pilgrimage*, 22.

[144] Day, *Selected Writings*, 240.

While Day was steadfastly opposed to capitalism, she was equally critical of the turn to the state as an alternative to the ruthlessness of industrial capitalism. In particular, both Maurin and Day warned of the dangers of responding to the needs of the poor by passing the buck to the anonymous forces of the bureaucratic state. For them this represents a failure to follow Jesus' mandate to respond individually to the concrete needs of those who suffer. The proper Christian response to the suffering of the poor lies in developing small communities and local bodies to respond to their needs. Day took this as rather obvious: "we all should know that it is not the province of the government to practice the works of mercy. . . . Smaller bodies, decentralized groups, should be caring for all such needs."[145]

This focus on small, voluntary, decentralized bodies appears to support a charity-based model of social action. Day insisted, however, that the transformation of the entire social order remains the fundamental goal of the Catholic Worker movement: "To feed the hungry, clothe the naked and shelter the harborless without also trying to change the social order so that people can feed, clothe and shelter themselves, is just to apply palliatives."[146] Thus, while Catholic Worker houses of hospitality offer charitable goods to the poor and the dispossessed, Day thought this work should be supplemented by the promotion of justice through protest, picketing, and the dissemination of Catholic Worker newspapers.

During Day's life this work for justice manifested itself in concrete ways. For instance, she advocated for solidarity with mistreated laborers by fasting from those products that were not grown in her region and were not produced under just working conditions. Like Berry, Day thought it was impossible to guarantee the ethical conditions under which items or products were produced halfway around the world; hence it was necessary to engage in the discipline of what Peter Maurin described as "regional living."[147] Again, localism represents one way to support practices of just economic exchange.[148]

---

[145] Dorothy Day, "More about Holy Poverty, Which Is Voluntary Poverty," *The Catholic Worker* (February 1945), 1–2.

[146] Ibid. See also *Selected Writings*, 91. Indeed, the most basic criticism Day leveled against the Catholic Church was that she saw in it "plenty of charity, but too little justice." Day, *Selected Writings*, 150.

[147] Day, *Selected Writings*, 230.

[148] According to Day, regional living is itself a form of voluntary poverty: "poverty means having a bare minimum in the way of clothes and seeing to it that these are made under decent working conditions, proper wages and hours, etc." Ibid.

Because of her commitment to a personalist approach to the transformation of the social order, Day maintained that what is needed to respond to an unjust social order is not a freer market or new federal programs, but rather saints: "until we begin to develop a few apostles along these lines, we will have no mass conversions, no social justice, no peace. We need saints. God, give us saints."[149] As with Berry's call for individuals to live their lives as a protest, Day called for a "permanent revolution" that would transform the social order through the practice of the works of mercy at the local level:

> we consider the spiritual and corporeal Works of Mercy and the following of Christ to be the best revolutionary technique and a means for chang-ing the social order rather than perpetuating it. Did not the thousands of monasteries, with their hospitality, change the entire social pattern of their day? They did not wait for a paternal state to step in nor did they stand by to see destitution precipitate bloody revolt.[150]

Thus the permanent revolution would not be achieved through violence or the mechanisms of the state, but through individual Christians who committed their lives to creating a social order "where it is easier for people to be good."[151]

This form of politics is anarchist. But it is not anarchist in a libertarian sense in which the state is resisted so that individuals can use their private freedom to pursue ends disconnected from the common good. Instead, it is an anarchic poli-tics that resists the state in order to accept a more radical form of responsibility that involves what Maurin calls "personal sacrifice." In this sense the approach to social change advocated by the Catholic Worker movement distinguishes itself from the liberal approach that works through the mechanisms of the state to create a more just society. According to Michael Baxter, the Catholic Worker movement represents a "radical" alternative to this liberal paradigm. Baxter ar-gues that where the liberal marches on City Hall in response to the problem of hunger, the radical responds concretely by feeding the hungry.[152] In this sense the Catholic Worker approach to social transformation differs from that of the civil rights movement, which when possible made use of the levers of the state to achieve social change.

---

[149] Ibid.

[150] Day, *The Long Loneliness*, 186; the longer passage is quoted in Zwick and Zwick, *The Catholic Worker Movement*, 52.

[151] Day, *The Long Loneliness*, 170.

[152] See *Voices From the Catholic Worker*, ed. Rosalie Riegle Troster (Philadelphia: Temple University Press, 1993), 517.

As in the case of Dorothy Day, the details of Martin Luther King Jr.'s life are well known. Born in 1929, King received a BDiv from Crozer Theological Seminary in 1951 and a doctorate in theology from Boston University in 1955. He led the 1955 Montgomery bus boycott and participated in the nonviolent protests in Birmingham in 1962. King is perhaps most famous for his "I Have a Dream" speech in the 1963 March on Washington and his pivotal role in organizing support for the passage of the Civil Rights Act in 1964. Although he is most often remembered as a leader in the civil rights movement, this interpretation ignores his consistent advocacy on behalf of the poor and oppressed in both the United States and abroad. In what follows I will describe his transition from a focus on civil rights in the United States to advocacy for international human rights, with a particular reference to his work to fight poverty from the mid-1960s onward.[153]

Martin Luther King Jr.'s commitment to racial and economic justice was rooted in his experience in the black church. For him the suffering and persecution of African American communities in the United States made the black churches uniquely qualified to speak out against racial and economic injustice. Moreover, he viewed the nonviolent techniques used by the early Christians in confronting the Roman Empire as an important precursor to both the civil rights movement and the opposition of American churches to the unjust economic and military commitments of the United States government.[154] King was more nuanced, however, in his opposition to American democracy than early Christians to the Roman Empire because he thought American democracy possessed ideals that bore some resemblance to the Christian commitment to the basic dignity of every human being. Thus, while he remained committed to the ideal of building an inclusive global community of racial and economic justice—the beloved community—King saw some overlap between this religious vision for society and the promises of American democracy.

In his speeches King blended the prophetic imagination of the Christian tradition with the propositions of American civil religion. This rhetorical strategy is powerfully presented in the August 1963 speech, "I Have a Dream," in which King prophetically criticized the present social order on the basis of an imagined utopian future. While the broader horizon of this utopian future is framed in terms of God's reign, King firmly situated this possibility in relation to the foundational commitments of American democracy, suggesting that the

[153] Thomas F. Jackson, *From Civil Rights to Human Rights: Martin Luther King, Jr., and the Struggle for Economic Justice* (Philadelphia: University of Pennsylvania Press, 2007), 1.

[154] Lewis V. Baldwin, *The Voice of Conscience: The Church in the Mind of Martin Luther King, Jr.* (New York: Oxford University Press, 2010), 99.

dream is "deeply rooted in the American dream."[155] The specific content of this prophetic vision is the call for Americans to realize the unfulfilled promise of the American experiment: that all human beings are created equal. As with any prophetic discourse, this work of imagining alternative possibilities for society is linked to a concrete call to action in order to make those possibilities realities.[156] Thus King speaks "the fierce urgency of now" and observes that "this is no time to engage in the luxury of cooling off or the tranquilizing drug of gradualism. Now is the time to make real the promises of democracy."[157]

Although this dream would find some partial fulfillment with the passage of the Civil Rights Act almost a year later in July 1964, it became increasingly evident to King that his commitment to racial justice would only effect real change if it was linked to a program for greater economic justice. On July 4, 1965, King gave another speech entitled "The American Dream," in which he acknowledged that the dream he spoke of in Washington in 1963 "has often turned into a nightmare."[158] King describes how he had encountered extreme forms of poverty as he toured the country, from ten or fifteen African Americans living in two rooms in Harlem to workers in the Delta region of Mississippi not earning more than six or seven hundred dollars a week. These encounters led him to argue that racial equality without economic opportunity is an illusion and that a class system that subjugates the poor is as "vicious and evil" as a system based on racial injustice.[159] At the end of the speech King proclaimed that while his "dream has been shattered," his hope remains: "I still have a dream that one day God's children will have food and clothing and material well-being for their bodies, culture and education for their minds, and freedom for their spirits."[160]

King was critical, in particular, of the way in which the biblical parable of Lazarus and the rich man (Luke 16:19-31) had come to represent the fundamental structure of social relations within the United States (and much farther abroad). In this parable Jesus describes a beggar named Lazarus lying at the gates of a rich man's house, full of sores and begging to be fed by the crumbs that fell from the rich man's table. Lazarus and the rich man both die, and the rich

---

[155] Martin Luther King Jr., *A Testament of Hope: The Essential Writings and Speeches of Martin Luther King, Jr.*, ed. James M. Washington (New York: Harper Collins, 1991), 219.

[156] See Walter Brueggemann, *The Hopeful Imagination* (Minneapolis: Fortress Press, 1986), 97–99.

[157] King, *A Testament of Hope*, 217–18.

[158] Martin Luther King Jr., "The American Dream," 4 July 1965, http://mlk-kpp01 .stanford.edu/index.php/encyclopedia/documentsentry/doc_the_american_dream/.

[159] Ibid.

[160] Ibid.

man (sometimes called "Dives," the Greek word for rich) is sent to hell for his failure to respond to the needs of Lazarus. King interpreted this parable: "Dives went to hell because he . . . passed by Lazarus every day and he never really saw him. He went to hell because he allowed his brother to become invisible. . . . Dives went to hell because he sought to be a conscientious objector in the war against poverty."[161] King saw the fact that people who live in comfortable conditions remain indifferent, unaware, or inattentive to the suffering of others as the major impediment to building a society committed to economic justice. In particular, he maintained that in American society the poor have been "shut out of our minds, and driven from the mainstream of our societies, because we have allowed them to become invisible."[162]

In response to this situation, King advocated for a revolution of values that would awaken "the dozing conscience" of humankind.[163] Like other thinkers examined here, King turned to the parable of the Good Samaritan as a paradigmatic example of the type of ethical vigilance needed to support this revolution. For him this parable describes an important example of the type of "dangerous unselfishness" that is needed if we are to take responsibility for the suffering of the poor.[164] In relation to the responses of the Levite and the priest, King observes that the Jericho road was dangerous and was called "the Bloody Pass. So it is possible that the Priest and the Levite were afraid that if they stopped they too would be beaten; for couldn't the robbers still be around? . . . So I can imagine that the first question which the Priest and the Levite asked was: 'If I stop to help this man, what will happen to me?'"[165] Then a man of another "race," the Samaritan, came by and got off his horse and aided the victim. He argues that the actions of the Samaritan suggest that he reversed the question asked by the priest and the Levite: "'If I do not stop to help this man, what will happen to him?' The good Samaritan was willing to engage in a dangerous altruism."[166]

[161] King, *A Testament of Hope*, 274.

[162] Ibid., 624.

[163] Martin Luther King Jr., "Draft of Chapter III, 'On Being a Good Neighbor,'" in *The Papers of Martin Luther King, Jr.*, Vol. 6, *Advocate of the Social Gospel, September 1948–March 1963*, ed. Susan Carson et al. (Berkeley: University of California Press, 2007), 478.

[164] King, *A Testament of Hope*, 284.

[165] "Draft of Chapter III, 'On Being a Good Neighbor,'" 482.

[166] Ibid. King applies the significance of this parable to his decision to side with the striking sanitation workers in Memphis. While the Jericho road is dangerous, he reflects, the critical question is not: if I help this person suffering on the side of the road what will happen to me, but "if I don't stop to help the sanitation workers, what will happen to them?" Quoted in Michael K. Honey, *Going Down Jericho Road: The Memphis Strike, Martin Luther King's Last Campaign* (New York: Norton, 2008), ix.

In "A Time to Break the Silence," King linked the parable of the Good Samaritan to the issue of economic justice:

> A true revolution of value will soon cause us to question the fairness and justice of many of our past and present policies. We are called to play the good samaritan on life's roadside; but that will be only an initial act. One day the whole Jericho road must be transformed so that men and women will not be beaten and robbed as they make their journey through life. True compassion is more than flinging a coin to a beggar; it understands that an edifice which produces beggars needs restructuring.
>
> A true revolution of values will soon look uneasily on the glaring contrast of poverty and wealth. With righteous indignation, it will look . . . across the oceans and see individual capitalists of the West investing huge sums of money in Asia, Africa and South America, only to take the profits out with no concern for the social betterment of the countries, and say: "This is not just." It will look at our alliance with the landed gentry of Latin America and say: "This is not just."[167]

In this passage King affirms the necessity of both individual compassion for those who suffer and the transformation of structures and institutional arrangements that continue to produce beggars. Thus he describes the need for a revolution of values at the personal level as well as a human rights revolution at the structural level.

In view of this analysis, King argued that it is necessary to move beyond the realm of American constitutional rights and into that of human rights.[168] His advocacy for the global poor was an outgrowth of his conviction (which echoes Day's commitment to the mystical Body of Christ) that "the rich must not ignore the poor because both rich and poor are tied in a single garment of destiny. All life is interrelated, and all men are interdependent. The agony of the poor diminishes the rich, and the salvation of the poor enlarges the rich."[169] Because poverty exists in "Indiana as well as in India; in New Orleans as well as in New Delhi," King argued that the war against poverty cannot be limited to United States citizens alone: "Cannot we agree that the time has come for an all-out war on poverty—not merely in President Johnson's 'Great Society,'

---

[167] King, *A Testament of Hope*, 630.

[168] Ibid., 58.

[169] Martin Luther King Jr., "The Octopus of Poverty," first published in *The Mennonite* (5 January 1965): 4; repr. in idem, *"In a Single Garment of Destiny": A Global Vision of Justice*, ed. Lewis V. Baldwin (Boston: Beacon Press, 2013), 118–19.

but in every town and village of the world where this nagging evil exists?"[170] Furthermore, King argued that the United States, as the most affluent and technologically advanced country in the world, is in a unique position to commit itself to "an international program of aid" to combat global poverty.[171] He comments: "there is nothing new about poverty. What is new is that we now have the techniques and the resources to get rid of poverty. The real question is whether we have the will."[172]

King saw a number of prevailing realities that prevented Americans from supporting programs to eradicate poverty. The militarism of the United States during the Vietnam era was one important factor. The United States fought endless battles abroad, but failed to fight poverty at home, spent thousands to kill "the suffering poor of Vietnam" but very little to bring the poor out of poverty in the United States.[173] Specifically, King pointed out that during the Vietnam War the United States spent $500,000 to kill each Vietcong soldier and $53 a year on each person living in poverty in the United States.[174] Thus, in addition to the fact that the American poor were disproportionately sent to fight on the front lines in the war in Vietnam, American taxpayer dollars were being directed toward a military that was killing poor Vietnamese soldiers rather than on bringing poor Americans or Vietnamese out of poverty. King concluded,

"   I know that America would never invest the necessary funds or energies in rehabilitation of its poor so long as adventures like Vietnam continued to draw men and skills and money like some demonic, destructive suction tube. So I was increasingly compelled to see the war as an enemy of the poor and to attack it as such."[175]

In view of the debilitating poverty at home and militarism abroad, King advocated for a reordering of national priorities that would lead to the end of the war in Vietnam. In particular, he called for the militancy of American society to be diverted away from Southeast Asia and redirected toward a war against poverty at home.[176] King framed this challenge in terms of the ultimate destiny of a nation before God. He argued that a nation that spends more on

---

[170] Quoted in *The Autobiography of Martin Luther King, Jr.*, ed. Clayborne Carson (New York: Warner Books, 1998), 262.

[171] Quoted in Michael G. Long, *Against Us, But For Us: Martin Luther King, Jr. and the State* (Macon, GA: Mercer University Press, 2002), 137.

[172] King, *A Testament of Hope*, 274.

[173] Ibid., 639.

[174] Ibid., 275.

[175] Ibid., 232–33.

[176] Ibid., 675.

the military than on programs that lift human beings out of poverty is approaching "spiritual death,"[177] and that at some point in the future Americans would have to stand before God and account for what they have done with their lives and for the spending priorities of their country. In the United States we will be able to say that we built enormous bridges, buildings that touched the sky, and submarines that reached the depths of the oceans. The God of history will respond: "'That was not enough! But I was hungry and ye fed me not. I was naked and ye clothed me not. I was devoid of a decent sanitary house to live in, and ye provided no shelter for me. And consequently, you cannot enter the kingdom of greatness. If ye do it unto the least of these, my brethren, ye do it unto me.' That's the question facing America today."[178]

King posed a series of challenges not only to the military priorities of the United States but also to its economic commitments. Like Dorothy Day, he stingingly rebuked capitalism, arguing that when poverty becomes a central issue it leads inevitably to questions "about the economic system, about a broader distribution of wealth. When you ask that question, you begin to question the capitalistic economy. And I'm simply saying that more and more, we've got to begin to ask questions about the whole society."[179] The problem with capitalism for King is that it is an economic philosophy rooted in a form of ruthless competition and profit-maximization that marginalizes any consideration of the broader values of equality or justice in the economic realm. He maintained that an exclusive focus on profit motives leads to an economic system grounded in an agonistic, "cutthroat competition" that leads individuals to become "more I-centered than thou-centered."[180] As I have noted, the market economy is an economic system that infiltrates every sphere of existence and forms persons who commit to its logic in an ethos of self-interest and pernicious individualism. King specifically argued that "capitalism has often left a gulf between superfluous wealth and abject poverty, has created conditions permitting necessities to be take from the many to give luxuries to the few, and has encouraged smallhearted men to become cold and conscienceless so that, like Dives before Lazarus, they are unmoved by suffering, poverty-stricken humanity."[181]

Again like Day, King promoted an economic system that moved beyond the stalemate between capitalism and communism. He supported the mixed system of social democracy because "the good and just society is neither the thesis of

---

[177] Ibid., 631.
[178] Ibid., 275.
[179] Ibid., 250.
[180] Ibid., 629–30.
[181] Ibid., 629.

capitalism nor the antithesis of communism, but a socially conscious democracy which reconciles the truths of individualism and collectivism."[182] He thought that truths would be reconciled concretely through "a radical redistribution" of both political and economic power.[183]

King worked tirelessly on the ground to make this redistribution a reality. Like Day, he sided decisively with labor and unions when they went on strike for a just wage and tolerable working conditions. In 1968 he was outspoken in his support of the 13,000 sanitation workers who went on strike in Memphis for safer working conditions. Furthermore, in October of 1967 King described his plan to organize a Poor People's Campaign in Washington, DC. He envisaged three thousand poor people from ten different cities coming to Washington and building a shantytown in view of the Capitol and the White House. These people would remain there and nonviolently disrupt the "business" of the capital until the United States government responded to the suffering of the poor. The Poor People's Campaign advocated for an Economic Bill of Rights for the Disadvantaged that called for $100 billion in spending over ten years (roughly $600 billion by today's standards) on education, employment, and housing assistance.

Martin Luther King Jr. would never see his vision for a Poor People's Campaign realized. By 1968 his approval rating in the United States had plummeted to 30 percent. This was a direct result of his steadfast opposition to the Vietnam War and his trenchant criticism of the American economic system. King realized that his post–Civil Rights Act commitments were not popular and that his advocacy on behalf of the poor placed him in conflict with powerful interests. In Chicago in 1966 he discussed the dangers these commitments entailed: "I choose to identify with the underprivileged. I choose to identify with the poor. I choose to give my life for the hungry. I choose to give my life for those who have been left out of the sunlight of opportunity . . . This is the way I'm going. If it means suffering a little bit, I'm going that way. . . . If it means dying for them, I'm going that way."[184] Tragically, these words proved to be prescient. King was assassinated in Memphis on April 4, 1968.

Both Dorothy Day and Martin Luther King Jr. sought the transformation of the social order as a response to the suffering of the poor. For Day the proper response from a Christian perspective was to initiate a communitarian revolution that would involve the retrieval of the radical personalism of Jesus and a response

---

[182] Ibid., 630. See Douglas Sturm, "Martin Luther King, Jr., as Democratic Socialist," *The Journal of Religious Ethics* 18/2 (Fall 1990): 79–105.

[183] Jackson, *From Civil Rights to Human Rights*, 307.

[184] Martin Luther King Jr., "The Good Samaritan," Chicago, 28 August 1966, epigraph in Honey, *Going Down Jericho Road*, ix.

to the suffering of the poor through concrete works of mercy. In particular, Day envisaged the Catholic Worker houses of hospitality and farming communes as seeds of a broader project of transforming the entire social order. In this sense her politics were anarchist and opposed all mechanisms of the state, even those policies, such as Social Security, that attempted to guarantee a basic standard of living for all American citizens. King similarly opposed some dimensions of American democracy. But he held out hope that a revolution of values could radicalize America's democratic commitments and make real its promises of egalitarianism and justice. Although the anarchic radicalism of Day differs from the prophetic radicalism of King, both witness to the type of "revolution" that is necessary to make the option for the poor central to the Christian life.

Conclusion

In an essay entitled, "1492—Through the Eyes of a European Theologian," Johann Baptist Metz describes his experience of traveling to Latin America and encountering the effects of European colonialism on its people in the deadened faces of street children "eking out the most wretched of existences" at the margins of society.[185] In response to this experience he poses a series of questions to Christians in the affluent world: "Can we Christians here in Europe, can the churches of our country, bear to look at these faces? Can we, do we want to, risk the change of perspective and see our lives as Christians, in the churches—at least for a moment—from the perspective of these faces? Or do we experience and define ourselves exclusively with our back to such faces?"[186] In view of the eighteen million preventable deaths from extreme poverty each year, Metz's challenge is critical for Christians in the developed world. The formation of Christians capable of engaging in the prophetic work of seeing the suffering of a crucified people as something for which they are responsible is a critical task for contemporary Christian spirituality. This is, however, only a first step in a spirituality that should lead directly to the cultivation of prophetic forms of life committed to justice for the poor. In what follows I will examine three different strategies for enacting that commitment to the global poor: charity, commutative justice, and structural transformation.

We have already examined the radicalism of Dorothy Day's politics of the "little way" as a response to poverty at the local level. This approach is praiseworthy for its attempt to follow the model Jesus himself employed to effect social change. The limitation of the localist approach defended by Dorothy Day and

---

[185] Metz, *Faith and the Future*, 66.
[186] Ibid., 67.

the Catholic Worker movement becomes particularly evident, however, in an age of globalization. In particular, apart from the work of the limited few who travel to impoverished countries and commit themselves to charitable activities in that locale (there do exist international Catholic Worker houses of hospitality in Mexico, the Dominican Republic, and Uganda), this localist approach represents an inadequate response to the suffering of the global poor. This is not to delegitimize this approach or to minimize its significance as an authentic Christian response to the plight of the poor at the local level. It is simply to point to one of its limitations as a technique of social transformation at the global level.

In terms of a charitable approach to poverty the alternative to this localism is to limit excess consumerism and adopt a simpler lifestyle. Peter Singer suggests that the money saved by limiting excess consumerism could be donated to global aid organizations like OXFAM and Amnesty International. As noted previously, Peter Unger has calculated that a donation of $200 would be sufficient to transform a sickly two-year-old into a healthy six-year-old. While this tactic lacks the personalism rightly advocated for by Gustavo Gutiérrez and Dorothy Day, it does represent an important way in which individuals in the affluent world can make a real difference in the lives of the global poor.

An alternative to charitable giving advocated for by Singer is the practice of microcredit lending, which has been made popular by Muhammad Yunus. Microlending is the process by which individuals in the developed world make very small loans to impoverished borrowers in the developing world who have no collateral and often lack a verifiable credit history. This gives the poor an opportunity to develop small businesses with funds that otherwise would have been unavailable to them. Thus an individual in rural India might be given a loan of $50 to raise farm animals and begin to participate in the economic life of his or her village. These loans have a high percentage of repayment (often over 99%) and various websites such as Kiva, Zidisha, and Lendforpeace now allow for peer-to-peer lending so that an individual in the developed world can lend money to a person halfway around the world.[187]

In addition to this charity-based approach to global poverty, the practice of commutative justice represents another important means of creating spaces of justice within the global economic order. This involves the cultivation of just exchanges between buyer and seller and the attempt to ensure that goods are produced under just and sustainable working conditions. The fair trade movement

---

[187] For a broader discussion of microlending see Muhammad Yunus and Alan Jolis, *Banker to the Poor: Micro-lending and the Battle against World Poverty* (New York: Public Affairs, 1999), and Douglas Hicks, *Money Enough: Everyday Practices for Living Faithfully in the Global Economy* (San Francisco: Jossey-Bass, 2010), 151–55.

exemplifies most clearly the practice of commutative justice within the globalized economy. This movement attempts to ensure that goods are produced under environmentally sustainable conditions in which laborers are properly compensated for their work. The most common fair trade products are coffee, tea, crafts, and textiles. For example, Fair Trade USA ensures that the coffee it certifies is produced by farmers who are members of a democratic cooperative, use restricted amounts of herbicides and pesticides, and are paid a just wage for their labor. In this way the fair trade movement contests the neoliberal market orthodoxy that views competition, and not the values of justice or fairness, as the most important feature of economic exchange.[188] While the fair trade movement does not venture an immediate, large-scale structural transformation of global capitalism, it does serve as a framework for organizing concrete forms of economic resistance to the injustices of the invisible hand of the market.

Finally, structural transformation and distributive justice remain central to the task of creating a more just world for the global poor. As with charity and commutative justice, this commitment to structural transformation can involve a number of different strategies. For instance, Martin Luther King Jr. criticized the priorities of the United States government in relation to military spending. In many ways the situation has only become worse since then. In 2012 the United States devoted $645.7 billion to military spending and only $30.5 billion to foreign aid. Additionally, in 2007–2008 the United States spent $700 billion bailing out the reckless and wildly profitable Wall Street banks, while cutting national poverty prevention programs, education, and foreign aid commitments. From a Christian perspective, challenging the unjust spending priorities of the United States is an important long-term strategy for transforming institutional structures that perpetuate various forms of social oppression.

This type of resistance, of course, need not be limited to the national level or be directed exclusively at the spending priorities of the United States government. As argued in the fifth chapter, the IMF and the World Bank have implemented neoliberal economic policies in the developing world that serve the interests of the corporate elite and not the interests of the global poor. For instance, IMF-mandated privatization of state-owned industries has resulted in the transfer of wealth from the public to private corporations. Thus the revenue created from the extraction of natural resources or the service of providing water to the public is directed into the pockets of private, international corporations instead of funding education and poverty prevention programs. Furthermore, the structural adjustment policies implemented by these international bodies have created situations in which poor countries have reoriented their economies

---

[188] Luke Bretherton, *Christianity and Politics* (Malden, MA: Wiley-Blackwell, 2011), 177.

toward the goal of repaying debts to the developed world rather than developing their own industries and infrastructure.

In response to this situation, one concrete step that could be taken is the cancellation of debts so that the poorest countries in the world do not continue to send twenty-five dollars out of their country for every dollar they receive in foreign aid.[189] As Pamela Brubaker puts it: "the poorest countries are siphoning off urgently needed resources for health care and education to pay the wealthiest countries and institutions interest on a debt that they have already paid three times over."[190] These debts should be canceled not only because of their questionable origins (they were imposed on these countries by the IMF and World Bank) but also because they create conditions in which it is virtually impossible for developing countries to implement the types of economic policies that alleviate extreme poverty.

Furthermore, there is a clear biblical precedent for debt cancellation in the Jewish and Christian celebration of Jubilee, an observance that reminded the Israelites of the type of society God expected them to build. Leviticus (25:1-55) instructs the Israelites to free slaves, share the resources of the land with all people, and cancel debts every seven years. This practice was resurrected with some measure of success in 2000, with a coalition of governments and nongovernmental bodies (led, in large measure, by Pope John Paul II and the Roman Catholic Church) advocating for the cancellation of over $90 billion of debts owed by the world's poorest countries. This type of work continues with various Jubilee organizations (Jubilee South, Jubilee USA Network, Jubilee UK, etc.) continuing to advocate for debt cancellation as a response to debilitating global poverty.

Distributive justice represents another important mechanism for responding to poverty. As Pope Benedict XVI has argued, demanding a more egalitarian redistribution of wealth at the national and international levels is a central task of Christians in an age of globalization.[191] At the national level this commitment to distributive justice involves advocacy for a progressive tax code and the redistribution of wealth in order to ensure that the poor receive basic necessities. It also

---

[189] Kristin Heyer, *Kingship across Borders: A Christian Ethic of Immigration* (Washington, DC: Georgetown University Press, 2012), 102.

[190] Pamela Brubaker, "Reforming Global Economic Policies," 127–39 in *Justice in a Global Economy: Strategies for Home, Community, and World*, ed. Pamela Brubaker, Rebecca Todd Peters, and Laura A. Stivers (Louisville: Westminster John Knox Press, 2006), at 131.

[191] Benedict XVI, World Day of Peace message, "Educating Young People in Justice and Peace," 1 January 2012, http://www.vatican.va/holy_father/benedict_xvi/messages/peace/documents/hf_ben-xvi_mes_20111208_xlv-world-day-peace_en.html.

entails advocacy for a just and living wage for workers, defense of labor unions, and the promotion of universal health care (which Benedict XVI describes as an "inalienable right").[192] Work on behalf of distributive justice is a more difficult task at the international level. But as we learned earlier, Thomas Pogge and others have offered important proposals about the ways in which the global poor could receive some compensation for their rightful stake in the natural world's resources.

While using the power of the state and international bodies to effect change is important, there have also been attempts to create and sustain business models by which business entities may hold themselves accountable to values beyond the traditional market imperative of profit maximalization. The Mondragón Corporation is the most prominent example of the attempt to create a business committed to distributist principles. The Mondragón model was developed by the Basque priest José María Arizmendiarrieta in 1941; his intention was to construct a business consistent with the distributist commitments of Catholic social teaching. Today the cooperatives of Mondragón employ over 100,000 workers and make up one of the ten largest corporations in Spain. Mondragón is employee-owned and -operated. Each year a general assembly of workers elects a managing director, but the assembly itself makes various decisions about the direction of the cooperatives.[193] This is the reverse of the structure of standard capitalist enterprises in which managers and CEOs make decisions about hiring and firing. Furthermore, where standard capitalist businesses focus on profit maximization and view employment as incidental to this profit-seeking activity, Mondragón makes stable employment its central goal.[194] The highest-paid-employee makes only 6.5 times as much as the lowest-paid employee (in contrast to the average rate of 273 to 1 in the United States in 2012).[195] Ten percent of all profits are reinvested back into the community in development projects. The result is that Mondragón workers report high levels of satisfaction with their jobs, and the local communities where Mondragón operates report lower crime rates, higher rates of education, and increased physical and emotional health.[196] While

[192] Sarah Delaney, "Pope, church leaders call for guaranteed health care for all people," *Catholic News Service*, 18 November 2010, http://www.catholicnews.com/data/stories/cns/1004736.htm.

[193] Richard Wolff, "Yes, There is an Alternative to Capitalism: Mondragón Shows the Way," *The Guardian*, 24 June 2012, http://www.theguardian.com/commentisfree/2012/jun/24/alternative-capitalism-mondragon.

[194] See the discussion of Mondragón in David Schweickart, *After Capitalism* (Lanham, MD: Rowman & Littlefield, 2011), 70.

[195] Wolff, "Yes, There is an Alternative to Capitalism."

[196] Cavanaugh, *Being Consumed*, 27.

this is only one concrete example of an alternative model for organizing labor by means of cooperatives, there do exist other models that create alternatives to the type of capitalism practiced by multinational corporations. For instance, Community Supported Agriculture, community-based banks and local credit unions, as well as various types of local cooperatives have attempted to create small-scale business models committed to a just and living wage, community development, and the flourishing of the community and environment.

These concrete actions—charitable giving, commutative justice, and structural transformation—represent important ways in which individuals in the developed world can respond to the challenge posed by Ignacio Ellacuría and Jon Sobrino to begin the process of taking the crucified poor down from their cross. While few Christians succeed in witnessing to the option for the poor with the radicalism of Dorothy Day and Martin Luther King Jr. or Mother Teresa and Archbishop Oscar Romero, it is nevertheless the case that each individual can contribute to the development of a more just economic and political order by either increasing charitable activity or supporting commutative and distributive forms of justice. Furthermore, these activities done on behalf of the poor not only accord with concrete moral duties but also help individuals in the affluent world express their relationship to the God of the Christian tradition who is a God of the poor.[197]

---

[197] Sobrino, *No Salvation Outside the Poor*, 33.

Conclusion

A Sacramental-Prophetic Vision

This book has examined environmental degradation and global poverty as interrelated crises that demand an urgent response by Christians. As we have noted, however, the problem we face is that there are cultural realities that obstruct individuals from seeing their responsibility for the contradictions in creation. In particular, I have argued that the market imaginary cultivates forms of life driven by the imperatives of growth, profit maximization, and conspicuous forms of consumption. These imperatives lead individuals to perceive the earth as raw material for industrial use and economic expansion and to view the suffering of the poor as irrelevant to their lives.

In response to this situation it is incumbent upon Christians to generate alternative visions of reality, visions that make it clear that God's will for the world is not that the environment and the poor should suffer unnecessarily. It has been argued that the sacramental and prophetic commitments of the Christian tradition provide Christians with important resources to respond to these crises and cultivate the sensibilities necessary to begin to heal the environment and to take the crucified poor down from their cross. Although the sacramental imagination and the prophetic imagination appear to stand in tension with each other in terms of their respective emphases, it is nevertheless the case that these two forms of imagination share the common commitment to a spirituality that is honest with reality—a reality that discloses itself as both beautiful and catastrophic, graced and unreconciled. The different spiritual exercises detailed in this work all support the formation of persons who can be honest with this reality and perceive those things that often are occluded from vision: the presence of God in the beauty of creation as well as the hiddenness of God in the suffering of the innocent. In this sense it is a sacramental-prophetic vision of reality that permits Christians to live more deeply in the presence of God (*coram Deo*) and to make that presence visible in a suffering world.

170

Index